Chapters
Of Our
Lives

Chapters
Of Our
Lives

Joe Lovett

To order additional copies of this book, contact:
Xlibris
844-714-8691
www.Xlibris.com
Orders@Xlibris.com
824189

CONTENTS

FOREWORD

I went to my fiftieth Carpinteria High School class reunion in 2017. I had a great time. I saw people I had not seen for more than fifty years. Fifty years! That is a lifetime. I was not even able to see everybody. The time that night went very quickly. On my way home to Northern California, I felt great regret that I had not stayed in touch with the people I had grown up with. I had great friends and very close relationships. I thought of a way to rectify this. I was going to write a book about those times.

When I got home and thought about an outline for the book, it dawned on me that I could never write a full book on my own. I have ADD, and it is hard for me to concentrate for long periods of time. Then it hit me. Having a few friends from my early days, I would try to convince at least forty of my classmates to each write a chapter. I enlisted the help of two of my friends, Terry Galvez and Cori Deaderick, to help me. I think they thought at first that I could not get forty classmates, some of whom I had not even talked to in more than fifty years, to contribute to the project. It became a legacy project for me. So I started on my journey.

I started by sending letters to all the classmates I had addresses for. I sent out sixty letters to classmates and followed up by calling as many as I could find phone numbers for, which was about fifty. Some people were not interested in writing a chapter. I understood this very well. I called as a virtual stranger to these people. Well, I have thirty-seven chapters. We have a book.

All the work for all this time has been well worth it. It is a great book. We have stories of happiness, sadness, and everything in between. I hope everybody that reads our book will feel the same.

I want to thank both Terry and Cori for their help. Special thanks to Linda Fryer and Thais Meyer for their help as well.

The Carpinteria High School class of 1967 would like to dedicate this book to our fallen classmates:

Rick Brister, Kris Brottlund, Randy Careaga, Randy Castile, Laurie Kavara, Louis Lytal, Darryl Mann, David Mendoza, Jack Moodhard, Jim Mount, Sue Moyer, Christine Muesing, Willey Norlin, Sam Putman, Bill Rocky, Gary Sanders, Bill Sargent, Don Seaman, Kevin Sears, Doug Walker, Ron Weatley, Bill Wheeler, Gay Williamson, Dolores Echeverria, Reynae Pearson, Janice Brown, Steve Smith

Joe Lovett
January 2021

IN MEMORY OF OUR 1967 GRADUATES
WARRIORS FOREVER!

CHAPTER ONE

Mark Campbell

MARK CAMPBELL

Riding the Revolution

The year 1967 was seminal for change. The '60s' social revolution was swinging into gear. The Monterey Pop Festival was blowing minds, just like the guitars of The Who and Jimi Hendrix. The road through Big Sur was filling up with hitchhiking hippies on a pilgrimage to a promised land. The summers of love stood out in contrast to the war in Vietnam, which loomed over the head of every eighteen-year-old male at that time.

The year 1967 was when I turned eighteen and graduated from Carpinteria High School and registered for the draft. I was one of a class of about 120. We were the last to graduate from the old high school in town. The following year, students would attend the new high school that was built north of town at the base of the foothills. We marched out in red-and-white caps and gowns with family and friends sitting in the bleachers of the old Memorial Field, where we used to check out the surf from the wooden press box during PE classes. Changes were coming to us all.

Growing up in the little coastal enclave should have been as close to idyllic as can be achieved. Set between the coastal mountains and south facing beaches, Carpinteria sits on a narrow coastal plain with a nearly ideal climate and a view of the Santa Barbara Channel Islands. This narrow strip of geography has kept Carpinteria a relatively small town with a distinct local flavor. In 1967, Carpinteria was still mostly a working-class town with jobs in agriculture and small businesses. There is a small state park in Carpinteria and there are some beachside apartments to the west, which in the 1960s gave the town an influx of summer, seasonal tourists. The tourist season now is year-round, and property values have gone through the stratosphere like other beach communities in California, altering but not quite burying the character of the town. It is still a place where most people know everybody. And did I mention the beaches? I was fortunate enough to grow up in that friendly, small-town environment during the postwar, baby-boom days of innocence. The ocean and the beach drew most of the locals to the shore often for fishing and cookouts down by the old boat ramp. My older brother used to launch his wooden, hollow paddleboard at the end of the street, two blocks from our house and paddle out beyond the kelp bed around the reef at Sandyland. The beach was a playground to me, and I found myself spending most of my free time there, recreating with friends during warm weather, or beachcombing by myself during a winter storm. By 1962, I had graduated from riding a canvas raft and a skim board to a gently used Santa Barbara Surf Shop surfboard. The new technology of foam and fiberglass made the boards just light enough for my 100 pounds to be able to manage carrying to the beach. I became part of a little band of kids that started surfing on our used longboard logs, catching waves next to the old fishing pier at the state park that attracted summer tourists (girls). We would hang around the lifeguard tower and watch Merv Larsen paddle out during one of his breaks and bust out his drop-knee back-side turns. Merv was one of those surfing, lifeguard watermen that we looked up to and aspired to be. We migrated eventually to the easternmost end of the main beach known as the Tar Pits. The state park had not yet expanded into that area that has since been paved for RV camping. Jeff White and Kevin Sears were lifeguards as well, winning dory-rowing events in lifeguarding competitions up and down the coast. Even though Kevin was in my class, his surfing and waterman skills were legendary by the time he was seventeen. Along with Jeff Boyd and others, he was leading the change of Carpinteria surfers. My little tribe of groms, which included Bernie Baker, Steve Johnson, and Matt Moore, settled in at the Tar Pits and occasionally ventured to Rincon, one of the premier surf spots in the world only two miles south of Carpinteria. We, like thousands of other teenage surfers along the coast, were unknowingly perfecting the California lifestyle that was becoming the blueprint for a whole generation. Bernie would go on to be a successful surfing photographer, journalist, and surf contest facilitator from his house and headquarters at Sunset Beach on the North Shore of Oahu. Matt, another waterman, is still one of the sought-after surfboard shapers on the coast. And Steve is still the most stylish surfer in the water, especially at Rincon when it goes well overhead. At some point, I had been granted membership into the Hope Ranch Surf Club, and I thought my life was complete. I got to wear the little club badge on my board trunks. I thought I'd made it. I got to join what I perceived to be a group of the surfing elite in the Santa Barbara area. At that time, surf clubs competed against each other up and down the coast, and status was the reward for winning.

However, by 1967 the writing was already on the wall for surf club culture. It was going to be a casualty of the sea change of late '60s counterculture. There were changes taking place in the world at large. Politics, protest, drugs, and the war were having a profound effect on the minds of members of my generation, and of course the same social upheavals were taking place quietly and not so quietly behind closed doors in small towns as well. The silent conformity of the '50s was being confronted by louder voices. The saving grace then as now was that surfing was an option for one who gravitated that way. It offered me its unique form of escapism and its inclusion into the ocean tribe. So it was in this setting that I graduated and entered adulthood with a Yater Spoon surfboard under my arm. I had two choices: stay at the beach, get drafted and possibly sent to Vietnam, or go to college and avoid the draft with a 2S or student deferment. Santa Barbara City College was the available option for a student with my spotty high school record. However, my parents had unearthed a college brochure from an obscure community college on Maui called Maunaolu College. My mom had married my stepdad when I was sixteen and they had honeymooned on Maui, and they came back with more than just a honeymoon glow. They described a magical place that was not really on anybody's radar yet. I think they also thought that getting me away from certain free-spirited influences around our town would be a good thing. That was the theory anyway.

The school was a two-year private college situated between Paia and Makawao on the slopes of Haleakala, the imposing, 10,000-foot volcano that makes up half of the island of Maui. Even by 1967 standards, Maunaolu College was a bargain at $600 a semester for board, room, and tuition. I had a bit of Social Security money that was available to me because of my birth father's passing when I was ten. As an added incentive to me, my parents had highlighted the part of the brochure that stated that a PE class in surfing was to be taught by a world-champion surfer. No instructor's name was given. So without much sense of purpose, I applied and I was accepted as a freshman for the fall semester of 1967. Still, I wasn't eager to leave behind the town, the people, or the beach that I loved.

Maunaolu College (sometimes written as Mauna Olu College) had its beginnings as the East Maui Female Seminary, a small school for Hawaiian girls founded at Makawao by Rev. and Mrs. C. B. Andrews and the American Board of Mission in 1861. The meaning of the word, Maunaolu translates in English as "pleasant mountain," "friendly mountain," or "mountain place." The school's buildings were destroyed by fires in 1869 and again in 1898. The building that still exists today was completed in 1900, and after many years, the small struggling school graduated its first class of six girls with eighth-grade diplomas. From that point, the school continued to grow with an emphasis on Bible study and home economics. In 1942, the campus was taken over by the military for the war effort. It was turned into a military hospital and headquarters. It served for a brief time as the Maui Community Hospital. At the end of World War II, the Maunaolu trustees, with the help of the H. P. Baldwin family, reacquired the grounds, and in 1950, they reestablished the school. Instead of an all-female college, they set up a four-year community college for students to complete their last two years of high school and their first two years of college. Through the 1950s and early '60s, the school struggled to keep its enrollment up, but by 1964, it was establishing itself as Maui's coeducational community college, reaching an enrollment of 202 students. In 1966, Maui Community College opened and began attracting local students away from Maunaolu. However, Maunaolu had started to attract students from the other parts of Hawaii, as well as from other states and other countries. By 1967, most of the students lived on campus. The student body was made up of students from Oahu, Kauai, and the Big Island of Hawaii. There were students from throughout the Pacific Basin, including Micronesia, Samoa, and the Marshall Islands. There were students from California, the Midwest, and the East Coast of the United States, as well as from the Caribbean. There were international students from Vietnam, Indonesia, and Sweden. Together it added up to about 200 students with about 30 professors, administrators, and support staff.

There were no direct flights from the mainland to Maui in those days. The United Airlines 707 took me from LA to Honolulu. As I flew into Maui on the interisland plane from Oahu, I saw the green carpet of sugarcane fields covering the valley floor, with occasional plumes of smoke rising from fields that were being readied for harvest. As I stepped off the plane, I was greeted by the strong, warm trade winds that blow through the valley almost daily. The college's Volkswagen bus picked me up, along with my board, and a few other students, and took us to the school, about twelve miles from Kahului, the biggest city on Maui. Maunaolu was 900 feet above the sea level. It was in the climatic transition zone where sugarcane fields gave way to pineapple plantations. If you continue to climb higher up the slopes of Haleakala, you will pass through many climate zones until you reach the summit, where it is almost arctic-like in its temperature and in the type of flora it supports. I was dropped off at the boys' dorm, known as Baldwin Hall: a 1930s craftsman-style horseshoe structure where the dorm rooms were fronted by a lanai that followed the horseshoe shape around a beautiful green area with a large monkey pod tree in the middle. A variety of avocado trees surrounded the dorm. It was located about a quarter mile from the main campus. I was feeling a little dismayed about some of what I was seeing. True, I could see the blue Pacific from this locale on the windward side of Haleakala, but it was a good six or seven miles down to the beach. With no car, that could be a problem. Growing up in Carpinteria, I was never more than a couple of blocks from the waves. I was also culturally not prepared for the difference between California and Hawaii. I was raised in a place where the 1950s and '60s infrastructure, like freeways and colleges, was still shiny and brand new. This was old Hawaii. The buildings were wooden and worn. And everything seemed to be wearing a coat of rust-colored volcanic dirt. I was not yet ready to appreciate the difference. I walked up the hill to the main campus. The main building, with its flagpole and large front lawn area, was situated on a hill with a dramatic view of the entire valley of Maui and the West Maui Mountains. It was a large, two-story, white Victorian structure that had classrooms, administrative offices, an assembly hall, and a dining hall. There were other smaller structures on the grounds including the girls' dorms and staff housing. When I sat down to my first meal in the cafeteria, I encountered another culture shock. The food in Hawaii was going to be different: two scoops of rice, a scoop of macaroni salad, and a beef/vegetable thing. Also, the dean of the school was making an announcement that coats and ties were required for Sunday dinners. The vibe I was getting was this school was not far removed from its missionary roots.

Feeling a little homesick and disoriented, I walked back to the boys' dorm. I noticed that there were a couple of people checking out my surfboard that I had left on the lanai. As I got closer, I began to recognize a celebrity from the surfing mags and movies I had seen, and I quickly started to fill in the gaps. Jeff Hakman was to be the "world champion surfing instructor." Jeff had been a fixture in the surfing media since Bruce Brown filmed this little thirteen-year-old kid surfing the giant waves at Waimea Bay in the early '60s. By 1967, Jeff was no longer that skinny little kid. He was well established as one of the premier Hawaiian surfers. In 1966, he won the prestigious Duke Kahanamoku surfing championship at Sunset Beach. Jeff had been offered free room, board, and tuition at Maunaolu in return for teaching a one-half-credit surfing PE class. After introductions, we talked boards for a while. He and his roommate, Leon Tompkins from Kauai, were just down the hall from my room. And Leon had a car, a '56 Chevy. Things were looking up.

The next few days were spent meeting roommates, registering for classes, and trying to come to grips with comprehending the foreign language known as Pidgin English. Classes started, and it wasn't long before I was in the van with Jeff at the wheel, heading down the mountain, past Baldwin High School to Hookipa Beach, the nearest beach to Maunaolu. A pickup truck loaded with boards and more students was behind us. Some of us more or less looked the part, but there were several boys and girls from places much more removed from a Hawaiian beach than California. Some were from New England, one was from Kentucky, and Inger was from Sweden. All of us were about to be baptized in the Hawaiian sun and surf. All of us came back to the school with sunburns, coral cuts, and smiles.

Connections were made, and rides to the beach became easier to arrange. One of my classmates, Leonard Brady, had a car. We called it the suck mobile, because of its struggles going up hills, but it ran, and we were spending more time surfing at Hookipa or bodysurfing at Baldwin Beach than we were in class. That was a large part of the reason I went on academic probation the first semester before getting my act together. I was enjoying Hookipa's trade wind right-hander on my Yater, as well as trips to the south shore with Leonard and our crew. Jeff organized a surf contest for the college, and I came away with a second-place trophy. Leonard would go on after college to form the company Island Style with Bernie Baker, as well as work for the Hollywood director John Milius.

From our vantage point on Haleakala, we could look down and see both the north and south shores. The south shore was more distant, and in the days before surf prognostication, the hint of white water at the Maalaea Harbor would lead us on many a goose chase. But there came a day in October when the north shore outer reefs came to life. Jeff, Leon, and I piled our boards on the Chevy and headed for the still little-known spot called Honolua Bay. For us, it meant driving all the way to the south shore and around past Napili to get there, a distance of about fifty miles. Road conditions and slow traffic made for a long commute. Honolua Bay is a small, stunningly beautiful bay that looks across the channel to the island of Molokai. The bay provides a calm, sheltered anchorage in pristinely clear water surrounded by lush green foliage. Most of the time, it is a snorkeler's paradise, but when the swell is right, it offers up one of the best surfing point breaks in the world. Parking on the cliff next to the pineapple field wasn't a thing yet, so we paddled out from the mouth of the stream where it enters the bay. There was one other car there. Renowned surfer Tiger Espere was with that group. Nobody was out yet. We all paddled out together across the azure bay. The waves were strong and well overhead, and between the wave size and the rocky cliffs that line the shore, I sensed that my Yater Spoon and I were badly overmatched. Surfboard leashes had not yet been invented, so if you lost your board, it usually washed to shore. Honolua's rocky cliffs, with its infamous cave, devoured boards at a frightening rate. I posted up around the bowl section toward the end of the wave and tried some tentative drops without a shred of confidence. Meanwhile, I had a good view of Tiger and Jeff. The memory of Jeff streaking across the outside wall on his G & S John Peck Penetrator doing a cheater five is etched forever in my brain.

As fall proceeded, there were plenty of windless or slightly offshore mornings at Hookipa. Those conditions can create some wonderful moments for being in the water and for surfing. We made more trips to Honolulu Bay, and we made other explorations down dirt roads and across ancient lava flows, looking for waves. We had to make sure to be back before the cafeteria closed; otherwise, we would have to be content with an avocado and some Wheat Thins in our rooms for dinner. Thanksgiving break rolled around, and many of the students from the other Hawaiian Islands, including Jeff, took the short plane ride back to be with their families. When Jeff came back, he had a new board. It was unlike anything I had ever seen. It was a three-stringer with the words "God is Love" penciled in small letters next to the middle stringer. It was made by Dick Brewer, shaper and guru for the new breed of surfers emerging on the North Shore and elsewhere. Not only was Jeff's new board shorter than the usual 9'-plus longboards of the day, at 8'6" it was also narrower than a standard board and drawn in at the nose and the tail. It was the first mini-gun I had ever seen. On subsequent trips to The Bay and elsewhere, I got to watch Jeff and a handful of others (it was starting to get a little more crowded) riding these new shapes. It was a new approach: more up and down on the wave and less trimming toward the nose. Before Christmas break, Jeff appeared with another Brewer, this one shorter still, probably about 8' long. I purchased his 8'6" and officially entered the short-board revolution. It was called a revolution because the future was swinging toward boards that were much shorter, lighter, and more maneuverable.

When Christmas break had come and gone and the second semester was about to start, I returned from visiting my family in Carpinteria. I learned that Maunaolu had another surfing celebrity. Jock Sutherland was enrolled at the school and partnering with Jeff to teach the PE class. Jock was also in the surfing movies and magazines of the time, making his name as a fearless charger at Pipeline and other North Shore spots. Jeff moved out of the dorm, and he and Jock found a house off campus in Haiku, where there were some memorable parties that I don't remember much about. As far as surfing instruction, I don't remember much about that either. I think the classes mainly consisted of us all piling into vehicles and going to a place like Paukukalo, near Wailuku, and Jeff and Jock paddling out. It was up to us if we wanted to paddle out too. This led to some attrition, but nobody drowned, and you couldn't ask for better role models. Jeff and Jock inspired us with their poise, grace, and sharing both in and out of the water.

After that semester, both Jeff and Jock parted from Maunaolu. They left behind a motivated surf crew. Our crew consisted of Leonard, Jay Mann, Erick Ahlgren, me, and anyone else who could fit into my 1963 red VW Bug with rack piled high with boards. We couldn't necessarily afford a new Brewer, but Les Potts was shaping boards in Lahaina. In the months and years following, we started making our own boards. There were a couple of old outbuildings at the boys' dorm where we started stripping the fiberglass off old longboards and reshaping the foam core inside into smaller and smaller designs and re-glassing them. It became a crude obsession. I reshaped that Brewer board that I bought from Jeff (God forgive me!). That board would fetch a handsome price today from any number of surfboard collectors, but its place in the history of surfing is where its real value would have been. Some of the boards the college had purchased for the PE class of '67 mysteriously disappeared. No workable piece of foam was safe. We tested each new shape at the usual spots, and some spots that aren't there anymore like the notorious Kahului harbor right slab, and the harbor left that was world class until they extended the breakwater in 1969.

Other celebrities passed through Maui and Maunaolu. The popular duo of Seals and Crofts played for students in the little assembly hall. Michael Clarke, drummer for The Byrds, was dating a pretty, young freshman. When the band Quicksilver Messenger Service was visiting Maui, they were given impromptu surfing lessons by some Maunaolu students at Oluwalu. Many Maunaolu students were present when Jimi Hendrix was playing and filming his movie *Rainbow Bridge* in a field not far from the campus. Timothy Leary, the famous New York psychiatrist turned LSD guru, was often spotted around the island. The magic of Maui was becoming known to jet setter and hippies alike.

During the late '60s, Maui became a sort of epicenter for spiritual change. By 1968, the hippie movement was starting to impact Maui. Communes like the Banana Patch near Haiku and the one on Big Beach at Makena were populated by young people looking to return to nature. The free thinking and the nudity ran head on into the long-standing missionary values of many Mauians. There were occasionally some very tense moments, and the results weren't always pretty. As surfers and college students, we were somewhere in the middle. We could look pretty scruffy by day, but at night, we clean up pretty good. The culture war was not as obvious at Maunaolu, but the last vestiges of its missionary roots were steadily eroding away.

Maunaolu had a mix of old and young professors. Some were rigidly old school and suspicious of the changes that were happening in the world. Some were openly embracing the new movement. All seemed to have a level of passion and love for where they were and what they were trying to teach. Class sizes were small, and because most staff and students lived on campus, there was a family-like feeling at the school. I learned to be a better student at Maunaolu, but still had no clue what I would do after my two years were up. Somehow, dumb luck interceded on my behalf once again, and during my sophomore year, it was announced that Maunaolu would be adding a four-year curriculum. Hallelujah! An extended stay in paradise fit nicely into my life goals. I finished my four years with a degree in English literature and a minor in anthropology. Not useful, but hey, I got to spend four years in a kind of glorified summer camp. And I did manage to parlay my degree into a teaching credential some years later. When I was a senior, it was announced that Maunaolu was being sold. It was purchased by United Stated International University. They had campuses in England, Mexico, and Africa. They also owned Cal Western University in San Diego. USIU would be turning Maunaolu back into a two-year college. Graduation was bittersweet. It was the end of a unique run. There were thirteen of us who graduated from Maunaolu in 1971. The ceremony was held outside on the stately grounds of the house where the president of the college and his family lived. We were the first and only four-year graduates from that college. Mike Malloy was one of those graduates. In his senior year, he got married and bought some property in Kyla, the upcountry area on the slopes of Haleakala. His three sons, collectively known as the Malloy brothers, have been an influential force in the surfing world since the late '80s. We seniors called ourselves the Edsels. Google it if you don't know what an Edsel was. Those four years saw a lot of changes. Music changed, culture changed, surfboards changed, and Maui changed. Hard to go back to Maui now, remembering how it was then, but change happens.

USIU operated Maunaolu for a few more years, ultimately shutting it down as they downsized their operations. I went to a Maunaolu multi-class reunion about four years ago with my family. There were students there from across the years. Some were before my time, some were after. All of us felt a shared bond. Just the act of surviving all these years brings people of a certain age together like members of a club. We were able to take a tour of the old campus. The boys' dorm was renovated and remodeled by a renowned LA architect. It doesn't have that worn look any longer. Its distinctive character was beautifully restored and preserved. It is now a very upscale retreat offering well-heeled guests holistic therapies while they enjoy the Valley Isle. I can't help but think that they might have found an old hash pipe or two under the floorboards during the renovation. The building on the main campus looks much like it did when I first saw it. It has gone through a few phases since the school closed, but now it is at least a school once again. It is a kind of trade school for high-school-aged kids from islands throughout Oceania. Many of those island cultures are struggling to stay viable in this changing world. These island students are being taught business skills that they might be able to take back to their communities and use in productive and positive ways. It was a strange, almost out-of-body experience for most of us to be walking around those old grounds, remembering faces, voices, and moments.

All of us who came of age in 1967 were experiencing a revolution. For better or worse, the changes were happening all around us. Thoughts, attitudes, mores, music, and styles reflected a huge societal shift. Youth went on the move physically and philosophically. We are still trying to sort out the repercussions of the Vietnam War on our politics and our unity as a nation. Maui got caught up in courting the tourist dollar at the sacrifice of much of its authentic aloha. But we also experienced a creative burst that led to new freedoms and innovations. The sport I love isn't just in California and Hawaii anymore. Thanks to advanced wetsuit technology, there are now surfing communities in Iceland and Alaska as well as other cold-water regions around the globe. The sport itself has spread to almost every coastal nook and cranny and culture on the planet. Does that mean it is now like McDonald's? History will of course be the judge. "The good old days" has a different meaning for everyone, and they always look larger in the rearview mirror.

Next year, it will be fifty years since I graduated and left Maui. I eventually settled back in California on the central coast. I still keep surfing and count myself fortunate to be able to do so. I settled into a satisfying teaching career and was lucky enough to raise a family, but that memory of Maui and the friends I made and that little college that sheltered me for four years has influenced all my life decisions to one degree or another. It occurred to me while taking that reunion tour of the old campus that Pleasant Mountain is not so much a place as it is a state of mind. Those of us who lived those times will carry it always in our hearts. Who knows? If my luck holds, I will return someday in spirit form, and I will haunt the old hallways of Maunaolu.

Mark Campbell ⟫⟫⟫————————————————————➤ Rincon

CHAPTER TWO

Diane Darcy

DIANNE
DARCY

My Adventure

By
Dianne Darcy

I was visiting with my neighbor, sitting on his front steps, when Richard rode up on his motorcycle. Who was this man that took my breath away? He reminded me of Clint Eastwood in a way, with his good looks and easy self-confidence.

I was immediately smitten with him as he was with me, because he introduced himself and asked if I was single. I told him at the time I was seeing someone, but he just smiled and said, "OK."

As it turned out, the boyfriend that I was seeing at the time came to pick me up that evening, and before he could knock on my door, Richard had come up to him from next door and said something to him that I was unable to hear. The next thing I know, Richard was standing at my door with a big smile on his face and asked if he could come in. I wasn't really interested in that other fella anyway. This was the beginning of the adventure I'm about to write about.

I was living with my grandmother on Dorrance Way, having come home after divorcing my first husband and left with two small boys. It was a shock to Grandma when after just knowing Richard for four days I moved in with him with my boys. I remember her telling her neighbor friend that I must have known him before and just not have mentioned it. Because it was out of the question that I would run off with this stranger after just meeting him a few days ago.

We moved into his apartment on Santa Barbara, and those were the days when a landlord could discriminate against children, so when they found out that my little ones were there, Richard was given notice to leave.

He worked for his father, who owned a company in Santa Barbara that installed acoustic ceiling tiles. One day he came home and said he sold his motorcycle and bought a truck. It was a brand new Ford

Ranchero with a shell on the back. Because we had to move, he had other plans for us.

He knew that I hadn't been out of Carpinteria much, so he decided to take me and the boys on a road trip. I thought that would be exciting, so he quit his job, we sold my car for extra cash and took off across the United States.

Leland was four years old and Brandon was fifteen months. Inside the shell of the truck was set up to be nice and comfortable for the little ones. We arrived at our first destination in Las Vegas, NV. All the light and hotels were amazing and exciting for us to see. We didn't do any gambling; we had the children and couldn't take them in the casino, so we stayed in a motel for the night. The next day, we headed out to no place in particular.

We drove into Utah, looking in wonder of the formations of earth and rock that centuries of wind and rain had carved out in such a glorious way. I was amazed at the color of the earth. I was used to the dark farmland and white sandy beaches of Santa Barbara and Ventura counties. I was in awe of what Mother Nature had done.

Onward to Colorado we went. This is such a beautiful state, but what really stood out for me was driving through the Rocky Mountains. It was a little frightening driving on those winding roads, but the scenery was breathtaking. Evergreens covered the mountainsides and wildlife was abundant. We saw a couple of elk not too far from the road and lots of squirrels here and there in the trees. It was evident there were skunks in the area; you could definitely pick up that odor.

After a while, the scenery became pretty boring going through some of the Midwest: lots of corn and wheat fields, nothing too interesting until we got to the East Coast. It was good to see the ocean finally again. We arrived in Virginia and took a couple of days to shake the travel out of our system. Richard and I decided to go out to dinner without the little ones, and lucky for us, the motel had a babysitter that we could hire. She was an Amazon, a giant of a girl! I asked to take a picture of her and the kids, and she obliged. However, holding Brandon, she slid down to one knee and I couldn't get the full effect of her size. Her hand was covering his entire chest. Wow!

We went through the Southern States, the Carolinas, Georgia, Alabama, etc. Stopping for breakfast in the South was a new experience for me. I ordered egg and bacon with toast. Something was on my plate that was completely foreign to me. This white stuff kind of looked like cream of wheat, but not really. I asked the waitress to come over and tell me what it was. Richard knew but wouldn't tell me. She said, "Them are grits, honey. Where y'all from?" That was my introduction to grits, which by the way, I loved. I still eat them to this day.

Driving into New Orleans, LA, I had an urge to try and look up my father, whom I hadn't seen since I was two years old. I told Richard that my dad lived here and I would like to try and find him. I went to a payphone, and as it turned out, there were only five Darcys listed in the phone book for all of New Orleans. Joseph Darcy wasn't listed, so I called one of them that was listed.

A man answered the phone, and I said, "Hello, my name is Dianne Darcy. I'm here from California, trying to find my father. His name is Joseph Darcy, who was married to my mother Virginia. Do you know who I am?"

The man on the other end of the phone said, "I'm your Uncle Frank." I asked if he knew how to get in touch with my dad, and he said yes. I told him that I was here in New Orleans with my husband and children for just a short time, so it was important to reach him as soon as possible. Uncle Frank took down the number I gave him, and in about two minutes, my dad called me back. We made arrangements to meet up with him after Richard and the kids and I freshened up in our motel. I couldn't believe it! I just spoke to my father! OMG! All these years later? I was two years old when my mother and father divorced, so twenty-one years later, I was able to find and connect with him with just one phone call? That caused a little resentment between me and my mother. We talked it out later and got it worked out between us. I know my mother always had my best interest at heart.

The reunion was great! He was so happy to see me and his grandsons. He used to frequent a little neighborhood bar and wanted to take us there to show us off to his old friends. Dad put some quarters in the jukebox, and Leland, who was four, danced with him. Joe was so proud to show off his beautiful daughter and his darling grandsons to his old pals. (I was pretty cute back then, folks.) We left the bar and went to Bourbon Street to take in the sights and get something to eat. Well, when you are in New Orleans, you *have to* have oysters on the half shell, which we certainly enjoyed. Fifteen-month-old Brandon was in his high chair, and I gave him a raw oyster to eat. You should have seen the facial contortions. It was hilarious! The next thing you know, he was reaching out with his little hands for *more*! We all just burst out laughing, and Dad said, "He's a true Louisiana boy."

We had a very pleasant visit, took some pictures, and then we got back on the road. I told my brother Jim that I found our dad, and when he and his wife and son moved back to CA from Washington, DC, they also went to see him. Our mother was not pleased about it, but that's life. I continued to write to Dad for several years after that until he passed away. The Darcy family notified my mom about his passing, but she didn't tell me until months later, so I didn't get to send my condolences.

Mexico was next on Richard's agenda. Those were the days that you didn't need a passport to enter the country. We crossed the border in Texas. I guess it was your typical border town, but it was a whole different world to me. The one thing Richard mentioned was that if we ever got into a car accident, to grab the kids and run. The police didn't care who was at fault; *everyone* would go to jail.

Our destination was Mazatlán. I had no idea how far that was; it turned out to be around one thousand miles from El Paso. The roads were fairly good, and as we were passing some of the men working on the road, I noticed a few of them waving at us while they took a pee! I couldn't believe it! It was no big deal to them! I had to laugh, and of course, we waved back. I told my mother about it, and she said that when she was in France, the men would just pee against a building on the sidewalk. Evidently, some countries just take it for granted, but this girl from Carpinteria found it to be very peculiar.

Entering some of the little villages, I noticed there were no sidewalks or walkways to the homes. There was no grass or shrubbery in the yard. Women would be in front of their house sweeping the dirt. I was impressed at how tidy they kept it, considering all the dirt.

Every time we stopped in a little town, suddenly we were surrounded by women and young girls that wanted to hold my kids. My boys had very blond hair, and I understood what *rubio* meant in Spanish. I didn't do too well in high school Spanish class, but I got by in Mexico, knowing a few sentences. At first, Brandon was a little apprehensive, but after several of these encounters, he got used to it.

As we drove into unfamiliar territory, it was obvious we weren't going to find a Fosters Freeze or an A&W anywhere, so when hunger set in, we stopped at what looked like a place that would serve food. Richard and I ordered tacos; the boys had something simple, cheese and beans in a tortilla. I asked, "Que es esto carne?" I think I asked the lady serving this food, "What is this meat?" All she said was "Si, carne." Well, folks, I have friends that unknowingly at the time had eaten dog or monkey and said it was "delicious," but as God is my witness, the meat in these tacos was the most disgusting thing I had ever had the displeasure of pushing over my tongue. I said to Richard that must have been a dead donkey they found lying on the side of the road. We didn't complain, just ordered *queso y frijole tortillas*.

The next town we came into was a little bigger with paved street and more populated. A school bus stopped and a dozen kids got off. They were all in school uniform, and I was impressed with how white their shirts and blouses were. They all came right over to greet us; I guess there weren't too many Americans traveling through their town very often. I asked them in Spanish if they liked school, then I asked if they wanted some chocolate. I brought a bag of Hershey's Miniatures with me and handed them out to these happy delightful children. I will never forget the joy on their faces when receiving such a small gift as a little chocolate candy.

As we traveled through the many little villages, it touched my heart at how friendly the people were. It was nothing at all like the border towns I'd been to, where everyone was trying to hustle money from you.

Richard wasn't fooling when he told me about car accidents in Mexico. We were in the parking lot of our motel when I heard tires squeal. A car didn't slow down and crashed into a woman sitting at a stop sign. Here came the police and arrested everyone, even the lady that got hit from behind! Richard said, "That's why I said run."

We traveled through what I would call jungle, or for a better explanation, dense foliage and vegetation. It was beautiful with poinsettias draping off the shrubs and trees. I could hear the sound of birds calling, but their cries were unfamiliar to me. I never knew what kind they were. I would bet there were parrots there among the trees. You get to know the particular sounds of the indigenous species you grow up with. These unfamiliar sounds and smells were an exciting experience for me.

We finally arrived in Mazatlán and got a hotel room right on the beach. The hotel was old but clean and comfortable. We took the boys with us for an evening swim. It was November, and the water was as warm as a bathtub. I was in heaven being in the ocean again.

I guess I was just young and naive when leaving my jewelry on the dresser in the hotel room, because when we returned, it was no longer there. I went to the hotel manager and told him what happened, and he said that his maid wouldn't ever take anything. I couldn't prove it, so it was just my loss. That was a lesson well learned.

We took in some sights and stayed a few days, then started our journey home. I was ready to get back to California. It was exciting to see a lot of the United States and Mexico, but I was tired of all the travel. We were on the road for about three months.

While traveling back, we went through Chihuahua, Mexico. I had to laugh thinking of the little dogs that probably originated there, or so I thought.

We finally made it back to the United States and ended up in Fountain Valley, where Richard's sister lived with her husband and twelve-year-old daughter. This was just around Christmastime, and we had fun decorating the house. My mother sent us a Christmas fruitcake. It looked really good, and the boys were begging for a piece. Although we hadn't eaten dinner yet, I let them have a slice. After a little while, I noticed Brandon crawling on the floor and falling over; Leland was passed out. I couldn't believe it! My mother had failed to tell me that she had soaked the fruitcake in rum for an entire month! This was done after the cake was cooked, so all that alcohol was soaked in the cake and my children were *drunk*! Needless to say, I was furious with my mom.

A few weeks later, Richard and I took a short trip to Las Vegas and got married. I wasn't too keen on the idea having been in a bad marriage before, but he was persistent saying he wasn't like my first husband, so I finally agreed.

It was nice of his sister to have us all stay there with them, but I was really homesick for Carpinteria. My grandma said that I could come back home and bring Richard and the boys. I was so happy to get back to my hometown. We were back in Carpinteria, on Dorrance Way. It seemed that life was going great. Richard loved the boys but wanted us to have a baby together. It only took a couple of months of trying when our baby girl was conceived. Now this was back in 1973, so they didn't have ultrasound back then. There was no way to know the gender of the baby. We did try for a girl though. I had a book that helped in a scientific way to make the odds in one's favor. We moved to Isla Vista into our own apartment and Jennifer was born on June 5, 1974.

I will close the story now with saying that this marriage didn't work out. However, God has blessed me with three beautiful children. I also have two granddaughters and a great-grandson. I'm living in Las Vegas now and would love to be back in my little hometown of Carpinteria.

CHAPTER THREE

Fred Naranjo

FRED
NARANJO

About Fred

My name is Fred Naranjo. I am a 1967 graduate of Carpinteria High School. I was born in Santa Maria, California, raised in Guadalupe, CA. My family and I moved to Carpinteria in 1962. Half a year at Carp Junior High, one full year at Carp High School, then moved to Santa Barbara. Attended high school there for one year then moved back to Carp in my junior year, then graduated in 1967. Right after high school, I went into the army, took my basic training at Fort Ord in California, then went on to Fort Polk in Louisiana. In this same year, I got the order for Vietnam, which is where I spent the next thirteen months. I was with the First Cav. When my time was up, I came back home then got assigned to Fort Hood, Texas (seven months). Next orders were to head out to Korea, assigned to the DMZ, after this tour I came back home and then assigned to Fort Carson, Colorado (one year). From there, I moved on to Germany (three years), best parties in my life! I was intrigued by the culture of Germany, took advantage of visiting places I knew I would never come back and see. I then came back to the States and was assigned to Fort Bliss, Texas. I was there for about a year and went back to Vietnam. This time around, I was not in a combat zone. After this trip, I came back to the States and went back to Fort Bliss, Texas. Next, I was shipped back to Germany for three more years. This time in Germany, I really loved it. I met many interesting people. Next trip after Germany was back to Korea. I enjoyed where I was stationed, a lot of Mexicans! I was then reassigned back to the States, to Fort Hood, Texas.

When I was in the service, I was in the infantry unit most of my tours. When I came back, I was on stateside duty, and I met a lot of interesting people and got into a lot of good, interesting fights. I had the option of staying in six more years to complete my twenty years or to get out. I chose to get out. It was no longer the same to me. In

1980, it was bittersweet. I was a free man out of the army, but also that year, my mother passed away.

When I got out of the army, I did nothing the first couple of months. I was then offered a job at AMPM on Casitas Pass Rd. in Carp. We would go hang out at The Palms, get drunk, and raise some hell. We would also go to Casa del Charro, which was owned by Joe Escarino. I worked at AMPM for about five years then moved on to work at the 76 Gas Station on Santa Monica. I worked there for twenty years. I quit there and moved on to work for Risdon 76. After this, I got tired of it and started at Vons Grocery Store. I decided I wanted to try somewhere else and transferred over to Gelson's in Santa Barbara. This was where I retired. Along the way, I had a daughter. She is the most precious thing in my life. With the life that I've lived, I wouldn't change *a thing*!

I met a lot of good people at Carp High School, along with a lot of jerk-offs. As the time went by, I did spend time in jail, got a few DUIs. That didn't stop me from living my best life. I just didn't want to listen to anybody who tried to tell me otherwise. I've had an interesting life. I've learned a lot as time went by; with the way I was to the people who really know me, I think they would agree that we *all learn as life goes on*. Now, as I am older, I can definitely say I got wiser and see things from a different perspective. I would like to thank Joe Lovett, Terri Galvez, and Cori Deaderick for putting this book together and to thank all the graduates from 1967.

CHAPTER FOUR

Brenda Stump

BRENDA
STUMP

Chapter of My Life

By Brenda Stump Duncan
Class of 1967

You know how many little girls love horses; well, I'm one of those little girls. During my sophomore year, my sisters and I were given a horse. Mr. Chan was an off-the-racetrack thoroughbred. I could not drive yet, so we would have to carry the Western saddle and tack from our house on Arbol Verde to the paddock next to the Standard Oil office on Carpinteria Ave. That saddle was very heavy, so we opted for a bareback saddle pad with no stirrups and a snaffle-bit bridle. I forgot to mention that we did not know how to ride at all. Chan at 16.2 hands tall at the shoulders. A hand is four inches, which made him 5'5" tall. We learned that we could cut through our neighbor Mark Campbell's yard then cross the nursery property, which made the walk shorter. Thank you, Mrs. Campbell. My sisters Marcia and Corinne Stump and I would ride/walk every day after school. One of us would ride while the others walked behind. We got our 10,000 steps in long before it became popular.

I remember Dad, Joe Stump, getting phone calls late at night from someone at the Fosters Freeze, telling Dad that our horse was wandering Carpinteria Ave. The patrons would make a human chain across the street to corral him until Dad could round him up and take him home.

I remember one winter it rained and rained and rained. The paddock was knee deep in mud. Thoroughbreds are very thin-skinned and chill easily, so Mother brought Chan home to live in the garage for a while. That was a great joy until we realized that we had to muck the garage daily.

I moved away to start my own ranch after graduation. It was thirteen miles north of San Miguel, CA. We had to have a water well dug, needed a generator for power, and had no phone service. My nearest neighbor was two miles away. I was conditioning myself for the COVID-19 back then and didn't know it. LOL

The winter of 1968–'69 was terrible. I remember the beginning of that winter very clearly to this day. The day started off quiet, with rain in the forecast. In the afternoon from my front yard, it was clear skies, but to the east over many rolling hills toward Parkfield, I saw massive black clouds hang over the hill and could hear a great orchestra of thunder and lightning. This was a very rare occurrence. Not too many minutes later, I heard what sounded like a street sweeper coming down the country dirt road at the bottom of our knoll. It was a sheet of water two or three inches high, covering the whole width of the road, followed by another wave of water on top of the first, then a third wave. I took off for the barn to lock up the horses, put away the chicken, and look for the dogs and cat. Armageddon must be on its way. That was the beginning of four 100-year storms. The storms wiped out the San Miguel bridge; the county road had ruts six feet deep. The ranchers tried to bulldoze the road to keep them open, but they were running out of options. The paved river road had wasted out above our place and below, stranding several families.

Easter Sunday 1969, another 100-year storm was predicted. If that happened, all the roads would be gone. Our nearest neighbor would send a message to his brother who lived across the dry creek from his ranch, now a raging river 1/4 mile wide, to ride his horse over the foothills toward Highway 101 to Camp Robert to get a helicopter to rescue all the neighbors. I was three months pregnant.

After four years, I started a new chapter in my life and moved back to Carpinteria and Santa Barbara with my daughter, Libby, who has cerebral palsy and is allergic to all pets. That was the end of my horse dream for a while.

My love for horses never died. Fast-forward thirty-eight years and you'll find me in Suisun City, California. Suisun, meaning west wind, is halfway between San Francisco and Sacramento. Suisun has many acres of open spaces. One afternoon on a drive, we followed Grizzly Island Road out to Rush Ranch, a Solano Land Trust property of 2,070 acres. The ranch was built 125 years ago. Flat-bottom boats would sail up the slough to load up hay and grain for the horses in San Francisco.

We learned that a program directed by Michael Muir, great-grandson of John Muir, ran Access Adventure, an all-volunteers 501C-3 program that enriches the lives of people with disabilities and other underserved members of the community by providing outdoor recreation, open space access, education and therapy, through a working partnership with horses. Our trolley seat 12 or using the hydraulic lift we can seat five power wheelchairs. We are also training the disabled to drive and compete in horse-driven events such as cones, marathon, and dressage. Stefanie Putnam, an international driver, was introduced to drive by Access Adventure.

We have met the most wonderful people throughout our service to the physically and mentally challenged. To watch a visually challenged person see a horse with their hands for the first time is awesome. We have traveled near and far, visiting Ronald McDonald Homes, veterans' homes, and care homes, bringing back old memories and new joys to our riders. Michael breeds horses, Stonewall Sporthorse, as part of our fundraising efforts. I have learned how to drive a team of draft horses, breed mares, deliver foals, and help train the foal to drive and ride. I'm still involved with Access Adventure and invite you to check out our website Access-Adventure.org.

Brenda Stump, 5 years old

Brenda Stump

Brenda Stump

Brenda Stump

CHAPTER FIVE

Thais Meyer

THAIS
MEYER

Thais Meyer

Who would have thought that a southern California girl from the "safest beach in the world," Carpinteria, who had never been around cold temperatures, snow, or icy roads other than a one-day senior snow trip, would fall in love with Alaska and its people? But that is exactly what happened to this beach-going, sun-loving '60s girl.

My dad had always been in the Oil Patch, and we moved many times during my growing up years. He had worked all over the world. And so it was that he and mom found themselves living in Kenai, Alaska. I was living with my sister in Oxnard the summer of 1967 after high school graduation. I had decided it would be fun to visit them for the holidays, all the time expecting I'd return to California in January 1968.

My cousin (by marriage) Linda rode with me for the drive from California to Seattle and flight from Seattle to Anchorage. We were met at the airport in Anchorage by my mom, who was beside herself to have her eighteen-year-old daughter back under her thumb.

It was snowing and blowing when the Western Airlines plane from Seattle landed at the Anchorage International Airport that November night. I was dressed for success at the time of Sunday best for air travel in November 1967. My legs and feet were frozen walking from the plane to the terminal. But I was so excited to be somewhere I'd never been before.

Kenai reminded me a lot of Carpinteria. It was a small town and everyone knew everyone else. Doors were never locked, and neighbors ate dinner with each other. I spent about a year and a half in Kenai and made some lifelong friends. We still talk and get together to this day.

Then in late 1968, my dad, Gil Meyer, was assigned to Singapore, where he was to supervise the building of the first ship-style mobile oil-drilling rig. He and mom (Wanda but everyone called her Mickey) moved to Singapore, and I became a resident of Anchorage. I worked downtown in the offices in the offices of Western Offshore Drilling and Exploration Company in the Frank Cool Building. My job was pretty much being a gopher: go for this and go for that. I'd do whatever needed to be done, at times going to the Anchorage International Airport to either pick or send out a package by air. During those many trips to the airport, I met Marion Lay. She was the base director of stewardesses for Western Airlines. She asked me one time if I'd ever thought about being a stewardess. To be honest, the thought never crossed my mind. But it sounded like fun. After weighing and measuring me (there were strict guidelines at the time), she asked for my address.

It wasn't too long that I received a letter and ticket from Western Airlines. I was to travel to Los Angeles for an interview. I wasn't offered a position at that time. My hips were 1/2 inch above the limit for my height. However, I ran into Marion again at the airport soon after, and I was on my way to another interview in Los Angeles. This time, I was offered a job and set up for training class. My hips must have gotten smaller. Ha ha.

It was the golden years of airline travel. I certainly was one of the lucky ones. But after training finished, it was announced that Western was closing the crew base in Anchorage. I left Western Airlines to return to Alaska. I was homesick and had a boyfriend I didn't think life was possible without. Ha ha.

A friend, Frank Cook, went to the Anchorage Athletic Club every day and knew Robert Reeve, who was founder of a family-owned airline called Reeve Aleutian Airways. He told him about me and Mr. Reeve told Frank to send me down to the Reeve Aleutian Airways Dispatch office near the airport and talk to his daughter Janice Reeve. Janice interviewed me and hired me as a stewardess with Reeve Aleutian Airways. I'd not even heard of this airline, nor did I know where they flew, or what the Aleutians were. Boy, did I learn fast.

The Aleutian Islands are a chain of small islands that separate the Bering Sea to the north from the Pacific Ocean to the south. They extend about 1,100 miles in an arc southwest, then northwest from the Alaska Peninsula to Attu Island. They are part of the circum-Pacific chain of volcanoes (often called the ring of fire). They were a factor in WWII when the Japanese landed on Attu in an effort to distract American forces away from Midway. The Aleutian Chain is the only site of combat on American soil during WWII. Its weather is uniform most of the year: high winds (thus the name Birthplace of the Winds), heavy precipitation, persistent fog. The shore is almost completely devoid of trees, the rocky shoreline rising abruptly to steep bold mountains.

Reeve Aleutian Airways was the only commercial airline to serve the Aleutians. Once leaving the villages of the Alaska Peninsula, the islands were site of different military forces. Most carried from the end of WWII as Alaska's strategic location became clear.

My first training flight after ground school was with Janice Reeve Ogle. She was the chief stewardess for the family-owned airline. She would become my sister-in-law in 1971 when I married her brother Whitham (Whitty) Reeve. She told me to meet her at the Dispatch Quonset on International Road at 6:00 a.m. We took the crew van to the aircraft sitting on the tarmac. I looked at the DC-6 and tried not to look surprised. It wasn't a jet; it had four propeller engines. The DC-6 would become one of my favorites to work. It was roomy, had overhead racks (not compartments), and heated floors. Oh, they felt so good in the cold wet wind of Aleutians. We went to Adak that day, with a stop in Cold Bay. Then we returned to Anchorage, with another stop in Cold Bay. We served a hot meal and drinks but *no alcohol*. Mr. Reeve would never agree to alcohol on his flights at that time. He didn't want "his girls" to have to deal with an intoxicated passenger. It was so fun, very different than I had expected.

Reeve Aleutian Airways also flew L-188 Electras (turboprop) and DC-3s. They were the last to fly the DC-3 on a commercial airline flight schedule. These were my favorite trips, three-day milk runs out the chain. One stewardess not only served the passengers in flight but also acted as station agent on the ground. There were several villages on DC-3 flights that didn't have airport facilities or station managers. The stewardess would make out airwaybills for freight, write tickets, and collect money for airfares, also make out

the manifest and weight and balance. All within a short ground time
of fifteen to thirty minutes. I would lower the door, which was also
the stairs, then lean out and yell to the crowd of people standing on
the gravel. I'd get the passengers separated from the ones with freight
to ship. Get the paperwork done, passengers loaded, and be on our
way. I would stand up in front of the twenty-six seats, which were on
an incline because the DC-3 was a tail dragger to give (yell, there was
no microphone) the before-flight briefing. We would stay overnight
in Cold Bay the first night and Dutch Harbor the second night. On
the third day, we would head back to Anchorage, making stops along
the way. These trips were scheduled for three days but could go on
for a week. It all depended on the weather. It was great fun, and I was
one of the lucky ones to experience passenger flights in aircraft that
would soon be retired from passenger routes.

I flew for Reeve for five years. Before I left, YS-11s were brought
into the fleet. My sister-in-law Janice and I did the Federal Aviation
Administration certification evacuation, which would allow RAA
to operate the aircraft commercially. Janice and I even set a record
for the evacuation of a full load of passengers. It was great fun, and
I enjoyed working for such a great company. But my marriage to
Whitham Reeve ended in late 1973. I felt it was only right that I leave.
I was asked to stay by Robert Reeve and by Janice. In fact, we all
remained friends. Even Whitty and I were close friends and still are.

When Western Airlines closed their crew base in Anchorage,
Marion Lay left Western Airlines and became chief stewardess for
Wien Air Alaska, another great family-owned airline. I made a phone
call to Marion and asked her if Wien would be hiring flight attendants
soon. She said, "Meet me at the Fancy Moose [a local bar] right
now." I did and brought with me my good friend and fellow Reeve
Aleutian stewardess Melody (Imelda) Larson (now Burton). Melody
had decided after hearing my plans that she would like a change too.
We walked in, sat down, and waited for Marion. She arrived a few
minutes later and tossed a couple of applications on the table and
said, "You're hired." Melody and I were both excited to start our new
adventure. Our training class began March 18, 1974.

After about a month of ground school training, we were flight attendants for Wien Air Alaska. We were given our wings at a ceremony. Because Melody and I had hopped straight over from Reeve Aleutian, we were put on the flight line immediately. The other in the class would go through several onboard training flights.

Working for Wien was the same as working for Reeve in many aspects and different in some as well. Same family atmosphere, we were a family of employees. Wien's flight network covered most of Alaska, except for the Aleutian Chain. We worked on mainly Boeing 737s, but we also had the two-day milk run with a twin turboprop F-27/F-227. All the aircraft could have any combination of cargo and passengers. Only one flight attendant was needed on the F-27/F-277, and from one (for twenty-six passengers) to three for a full load of passenger seats on the B-737.

It was great fun. One flight, Melody and I were working from Nome down to Fairbanks. Captain Ace Dodson was in command. We took off from Nome and lost all the hydraulics. The flaps and landing gear were down (for takeoff lift) and we would be flying dirty all the way to Fairbanks. An hour flight would take more than two hours. We were going to be low on fuel and perhaps need to make a landing at a small airstrip somewhere along the way. The cockpit crew was busy assessing and planning for what might be an emergency landing. The problem wasn't landing at a small airstrip; it would be trying to take off without much length. We made it to Fairbanks, landed safely, and then promptly ran out of fuel on the tarmac. We had to be towed to the gate. However, we all breathed a sigh of relief.

In the late 1970s, Wein expanded their route map to the Lower 48, or the Continental States. We opened a crew base in Seattle. We were now flying to Salt Lake, Portland, Reno, Albuquerque, Phoenix, and Denver out of Seattle. I transferred to Seattle. Seattle was and is my favorite city. I lived in a condo I'd bought a few years before in Tukwila. But again, my heart was in Alaska. Soon another flight attendant in Anchorage asked me to switch bases with her. I went back to Anchorage.

During that time of airline mergers, bankruptcies, and corporate raiders, a new owner borrowed money from the corporations in Alaska with the promise of keeping the airline in business. This new owner started selling off the airports and facilities, and he literally sold all the assets until the airline was declared bankrupt. The employees found out we would be jobless on the local TV news in November 1984 after flying for fourteen and a half years. The greed of one man had put countless Alaskans out of work and left a void for air and freight service to the people of Alaska. It was devastating. There were attempts to bring Wien back. We picked up Bureau of Land Management charters out of Boise, Idaho, flying firefighters across the country the summer of 1985. Flew gambling charters out of Oakland, California, to Reno in the fall. But in the end, Wien was gone.

To this day in 2020, the Wien Air Alaska family of employees gets together for reunions. The last one was a few years ago. They are always held in Anchorage or Phoenix and are always well attended.

During this time, I planned on moving back to California. My parents had moved to Santa Paula, California, during Dad's last few years working in the oil patch with Atlantic Richfield. He was superintendent of offshore drilling, and his office was in Santa Barbara. I was the only one in Alaska by that time. Just before I put my home in Anchorage on the market, Janice Reeve (Ogle) came by. She wanted me to come back to work for Reeve Aleutian. They were adding to their route schedule and buying B-727s. They would operate flights out of Anchorage to Russia. It sounded great but I hesitated. I was thirty-eight. Did I want to take a chance of the same thing happening to Reeve as happened to Wien? Deregulation was having a devastating effect on airlines. They were dropping like flies. I decided that my flying career was over. I'd loved it and never considered it work, met people and made friendships that would last a lifetime. My flying years were during the golden days of aviation, when customer service was a priority. The passengers of that time weren't really aware that stewardesses/flight attendants were required in the cabin by the Federal Aviation Administration to evacuate the aircraft in an emergency. We received rigorous training with yearly recurrent classes on safety. Instead, the airlines competed with in-flight service. First class and coach were promised to be heaven on earth. Typically, it was!

So to Santa Paula I came. At first it was difficult. What kind of job could I apply for? I'd never gone to college, but had worked since my high school days. I decided to go to what I knew best, the aviation industry. I applied for ticket agent at Horizon Air. I was now working for Horizon Air, and when Horizon closed their counter in Oxnard, I transferred to Southwest Airlines as a ticket agent at the Oxnard Airport. I had taken the Civil Service Employment test months before and passed. There was a hiring freeze during that time. But a few months later, I received a call from Point Mugu NAS with a job offer in the Administration Office of Supply, thus my Civil Service career.

In 1987, I met Steve Beshirs. We were neighbors in Santa Paula. Our little compound was made up of seven houses, which were rentals owned by my cousin Terry's wife Bethene's parents. We started dating and were married January 30, 1988. We were married on the top of South Mountain, which is the south side of Santa Paula. We and some friends rode our horses to the top of the mountain on old Union Oil dirt roads. Some family along with friends made the drive up the mountain. The preacher was a good sport and sat on the horse we'd brought with us to marry us. It was a hoot. We rode back down to a small reception in the loft of the local Mexican restaurant La Cabana.

We took a trip to Idaho the next winter and made the decision to buy a home and relocate to Emmett, Idaho. This is where our daughter Cara was born in May 1991 at St. Luke's Hospital in Boise. I was one week from my forty-second birthday. She was and is the best gift I've ever been given. I didn't have a clue about how to care for an infant. I worked for the US Forest Service Emmett Ranger District of the Boise National Forest. Outside of flying, it was my favorite job. My job title was information officer. Rented cabins, sold Christmas tree permits, firewood permits, etc. And in the spring, the parks ranger and I would take our horses up to ride and open the hiking trails. It was great fun and some wonderful people to work with.

My husband Steve was still working in California as an ironworker. He would work a couple of months them come home for a while. But with Cara on board, we wanted to be together. We moved back to California, this time to Bakersfield. We bought a little house out in Rosedale, and I worked for the Veterans Administration. We enjoyed our time there but worried about raising Cara in the city. We decided to follow Steve's cousin and wife to a small town in northeast Texas. The community was called Rosewood. It was *hot* in the summer, which was from anytime in May till October. Humidity was at the drip stage, 100 percent usually. The Piney Woods was beautiful: rolling hills covered with trees, farmland, and cattle.

Cara was two years old, and she would start and finish her K–12 school years at the Harmony ISD about a mile from our house. She was active in everything: volleyball, softball, cheerleading, Honor Society, Student Council, FFA, and FCA (Fellowship of Christian Athletes). She kept us busy, and although she didn't keep us young (laughing), she gave our lives a new and deeper meaning. After high school, she went to college and graduated with her degree in Nursing/ RN. She works in pediatrics, which she loves. And us? We are just so proud of her.

The heat and humidity were too much for us old folks. We are back on the West Coast, right where we started in Santa Paula. We love the climate and being near friends and family, except Cara, of course.

Carpinteria is just up the road a few miles. There are walks on the beach or the bluffs, burgers at The Spot, dinners at the Palms, and get-togethers with long-ago classmates who are my forever friends. It's been a wild and crazy ride, but I wouldn't change it for anything.

Thais Meyer & Joanne Hinson after
Homecoming Parade 1966.

Thais in Reeve Aleutian Airways uniform 1969.

Anchorage Int'l Airport on the stairs of a Wien Air Alaska B-737 with Ray Peterson,
President WAA,Thais Meyer, & Rita Maser celebrating 50 years of service to Alaskans, 1974.

CHAPTER SIX

Cori Deaderick

CORI
DEADERICK

Memories

Just like the song "Memories," I do believe they are pressed between the pages of our minds. Some may return and some chose not to return.

On July 25, 1949, I was born Corinne Lee Deaderick in Flagstaff, Arizona. My dad was working for his Uncle Jim selling earthmoving equipment (John Deere tractors). My dad loved Flagstaff and the four seasons, but my mom wasn't too keen on the winters there with a baby. She would hang my diapers on the clothesline, and they would freeze and come back and slap her in the face. No dryers back then. So after plenty of thought, my dad asked my Uncle Jim if he could have the same job in the San Diego location, and we were soon on our way back to California.

My parents bought a new home not far from San Diego State University. About a year after we moved in, my sister Allison was born nine days before my third birthday. On that birthday, I got a John Deere tractor instead of a tricycle, and I loved that tractor!

I went to kindergarten and first grade at Montezuma Elementary School, and after I finished first grade, my parents started looking for a bigger house and maybe one closer to where my dad worked. They rented a house for the next year, and I ended up in another school named Stephen Foster Elementary. I only went to second grade there, and I remember becoming a Brownie and loved wearing the uniform to school and selling the Girl Scout cookies. I even had it on the day of our school pictures.

One of the biggest memories I have living there was I got the measles, and after going to the doctor, the next morning I woke up with a "QUARANTINE" sign on my bedroom window, which faced the street. Only people that had measles could come into the house.

Soon my parents found a new house that was just being finished in the town of Fletcher Hills not far from El Cajon. It was kind of *Country Life* there: no big town that I can remember, just a large shopping center, a gas station on the corner of the street that went up to our house, and a drugstore down on Fletcher Parkway. I remember getting a black Hula-Hoop with a yellow stripe at the gas station when my dad filled up his El Camino during the Hula-Hoop craze!

That summer, I turned eight and my sister turned five, and we moved into the new house, which was big. It had three bedrooms, *two* bathrooms, and a basement that was not finished.

Our backyard was a *big* canyon with no fence, lots of tumbleweeds, cactus, tarantulas, and *yes*, of course *rattlesnakes* along with the other kinds of snakes! My dad gave us a good schooling on what the different snakes looked like. We would occasionally find a snake sunning themselves under our swing set, but most of those were king or garter snakes.

Our first Christmas in the new house was amazing. My mom and dad picked three huge tumbleweeds that were graduated in size and spray painted them white. Dad put a post into the ground and slipped the painted tumbleweeds over it and made a snowman. He also made a hat out of tar paper, and the rest of Frosty was up to my mom. He was about eight feet tall when he was finished, and my dad put a spotlight on him. Soon, lots of people were driving by at night to see him. He was cool!

In third, fourth, and fifth grade, I attended Fletcher Hills Elementary. I loved that school! We learned to memorize plays and usually performed them around a holiday. They also had a great music program with an instrument we learned to play called a Flute-O-Phone! My grandkids call it a recorder. I still recall some of the songs we learned to play from our songbook.

Of course, the playground was the best time ever! The swings, the bars where we hung by our knees and would turn over and over again on one or both knees, then there was the Dead Man's Drop and the rings we would climb through with shorts under our dresses so no one would see our panties! Then there was the best game of all: chase, when boys would chase their favorite girl! I had one of those special boys that chased me all the time. I think he got in trouble from my third grade teacher a few times. I do have a scar on my right knee where I fell on a rock while he was chasing me. It left a scar that now when I look at it, those memories of that special boy, Jeff Brown, come back like yesterday.

One Saturday night, we had a scary thing happen. Our family went to the drive-in movie theater, and when we got home, my dad pulled into the driveway next to his El Camino. When the car lights shone on the garage door, my dad saw a small hole in the door. He got out of the car to check it out, and when he opened the door, he found a bullet casing on the floor of the garage. He looked at the location of it and measured it to the car, and if we were home, it would have hit the gas tank! The police came to check it out in the morning, and if my memory serves me correctly, my dad mentioned to the policeman that there was a man at work that he had problems with. It was something about being part of his Uncle Jim's family business and they didn't get along. Nothing ever came of the bullet incident again, but my dad wasn't happy at work anymore; looking back, he seemed depressed.

About a couple months later, I came home from school to see my dad being ushered into his father's car by my Uncle Moe, his brother. I ran to see what was going on, and my dad kissed me and told me to go in the house and he'd be back soon.

I went into the house and saw my mom sitting on the floor by an antique chair she was recovering, and she was crying. All she told me was, Daddy was sick and Grandpa and Uncle Moe were taking him to the hospital to get better! I was too scared to ask any more questions.

In a week or so, my mom got a job working for my friend Sherry's dad, who was a doctor. Next thing I know, my mom's sister and her family of four children were moving in with us to help my mom with the house. I didn't know then, but there were payments to be made. My Uncle Tex turned our garage into a bedroom for all of us four girls, and the two boys got my room. When the lights were out, I could see light through the bullet hole, and I sometimes worried that another bullet might come through the door again. I think we stuck ABC gum in the hole.

I later heard my mom tell my aunt that my dad had suffered a nervous breakdown. Finally, in the summer after fourth grade, my dad came home to visit, and I could tell he didn't like the changes to *his* nice new house.

Dad ate lunch with us, and he told us he wanted to sell our house and move to Carpinteria, where my grandparents lived. I got sad thinking about going to another new school! Soon the house was up for sale! There was a couple that lived down the hill from us that wanted to trade houses and some money for ours, and the realtor agreed it was a good deal.

After the move and holidays were over, my mom put the house up for sale. It sold quickly, so by the time escrow closed, Allison and I had about seven to eight weeks left of school. I couldn't even finish fifth grade, and I was bummed.

On a Saturday morning, the moving van showed up and was packed by noon and headed to Carpinteria. Now it was time to load the car. We had a bird, cat, and dog to get ready for the trip. I did have some friends on my grandparents' street because my sister and I and some cousins used to stay with them for two weeks every summer— Rodney Browning, his sisters, Gary Sanders, and Janet Daniel, who moved after sixth grade.

Just as we were finished packing, a car pulled up to our house, and Jeff Brown, the special boy who chased me, got out of his car and brought me apples for the trip and to say goodbye. I was sad and said, "Thank you," and we talked for a few minutes in our garage. He started toward his car; all of a sudden, he came running back and kind of slid into our garage toward me in his Wallaby shoes, kissed me on the cheek and said, "*I love you*," ran off and got in his car. And we got in ours and we watched each other drive away and I started to cry, thinking I would never see or hear from him again. But I did see him again our senior year. He called me, and he was in Santa Barbara, participating at UCSB in a speech-and-debate team event for his high school. We reconnected about eighteen years ago via Classmates and now email and text all the time. We laugh about the apples he brought that last day!

It was about a 4 1/2 hour trip to Carpinteria, and I couldn't wait to see my dad again. We moved into my great-grandma's house while she was recuperating from a broken hip in a nursing home. When she got better, we moved out to the family ranch on Foothill Rd. Ten acres of lemons and avocados was a great time for us. We played hide-and-go-seek at the cemetery at night and rode our pony during the day.

On Monday, my mom took us to Aliso School to register, and when we went into the office, she knew the principal, Mr. Slocum, from Santa Barbara High School. He then took Allison and me to our classes. I remember when the door opened, I saw Jory Small, Thais Meyer, Victor de la Cruz, Larry George, and others, but I had never seen a Hispanic person *ever*! I was a little scared! I do remember being very far ahead of the class, so I got extra work from the teacher. The one thing Aliso School had that we didn't have in Fletcher Hill was the Junior Olympics, and Jory Small and I loved those dashes, the 50-, 75-, and 100-yard. I also loved the pull-up or chin-up bars, whichever you call them. I even beat the boys by one pull-up, 16 to 15! I believe the next week was the last week of school for summer vacation and then it was on to Canalino School for sixth grade.

At Canalino, I met the friends that would go on to junior high school and high school with me. One thing I remember in sixth grade was Tommy DeAlba taught me how to throw a football at recess! I bet he doesn't remember that!

During seventh grade, Jack Moyer asked me to go *steady* and gave me a green-and-white St. Christopher, which I still have. We had an English teacher, Ms. Carmichael, whom my grandpa told me that he dated, and she taught my parents at Santa Barbara High. At the end of seventh grade, I tried out for cheerleader, and I actually made head cheerleader along with some of my best friends. Not long after that, it seemed like we were in high school. I had a boyfriend, Bobby, in eighth grade throughout ninth grade. My girlfriend Colleen Olszewski dated Bobby's brother Ralph, and we were lucky enough to see the Beach Boys at the Roller Gardens in Oxnard at a Battle of the Bands. It was so much fun!

Then Colleen and I were invited to go to Lake Nacimiento with the Walshes. That was a blast, learning how to double ski. I never forgot how.

At the end of ninth grade, Colleen and I tried out for junior varsity cheerleader; only three could make it, with an alternate. I was lucky to make head cheerleader again, and the other two were Colleen and Peggy Puentas.

Then my junior year, the principal decided we needed some song leaders for the first time at Carpinteria High. I made that squad too, along with Terry Galvez, Wendy Bliss, Linda Pino, Silvia Medel, and Reynae Pearson. That was a lot of fun and different from the cheerleading.

My senior year I didn't try out for anything. I took Work Experience and got out of school at noon and worked for Dr. Prather, the local eye doctor, which set me on my path to business college.

I had a couple of boyfriends in high school that were kind of serious at the time. One was G. G. Colson my sophomore year, and he went into the navy when he graduated in '65. My junior year I dated John Opple, and after he graduated in '66, he left for the summer with Don Chrisenberry to work at some lake. We kept in touch, and unfortunately, after they carne home to go to college, John and Don were in a tragic car accident and neither survived.

Then I met a nice young man, Allen Pinoli, my senior year. He worked in the refrigeration and heating trade for a big company in Santa Barbara. I had met him working at my dad's gas station. We dated my senior year and through that summer, and I knew he was *the one*. We became engaged in August, and I started business college in the fall along with JoAnn Hinson. Allen and I talked about when we wanted to get married, and the draft came calling even though Allen had surgery on both elbows at thirteen or fourteen years old and he was considered 1Y not 4F it meant (in case of a national emergency). We decided to get married in Las Vegas to speed things up to avoid Vietnam then I found out I was pregnant and the draft left us alone after a letter from my doctor. In May of 1968, we had our first daughter and we named her Stacy.

Two weeks after Stacy was born, Allen and I went to have dinner with my parents. Wow, did I get a surprise! After twenty-one years of marriage, my mom left my dad and took everything but the den furniture. I didn't know where my mom was for three months, and she finally showed up at our apartment to see Stacy and we learned she was now with Jim Moore, Terri and Matt's dad. They soon married, and Terri and Matt became stepsister and stepbrother to Allison and me.

Allen's parents owned some apartments, and we lived in one for two years and then we bought our own house. In August of '71, we had our second daughter, Sally. Then Allen and I started Pinoli's Refrigeration/Heating & AC in 1974.

Then one day Allen bought a boat and only *one* single ski and vests for everyone to use. Our first trip was to Lake Shasta, and we took our teenage neighbor Robin and her friend to help with the girls. Oh what a trip that was!

Allen didn't know how to ski, and I only had skied twice: once when Bobby taught me and once in Mission Bay in San Diego. I was now twenty-two, trying to remember what Bobby taught me at fourteen on double skis, not one. I did remember that we were all skiing by the end of the first day but, Allen ended up with a bruise on the inside of his thigh from doing a *cartwheel* in the air while turning as he yelled at me to straighten out the boat. I can still see him in the air to this day. We had the normal fights at the launch ramp like most couples do, and it got real *old*! We had the boat for a few years and then I found out I was pregnant again, so we decided to sell it.

On December 17, 1975, we had our third daughter, Shelly. There was four years in between her and Sally, and there was no way I was going to have one baby at home with no one to play with while the other two were in school. And three is *always* a crowd anyway. So after reading a magazine article on how to choose the sex of your child, I decided to try it and see if it worked, not telling Allen what I did and I don't think I ever did! Not long after my experiment, I found out I was pregnant; of course, he was a little *heated*!

Then in August of 1975, we lost Allen's dad Primo to cancer at fifty-five, and the last thing he said to me was "I'll never see the baby." I said, *"Yes, you will!"* He died the next week! I knew then the baby was a boy! I knew God would replace what he had taken from us.

On December 15, 1976, the doctor sent me to the hospital seven weeks early, and one hour after checking in, our *son* was born at 4 lb. 5oz. The experiment worked! We named him Allen Primo after his grandpa. Small but healthy and came home Christmas Day! Allen was ecstatic to say the least. I just found out that Shelly and Allen are called Irish twins because of being the same age for two days. We added onto our house and lived here for two more years and decided a change of pace would be good for the kids.

In 1979, we bought a home in the Santa Ynez Valley, where schools were smaller and life was a little slower than Santa Barbara. By this time, Stacy was nine, Sally six, Shelly three, and Allen two, a great time to move. A big house on 1 1/4 acres.

The kids soon joined 4-H, raising animals to show at the fair. We bought a Shetland pony and he was a stubborn old boy. Then we were given a beautiful paint horse named Lightning because he had a lightning bolt on his side, and the pony was sold. Stacy and Sally loved Lightning and rode him every day and in our little parades. And *yes*, my kids became Pirates!

It was about this time we all lost Grandpa Jim (Terri and Matt's dad) to kidney disease at fifty-two. It was so sad, especially for the kids; he was the best grandpa *ever*!

I thought life was good. The business was doing *fantastic*, and Allen had bought another refrigeration business in Solvang from a good friend of ours. Stacy was graduating eighth grade, Sally was going into sixth grade, Shelly was going into first grade, and Allen into kindergarten, and Cori was doing a lot of cooking and laundry!

I stayed with Allen for three more years trying to make it work and to figure out what I was going to do if it didn't. Allen and I were invited to a big wedding and Allen was deer hunting (of course), so I took the kids. After dinner, I took the kids home.

After returning to the wedding a nice young man (Scot) came up to and told me he would like to buy me a beer if I could teach him how to Swing Dance. I said, "Sure!" So we danced and he didn't need much teaching.

I kept seeing Scot in the strangest places after the wedding. He showed up at the acre next door to our house and told me he owned it and was going to start building a house in the next year or so. He is a cabinetmaker by trade and had been building spec houses around town.

Again, Allen was off hunting, and Scot showed up to his property on a Saturday morning as I was loading dolls and other things that I made as a hobby into Allen's El Camino to sell at Los Olivos Day in the Country. He offered to help me load some boxes, and I thought that was nice. At the end of the day and all packed up in Los Olivos, I went to buy a beer to sit with friends and visit, and there he was again. He bought me a beer and we talked. Of course, I was flattered by the attention. I finally asked how old he was and he said, "Twenty-two." I almost choked my beer. He looked at least thirty with a mature mustache. I volunteered my age (thirty-six) to scare him, but it didn't faze him. If the phrase was around back then, I would have been called *a cougar*.

I took Stacy's job cleaning motel rooms when she went to City College. Allen wasn't pleased, but I had to start working somewhere. The kids were now the ages that it would be easier to manage after a divorce with school etc. It was now time to serve Allen with divorce papers! Then I started cleaning houses too, and one of the houses belonged to the man that invented the Hula-Hoop! He also invented the roll-on deodorant and the soaker hose.

I got a call from my dentist's secretary about a job opening with the local orthodontist. I had an interview and got the job. It was only one day a week and later another day. After I told people where I worked, there became more patients. So as a thank you, he put braces on Allen for free. I loved that work, but after three years, he started to retire and only needed one girl.

I started selling my handmade dolls in a local drugstore and to a Craft House Party Business. Then I was asked to make wedding gowns and the wedding party's gowns; that soon became a job. When the time came for all my daughter's weddings, I was blessed that they wanted me to make their gowns and the wedding party dresses.

Allen remained with another woman in 1986 after our divorce was final. Sally decided to live with him after he offered her a car. I still was seeing Scot, and after about a year, he moved in with me and we married eight years later.

I got a job as a secretary for a friend of Scot's and worked for him for about eighteen months until I went to a chiropractor and he broke my neck. I had to have surgery, and after two years, I found another orthodontist to work for. Then I needed a second surgery on my neck in 1996, so I had to quit my job.

In 1998, I now had four grandchildren and Scot and I opened a coffee shop in Solvang. We had the shop for five years until I got sick from black mold in the building so the owners bought us out of our lease and changed the name of the hotel where our coffee shop was.

In 2007, daughter Shelly had another son and Sally three days later had a set of identical twin girls and my son Allen got married at the age of thirty. My oldest daughter Stacy married Chris Ames from Summerland, a nephew of Gilbert Ames, who graduated from Carp in 1965. I now had seven grandkids. I did a lot of babysitting and staying with Sally and the twins because her husband is a stuntman and would be gone on movies for months at a time. He was famous for driving and jumping the General Lee on *The Dukes of Hazzard* and many other driving stunts in movies, like *The Fast and the Furious* movies. Sally became a stunt driver also and did some television commercials.

In 2008, Allen and his wife welcomed my eighth grandchild, a little girl, Presley. I now had another grandbaby to watch when her mom went back to work. Then three years later, Allen and Cammy had a little boy, Allen Jr. He is my ninth grandchild and the last. I am so fortunate to have all my children and grandchildren living around me, and I can see them any time.

This now brings me to Labor Day Weekend 2013. Scot and I had taken my daughter Shelly, her son Tucker, and a friend to Lake Nacimiento to waterski and to teach Tucker how to kneeboard. I hadn't skied or taught anyone to kneeboard in years and I was now sixty-four with arthritis in my hands, and Tucker was begging me to go first! I jumped in the water and looked at the boat, wondering how in *the hell* I was going to get back in! Ha! Then Scot threw the rope and ski, and after two tries, I got up and it was great. Tucker was so excited. Then he got in the water with me and the kneeboard. I showed him what to do, and off he went. He now surfs, so we need to go visit brother Matt. Everyone had a blast skiing.

Scot came home from work on Tuesday, cracked open a beer, and started watering his garden, and the neighbor boy came to get paid for feeding our animals. Scot went into the garage to get the money out of his truck and didn't come back. I went looking for him, and he was on the floor, trying to get up. I looked at him, and the left side of his face was sagging. I made him get in the car and it took me two minutes to get to the hospital. He had a massive stroke on the right side of the brain and paralysis on the left side. He was in the ICU for twenty-one days. Then he was in rehab facilities before he came home.

On Scot's first weekend home, I got a phone call from Joe Lovett, whom I hadn't seen since graduation, and he was coming down my way and wanted me to get him a room in Solvang so we could get together. What a great weekend that was, and it took the stress of Scot being home from the rehab hospital for me. I even called my sister Allison (who was Joe's girlfriend our senior year) to come over and didn't tell her Joe was at my house. When she realized who he was, she was so shocked. It was a nice reunion!

Five months later, Scot had to have brain surgery, and about three years after that, I realized our marriage was never going to be the same as we had grown apart. So after thirty years, we were divorced, but we're still close. I moved in with my daughter Shelly and waited for an apartment complex to be finished in Santa Ynez, where I now live and love it!

I now have a great-grandson from my oldest grandson. Kelsea is expecting my first great-granddaughter in July, and her husband is also in the army. Kelsea has a sister who is engaged also to a young man in the army.

Three generations

1983 with kids

Thirteen years old, junior high

Cory's dad Jack
1946 Wake Is.

CHAPTER SEVEN

Bernie Baker

BERNIE
BAKER

Bernie Baker

My stepson Kalani just turned twenty last week, and we were talking about his life *now* vs. my life when I turned twenty-four and had left Carpinteria for Hawaii. I had a great job (what now seems like an eternal lifestyle) and all the joys of growing up surrounded by the sport of surfing. I asked him what his best class in high school was as I was going to write this piece with the same thoughts. His was language arts, here at our local charter high school (thank you, Mr. Glasser at HTA). Back at the old Carp. High, mine was a mishmash of English, journalism, and Mr. Dowling's print/photo classes (industrial arts?). *Those* classes alone guided me through high school, into two years more of journalism at SBCC and on to my future "career" as a staff writer and senior photographer at *Surfer* magazine with a position that, if last issue's masthead holds correct, I still maintain, minus the salary!

I had already taken my writing skills from those classes plus some goofy, natural ability to jot down notes and construct a proper sentence and sent out a couple of stories surrounding surfing in our area, and I found myself published almost instantly. I remember Lorenzo, our mailman in Concha Loma, bringing me the envelope with my first buyout check for a photo, with no words: $25! I didn't even have a checking account; my mom had to deposit it into hers. A new Volkswagen Bug was around $3,000 and I think gas was around twenty cents a gallon back them. That check was like a thousand bucks to a junior in high school, but that's where and how it all started: a single shot I had taken—thanks for the drive, Mom—to Hendry's Beach near the Mesa. I shot it on Tri-X black and white, and they printed it for me at Anderson's on State. Are they still there?

So grounded with a couple more years of surfing (and a camera and lens stuffed under the car seat of my Karmann Ghia) and at the end of my second year of city college, I knew I had to head out to do a really big story with great photos to match. My parents had driven my sister Marylou and me across America at least three times and my mom always had her Kodak Hawkeye at the ready, so I think that's where I got the interest from. I turned twenty-one on the island of Barbados, halfway through a six-month journey across the Caribbean, South America, and up Central America and Mexico to the border and home. I remember I was sick as a dog with the flu when I got home, but I had pulled off the trip of a lifetime, hand carrying six months of exposed slide film and folder full of notes and scribbles.

I drove down to Dana Point a week later, spent a week in their offices, editing shots on a slide table and hacking out words on an IBM Selectric. A couple of months later and that issue of *Surfer* was out. Titled "Perils of the Tropics," eleven pages with those scribbles plus those color photos of surfing locations never seen before. I think it was probably the longest travel piece they had ever run, but I was already aiming beyond the stars for a new direction, the next assignment. And this is where my classmate Mark Campbell comes into the scene. Mark had gone off to Maui to start junior college classes at Maunaolu College above the sugarcane town of Paia and had written the gang a letter to let us know what was going on there. His letter started with the word *fantastic* underlined twice, then paragraphs of wave stories and people stories, all about Maui. I don't remember any of it. I just—to this day—remember that one opening word: *fantastic*! That was it. I checked out of classes a week later, packed what I needed (or thought I needed) to survive, promised my mom and dad I would be back to finish in six months. Within three months of arriving, I had a job offer as a full-time staffer at *Surfer*, a monthly paycheck and a shared house with two friends right at Sunset Beach for $500 a month divided three ways. I never looked back, never finished college, and now, here I am with a kid taller than me, knowing more of Instagram and TikTok than me, and he's already been to Tahiti twice. Yep, it's been a most amazing life and journey with so many travels and adventures—a couple of Indiana Jones sidetracks too. I could write a trilogy. I could TV script it for Netflix for five seasons or dump the whole thing on *National Geographic* and tell the guys trolling at Wicked Tuna to take a break. If we can get through this crazy pandemic, I want to take Kalani to this cluster of islands just north of Bougainville. I want him to see.

I have been linked to *Surfer* magazine's masthead since 1972. I have been involved with professional surfing in Hawaii since the mid-'70s. I've had my finger on the pulse of North Shore surfing for over thirty years. Obviously, I was a surf photographer, contest director, and journalist. But above all that, I like to think I'm a nice guy, as most anyone who knows me will attest. My first trip to Hawaii was in 1968, and that was a summer vacation coming out of my senior year of high school with three friends of mine, and we spent the summer in the islands. A really good friend of mine whom I ended up going to college with, Paul Kobayashi was from the Big Island. Paul's mom was the postmaster at the time. They invited us to come over and spend the summer surfing the Big Island, and it was Kona. She invited us to stay the summer that year. I got a job as a deckhand on a billfishing boat during the International Billfish Tournament over there, which by the way is into its umpteenth year, sixtieth year by now.

My first winter at the North Shore of Oahu was the winter of 1971 at Rocky Point with Kenny Thatcher and a whole group of guys that were from Southern California; I just spent the whole winter surfing. I spent the winter surfing and shooting photos. I spent that winter getting adapted to what in Hawaii was about. I think I probably came out of that winter knowing that I would return as soon as possible to actually put down roots and live here and maybe either finish college here, which I did in Santa Barbara. As soon as I got out of school, I was straight back over here immediately.

Some of the biggest changes were to the North Shore of Oahu. You know, the biggest change on the North Shore of Oahu—it's funny. I remember when Lopez used to call it the Wild Wild West. But uh, you know, the first decade or so, you could say that the North Shore was just a suburb of Honolulu. It's not so much the North Shore has changed; it's that everything around it has grown. The freeway came in all the way to Wahiawa in 1977. So you have a pouring over of population that's obviously going to change any community, any village, or any town. We live out here, and that makes us a suburb of Honolulu. The North Shore has changed radically just because of the population base on the other side of the hill.

In the mid- to late 1970s, professional surfing started to get traction, especially over here. Randy Rarick and I got together in 1975 in the parking lot of Surfride Hawaii, and Randy was running the IPS and doing the World Tour as it was threaded loosely together back then. He wanted to do something bigger and better for Hawaii, because this was our home. He and I sat in the parking lot that afternoon in the late fall and put together a project ultimately called Pro Class Trials, and what it was, was the trials for the two events that were taking place over here at the time in the winter. He also had an idea for putting together a larger series in the mid-1970s. This was also a part of IPS, which today we turned into the Triple Crown. The idea grew and grew and grew every year. I remember the first year we had 40 guys in both of the Pro Class Trials, and then we went to 120 in the third year. It has gone bigger and bigger every year.

Photos by Bernie Baker, of stepson Kalani Riveo

CHAPTER EIGHT

Benjie Medel

BENJIE
MEDEL

Life in Carpinteria

For a good history lesson on the town of Carpinteria, one could go to Jim Campos, class of '66, and Carpinteria native. He now writes a weekly column in the *Coastal View* about old-town Carpinteria. Jimmy and his brother Artie were playmates of mine when we were in elementary school. Along with Tommy Moreno, Dan Lionello, the DeAlba boys, David Granaroli, we were the kids who lived on Foothill Road. What can be said about those days in the early '50s? We were innocents living on beautiful acres and acres of lemons and avocados. Like many baby boomers, I had a father who had just seen WWII and all its horrors. He had been in the navy along with his two brothers, Henry and Lou. When he came home to his sisters, they all moved into a house together. Their mother had passed away before the war, and their father had taken another wife. The Medel children began their new lives together. Each of the brothers found work in the agricultural field. They each had large families, choosing to live in Carpinteria. Our grandparents and their families had come to "the North" early at the turn of the century from Mexico. Some came reluctantly. My grandmother Juanita came from a proud family with her husband to avoid the strife going on at the time. Pancho Villa was recruiting young boys to help in the fight. His method was just to grab them forcefully, and they were never seen again. My mom told me how hard it was for her parents. They wanted to be in Mexico, but it was too dangerous. There was a great influx of people coming into California and other states.

My dad's first job was spraying the lemon trees, for preventing the wrong insects from destroying new growth. While working one day, a ranch owner, Harold Cadwell, who was looking for a ranch foreman, was introduced to young Albert, and hired him. My father and mother moved into the little ranch house where the foreman lived. It was called the Mont Val Mar Ranch. That's where my sister Sylvia, my brother Lou, and I were born. Dad worked there five years until one day, another ranch owner, Erno Bonebakker, asked his foreman, Sal Campos, where he could find an experienced foreman. Sal recommended my father, and after a while, we moved to the bigger Gale Ranch. I was almost five years old, ready for kindergarten. The new Canalino school was almost ready for opening day, but not quite, so I was sent to Aliso school. It wasn't long before we moved into the new Canalino kindergarten schoolroom. My teacher's name was Mrs. Kroenke. Jeff Boyd, Emily Milne, Wendy Bliss, Tom DeAlba, Esther Cerday, Jack Moyer, and others were my classmates. I had to walk to school when I was five. The path was about a mile long for me. One day when walking home from school, I started feeling like I was getting a stomachache. I realized I was going to have to go to the bathroom, but I was too far from home and it wouldn't wait, so I ended up walking home with a lump in my shorts. I remember crying all the way home.

My mom was pregnant with my sister Kathy when I was five. I remember no one would take me to school so I would usually walk. Back then was different: not so many cars and they drove slower and everybody knew everyone else. I don't think there are too many five-year-olds today who are allowed to walk by themselves.

As Canalino School was completed, we were filling the classrooms from grade to grade. I remember Kevin Sears and I would ditch class in the sixth grade when we were at lunchtime. Kevin had the same idea. We didn't like math class, which was after lunch, so we would walk off the school grounds with our lunches in hand and go to a place that we knew, not too far from the school. It was a drainage tunnel made of concrete, and it went under the road. We would find each other there inside the larger tunnel and eat our lunches. That was how Kevin and I were similar. He was a good friend, always.

Sometimes, my dad would take me up to see Mr. Castiles's chicken ranch to get fresh eggs and chickens to raise. That's where Randy Castiles lived, up in Gobernador Canyon. We ran around and played while the men talked. Randy was a good friend for many years.

Sometimes, I'd get to go over to the ranch where Tommy DeAlba lived, and we would play down in the creek by his house. Living away from town, where many of the children lived, made us different. Ranch kids had lots of freedom to run and get lost in adventure around the many trees and hills. Neighbors were usually far away. It made me grow up independent. Of course, I'd make it home to eat, but often the triangle would be clanging and I'd be far away when I would hear it and go running home.

I drove a tractor when very young, got my license when I was sixteen. My dad gave me his 1946 Plymouth and he got a new car, a station wagon, because Mom had more children. I drove to the high school and afterward went cruising with my friends in the back seat. During the '60s, there was always talk about the war going on in Vietnam. From the time I entered high school, the war in Vietnam was in the news, which I didn't pay much attention to, because I was having too much fun.

But by 1966, I knew there was a draft, and I had a number that eventually would get called. Life went on, and that next year, I met a girl at a dance at the Veterans Memorial Building, sponsored by the boys' club called the Royal Jesters. It was the end of the school year, summer of '67, later to be called the Summer of Love.

I went to the dance with Fred Naranjo, who had a bottle of sloe gin. I never drank before. But before the dance, Fred handed me the bottle, and I took a drink, and another.

We went inside to a noisy hall, band playing, and I saw Helen Mendez. I didn't know who she was. We danced and stayed together until I took her home. Years later, after returning from Vietnam we met up again, and eventually married. We had two children before our divorce in 1980. If we had stayed married, we would be celebrating our fiftieth. But we didn't, and I got custody of my seven-year-old son. My daughter stayed with her mother. She was nine years old at the time. We stayed close, sharing custody and making the children as comfortable as possible. I was working for Safeway. I stayed with the company for thirty-one years. Our children attended Carpinteria schools all through high school.

The year I spent in Vietnam had a profound effect on me, only because I became drug addicted. There was a guy who handed me a cigarette, which I smoked, having begun smoking in the service, but it wasn't a cigarette. It was *cần sa*, the Vietnamese word for cannabis. The vendors sold them in nicely rolled packs just like Marlboros. This became common to me, and that's how I came home, dependent on the opium, speed, cannabis, heroin, or whatever there. Our society was changing during the war and after: people were protesting, rioting in the streets, all over the country, more and more drugs, people buying guns. The influences on the soldiers coming home caused upheaval. At the time, we weren't concerned with PTSD. It was unknown. But among the soldiers coming home were many men and women who joined the protestors screaming for an end to the war.

The times were a-changing. The politicians weren't able to change the system of corruption; in fact, the government made it worse. Black people were still not considered equal, poverty was skyrocketing, riots, killings, all recorded and played on national TV. Vietnamese were pleading for mercy from the devastation of their country. It was very difficult for me to see the people in Vietnam trying to live as normal a life as they could while running from bombs, strafing runs, and losing their young boys. Yes, they would appear innocent in the daytime, but at night, they changed into fighters, grabbing rifles to kill Americans.

I often asked myself what I would do if our country were invaded. I'd be just like them probably. I had some close associations with some Vietnamese that I knew as papa-san, mama-san, and baby-san. I lived among some families while there because I had a position that allowed me to live off-base, in an area considered safe enough for Americans. I lived on a street called Nguyen Van Thoai with some other servicemen. We were in a support group called Military Assistance Command, Vietnam (MACV). It was housed in a big concrete building outside Saigon, close to Tan Son Nhut Air Force Base. Many Vietnamese citizens worked for the US military command. Many ordinary citizens had special passes or ID cards that let them into the base daily to do their jobs helping the military of the

United States: mostly cleaning jobs, but also the ARVN, the army of South Vietnam, being trained by the US Army. So I had lots of time to communicate with these citizens of nearby areas cleared by the US Army. I blended in with them; they thought I looked somewhat like them. It was very interesting to speak about how they felt about us. They understood about the North and how intent they were on unifying the country. They just wanted to live in peace. They had only known war. First the Chinese, then the French, they were always fighting for their independence. Now the Americans were there. They weren't too sure what we wanted, but there we were. Sadly, the military advisors that were sent to analyze the problems in Vietnam and how the country would react were not able to judge the political situation accurately at the time. There were lies spoken by both sides, and Americans were thrust wrongly into an unjust war. There was never going to be a winner, only more destruction. The rest is history. Many men and women served our country, but without the just cause. It was an unjust war long ago, but not so long ago that we can't learn valuable lessons from it.

Anyway, life went on and over here in Carpinteria. I read about the flood of '69, the New York Mets winning the World Series, man on the moon, Joe Namath and the Jets winning the Super Bowl, all in 1969, the year I was stationed in Vietnam from January to Christmas Day.

I came home with some other guys on Christmas Day, landing in an airport at night in San Francisco. No fanfare, no welcoming home, but it felt good to breathe clean air. It was always so stinky in 'Nam.

My favorite smell is lemon blossoms, and it's that way because of the memories growing up fairly independently, not man neighbors, and I still appreciate quiet in my day. I favor camping for all it offers in quiet nature, with worries melting away.

Am I the only one still stuck in the past? It's our past. We lived it during that time between peace and war, easy living and hard times. They all blend together, and knowing that some people my age understand how it was, then and now, makes me aware of the many friends we have had and seemingly lost, until a reunion or something brings us together and we realize they weren't lost.

The past is the past, we hear. But it brings back flowing memories that only we knew, having lived through it.

Now, our parents are gone. Dad died at home, in his room surrounded by his seven children and wife of sixty-five years, Carmen. We managed until Mom got sick one day, complaining of pain in her stomach. She died one week later in Cottage Hospital, just seventeen months after Dad. I hope a lot of you readers know what I mean when I say we felt like orphans. We had them for so long among us, we were fortunate—very fortunate. I needed my dad. I need my mom, still. Feelings come out, time goes on. I got used to the idea but can't stop going to the cemetery to trim around the gravestone with Dad's old lawn clippers. I realized how dependent I was on them all this time.

My two children are Michelle and Brian, born in 1972 and 1974. Michelle married Rob Durtche. Brian married Christina Martinez. They each have three children. Michelle has two girls: Natalie and Emily, twenty-six and twenty-one. Son Jacob is eighteen. Natalie is a second-grade teacher at Our Lady of Mt. Carmel School in Montecito. Emily is a student and works part-time lifeguarding at the community pool, or at Jr. Lifeguards training with the local youth. Jacob will begin his EMT training next week. He also was a lifeguard.

Brian's had all boys: Ben III, Gabriel, Samuel. Ben's at Chico State in his third year. Gabe is attending SBCC. Sam is beginning seventh grade.

I've been married to Heidi since 1992. We've had no children, but the grandchildren always call her Nana Heidi.

I'm so glad I got to live in Carpinteria, in the orchards, quietly learning from nature just how wonderful life can be. My grandparents knew, because they had family who had come before them and told them of the nice, quiet town by the sea, with good soil for growing crops. Many generations before them had lived here when it was part of Mexico. It's our land: Carpinteria.

Benjie Medel's fourth-grade class, Canalino
School, Carpinteria, 1958

Top Row L-R: Cindy White, ___, Shelley Milnc,
Wendy Bliss, Cathy Sylvester, Jory Small, Linda
Hurd, ___, Sue McGillivray, Emily Brown
Bottom Row L-R: Jim Rockwell, Jack Moyer, Gary
Sanders, Benjie Medel, ___, Jeff Boyd, Gregg Floyd

CHAPTER NINE

Joe Lovett

JOE
LOVETT

My Story

When somebody tells you they grew up in a great place, you tend to take that with a grain of salt. Well, I can tell you I grew up in one of the greatest places in America for the time. It was 1959 and I was just ten years old. I moved to Carpinteria, California. For those who don't know where Carpinteria is, it is about twenty miles from Santa Barbara, California. As anybody who is familiar with the southern California coast knows, this is one of the most beautiful parts of the California coast, if not the most beautiful. There were two elementary schools. I started at Aliso. I met my first friend at that school. He is still my oldest and dearest friend. I remember one day when we were outside at recess, Steve picked up a bug of some kind and ate it. I almost puked. I asked him what he was doing, and with a straight face, he said, "We need to get used to eating bugs so when the end comes, we can survive." Even at a young age, I said to him, "I am not going to eat any bugs."

I was not a very good student. I would do just enough to get by to get to the next grade. I remember we were given the task of doing a report on a subject of our choice. I picked the subject of monkeys. I did not write anything. Well, to my surprise, our teacher wanted some of us to read our report to the class. Well, just think of what I felt when our teacher called on me. Since I did not have anything written down, I just started talking about monkeys. I was always looking down at a blank page. I can't remember what I said, but our teacher told the class that my story was very good. I had about forty-five minutes left in the class. When others were reading their stories, I was writing mine down. I turned it in and got a C+ for the report.

When I was thirteen years old, we moved. We moved to a new mobile-home park. The best thing about moving was that we now lived 1/4 mile from the beach. I never knew anything could be cooler than living that close to the beach.

I got a part-time job cleaning a dry cleaner's in town. Downtown Carpinteria was only ten minutes by car. By the way, I did not own a car, and I did not have a license. My mom had to take me to work. We had to go early so I could get done by 8:00 a.m. to get to school on time. By the way, my mom had to take me to school as well. I do remember while at work one morning, I had to pee. I went to the bathroom, and when I was done, I zipped my fly, and halfway up, I got some foreskin caught in my zipper. I wanted to scream in pain. My mom was just outside the door; I could not scream. I was in major pain. I did suck it up and got my zipper undone.

I saved my money and bought my first surfboard. It was 9'10" Gordon and Smith. It had thin redwood slats running down both sides of the board. It was great. It was the best thing I ever did. I would go to the beach as often as I could: after school, weekends, sometimes during school hours. I was able to stand up on my board the very first day. It is the greatest sport ever invented. Surfers from Carpinteria were some of the best in all of southern Cal.: Jeff Boyd, Kevin Sears, Mark Campbell, and Chris Blakeslee, to name a few. I was not in their class. Kevin Sears was one of the best surfers in California. I am seventy-one years old, and I still watch surfing on TV whenever I can. The waves at the beach down from my house were not that great. Sometimes the waves got to 4' to 5'. As a freshman in high school, I was not that involved with girls. My first crush was a girl whose family would come to Carpinteria for the summer. They were from Bakersfield, CA. She was very good-looking and was a sophomore in high school, so I win sky high. She thought I was all that because I surfed. We would spend all our time at the beach. We would stay at the beach all day and some of the night. At that time, we were still able to have beach fires. By the way, I was not that great a surfer. But I did surf and that was enough for a great summer love. My time in high school was the best time of my life, I thought at the time. I had girlfriends throughout high school. I found myself breaking up with the school girlfriends when the summer came. In tenth grade, I looked forward to the summer because that's when all the tourists would come to Carpinteria for vacation. Most of those families were from the valley—that is, the San Fernando Valley. It was great. They would bring their daughters for the summer on the world's safest beach. I was for that all the way. The second half of my tenth-grade year, I fell in love with a girl I had known for years. Her mother and my mother were good friends. We would go on camping trips down the coast for the weekends. It was great fun. She was the prettiest girl in our school. She had tan dark skin, great eyes, and she dressed great. I was overboard with her. But when the summer came, I was in summer mode. Our junior year, we were back on track. At the end of our junior year, she would not deal with my childlike antics anymore. She broke up with me. At the time, I did not think she would break up with me. I was a little cocky at the time.

My senior year of high school, my parents opened a takeout chicken business. My mother, bless her soul, named the business (are you ready for this?) Quick Chick A Go Go. You got it right: Quick Chick A Go Go. We used a technique called broasting, which is deep-frying the chicken under pressure. We sold a lot of takeout chicken. My father had a bit of a drinking problem. His main job for the business was to bread the chicken. He would do this in the morning before we would open. The liquor store would open around 9:00 a.m. He would go almost every day and buy a fifth of vodka. He would then come to the store and start drinking and breading chicken. He did not buy a mixer for the vodka. He would use orange crush out of the soda machine. By 1:00 p.m., he was soused. He did not come out to the front of the store. One time he did come out to the front. It was dinnertime, and one of our best customers came to order two buckets, with coleslaw, potatoes, and drinks. The total bill was about $25. That was a big bill for that time. The customer was getting a little frustrated because it was taking longer than he was used to. He said to me, "What is taking so long?" My father came running out to the front, totally drunk, and said to the customer, "Get out, get out." The customer never came back to our chicken store. One Friday night, I was working, and I had told my dad that I had to leave early because I had a date with my fifteen-year-old girlfriend.

She was great. My father told me if I left early, I was fired. So I never worked for my father again.

My high school years were great. I did have some identity issues, however. I played high school sports. I was pretty good in all sports. I played football, track and field, and basketball. Since I surfed, I also was involved in doing some drugs. Drugs of choice at the time were weed, LSD, and meth. My friends that hung out at the beach were all loadies, meaning most of them took drugs. Most of my friends that I played sports with were straight. Most of my loadie friends hung out together and did not hang with sports guys. None of my sports friends hung with my loaded friends. I was popular in school, so I got invited to all the parties, both from stoners and straights. At times, it was difficult to separate the two. I never did drugs in front of my straight friends. That's all I did with my loadie friends. I surfed, smoked dope, did LSD and some meth. Oh, I played high school sports as well. There was one time before a football game, I offered some meth pills to my teammates. I think around six of us took some meth before the game. For good or bad, we did win. Don't know if it was the meth or that we were better.

I did have two real girlfriends through high school. My first was a sophomore that lasted two full years. We did break up, however, for the summer both years. My last year as a senior, I fell for a freshman. She was the sister of one of my friends. I thought she was my soul mate. At that age, I think most young people think they have found their soul mate. After graduation from high school, she broke up with me. She did not want to have a steady boyfriend with so much school left in her future. I did love her. But she was right; she should not have been tied to me with so much left for her. I graduated in 1967. The Vietnam War was at its highest level. Carpinteria was a very small town. We knew who had been drafted or had joined the military. We had lost two friends in our town from a car accident. Everybody knew them. One day, I read the paper, and it said that someone from our town was killed in Vietnam. He was two years older than I was, but I knew who it was. It was devastating. He was just eighteen years old. His name was Jim McDonald. He was in Vietnam for less than two months. He was drafted into the army. I did not want to get drafted, so I decided to join the air force, thinking I would have some choice in what I would do in the air force. Well, I was wrong. One year after I went into the air force, I was sent to Vietnam. I am not going to share my whole experience, but I will tell you one story. When I arrived in Vietnam at Da Nang air base, I had to go to the flight desk in the Da Nang air base terminal. It was really a large Quonset hut, but you know what I mean. I boarded an Air Force C-123. For those of you who have no idea of what a C-123 is, I am going to give you the short answer. It is a cargo plane. It also served as a troop carrier. This aircraft had two props and two jet engines. In Vietnam, pilots took off very vertically once they got off the ground. That helped stop the enemy from shooting at them. When we were making our final descent into Pleiku AB, I could feel the hydraulics from the landing gear. When that happens, the wheels should be coming down. Well, that did not happen. I had not been in country for more than two hours, and I thought it was over. Well, the pilot went back around and tried the landing gear again. Whoops, they did not work. I did not know at the time that the crew chief could bring the wheels down manually. He did on the third pass, and we landed safely. I came home a year later and started my life as an adult.

Joe Lovett, Bobby Walsh & Steve Smith

Joe Lovett & Linda Pino Junior Prom

Joe Lovett Surfing

Joe Lovett 1975 at Air Force Base Alconberry, England

CHAPTER TEN

Shelley Milne

SHELLEY
MILNE

A Life in a Couple of Big Stops
and Many Mini Ones

I lived in the same farmhouse on Gobernador Canyon Road with my parents, brother, and numerous dogs for the first seventeen years of my life. I attended six months of kindergarten at Aliso School, moved over to Canalino for the remainder of the year. My kindergarten teacher was my granddad's cousin, so goes my relationship with the town. The school district kept adding wings to the school. As my classmates and I reached the end of Wing 1, construction finished on Wing 2. The pattern repeated itself until we finished sixth grade. Finally, we graduated from Canalino Elementary School and were able to move on to junior high at the old Main School (which was my parents' grade school). At last, we reached the high school (also attended by my parents, aunts, uncles, brother, cousins). My family even shared the same English teacher, Margie Holmes. As happened to my relatives, I graduated from high school.

At this point, I decided it would be good to look for a different climate and see what else the world had to offer. I moved to Salem, Oregon, and attended Willamette University for four years. I gained new friendships (many of whom are still in my world), attended interesting classes, experienced snow and a lot of rain. At that time, even Carpinteria had more restaurants than Salem, so my friends and I traveled often to the coast and to Portland for a bit of excitement. I achieved a degree in history but did not want to teach, so I was educated but unskilled (except for summertime jobs). A friend, Susie, and I closed our eyes, put a finger to a US map and landed on Phoenix, Arizona.

We were in Phoenix for three months from August through October (not the brightest of choices). We witnessed marvelous thunder and lightning storms, tried selling funeral plans to old people (it stuns me that I am now in the age group that targeted), tried exercising by playing tennis and walking around the city but the heat was not pleasant. One dark night, we turned in our apartment key, loaded up our cars, and took a month driving to Oregon. We took a week to visit Mom and Dad in Carpinteria—the day we arrived, we saw a wisp of smoke in the mountains. The fire burned during our entire visit, even necessitating a rapid evacuation from our home in Gobernador Canyon down to the beach area. By the time we moved on, the fire was under control.

We ultimately landed in Portland, rented a house without any furniture, and proceeded to look for work. By December, Susie had joined the Peace Corps and served in Thailand for the next three years. I stayed in Portland, working at Penney's and Nordstrom's before a college friend, anxious to get out of her parents' home, begged me to move to Eugene and be her roommate.

So in 1973, I landed in Eugene, found a job, met my future husband, and established a life. And like my parents, I have lived in the same house for the past thirty-four years.

Aside from temp work when I first moved to Eugene, I worked at only one place for thirty-plus years. At that time, it was known as the Oregon State Scholarship Commission. We oversaw the State Need Grant program, administered scholarships as well as the state guaranteed student loan program. For the most part, the age group of the staff was in the same generation. We enjoyed one another, and we were working for a good cause (financially enabling students to attend college and/or proprietary schools). Turnover was small— friends made then remain friends today.

Tom joined the commission staff in 1974—he worked with the State Legislature, drafting presentations, working on annual budgets, and explaining program complexities to the world of financial aid. As we worked in separate departments, we saw no problem developing a relationship. He was also a California native (east Palo Alto), though he went to college on the East Coast. We were married in 1976, and we adopted our first son in 1984 when he was twenty-three months. We adopted our second son in 1985 when he was two days old. Both times, it was a true learning experience starting from scratch.

Even after the adoption of our sons, I kept working full-time. I oversaw the department dealing with default prevention of state guaranteed student loans, which allowed me to travel to national conferences to learn about new regulations, discuss issues, and socialize. I was able to travel to Dallas, Fort Worth, Austin, New Orleans, St. Louis, Savannah, Tampa, Washington DC, Indianapolis, and so on. This was a treat because annual vacations from work were initially only two weeks—travel meant trips to Carpinteria and the Bay Area (Tom's family), so the business trips were my opportunity to see the country. On the occasions when Tom would travel for work, I would have the pleasure of holding down the home life. Together, we were able to support each other in managing the kids, the home, the dog, and our various work duties.

Ultimately, the work of student financial aid changed, and the student loan programs previously held by state agencies were transferred to the control of the federal government (and serviced by private collection agencies). Luckily, even though I had not attained normal retirement age of sixty-five, I had worked for the State of Oregon for a full thirty years. I retired in 2003. After a celebratory retirement trip to Great Britain with my mom and her two best friends, Martha Hickey and Jane Bianchin, I was asked to return to the agency as executive director. Given all the changes, there were many layoffs to be made, and the powers that be thought I could complete the task at hand. I did but it wasn't fun. Truly, it was time to re-retire. That was in 2004.

I do want to say that there were no better traveling companions than my mom, Jane, and Martha. As the designated driver, I also accompanied them to Holland for two weeks. They set the standard for how to have a good time during any kind or travel.

While still working and before children, Tom and I began running with friends from work. Many people in Eugene were getting into running, and interest was high. Steve Prefontaine was competing for the University of Oregon, and track events were extremely popular. Tom and I were never at a loss to find running partners or participate in competitive races. We participated in many 10K races, but the most fun was the Roseburg to Coos Bay team race (six members to a team, and three segments per runner); the course was on lonely roads into the hills and over to the coast. Once the kids came along, preschool, school, PTA, Little League of every sport, full-time work, and so on, free time and enthusiasm for running disappeared.

Once life was more manageable, I took up competitive walking. I participated twice in the team relay, Portland to Coast (my favorite leg was at 2:00 a.m. on a beautiful stretch of mountain road leading to Seaside). I then thought that maybe doing a marathon would be fun. In 2001, a friend and I signed with a female coach to train with a group of women (and paid $100 each for the pleasure) for nine months with the goal of walking the 2001 Portland Marathon. My friend Mary and I connected with three other women who also paid those big bucks to train. When one is walking, one can talk in complete sentences (running makes carrying on lengthy conversations more difficult). The five of us learned a great deal about one another over the many hours of training. When it came to the race, we walked together, stayed together, and completed in our desired time of six hours. That was our only marathon—we did it well, so why chance another? Through the last almost twenty years, we have competed together in many races (half-marathons, 10Ks, and the local Butte to Butte) and we still try to meet every Sunday morning for a good walk. Our conversations early on were about children in school, divorces, and work, but now they have morphed into concerns about parents, death, and health worries.

In addition to walking, I have now taken to hiking. A friend and I decided that it would be fun to ask six other friends to hike the trail along the Rogue River. In an effort to hike the forty-six miles of the Rogue River trail without any embarrassment, we trained for several months on local mountain trails. We also traveled to the Metolius River and hiked in the Jefferson wilderness. The best thing we did was sign up with a river raft company, Orange Torpedo, to track us from their raft. They also hauled our gear, provided our wine, and met us at each night's lodging—best thing we ever did. Still hiking.

I also want to emphasize how important my friends have been to me. They have helped me weather the storms of adulthood as well as thoroughly enjoy the good times. Wendy Bliss MacMurray has seen me through nursery school at the Hale's house in Lillingston Canyon through high school and life beyond. It is good to have friends. I highly recommend it.

Tom has always been very patient with my training and travels. While the boys were still at home, he would be the caretaker while I traveled, ran races, or worked overtime. After the boys left home, he would still take care of the home and mind the dog. We have managed to work in some trips together: China with the Carpinteria Chamber of Commerce, Egypt with a college friend and her husband, Scotland, England (timed it for the Goodwood Festival of Speed), Vancouver (BC), as well as Boston, DC, Seattle, and the Carmel area for the annual Concourse d'Elegance. We had other plans, but they have been set aside for the time being.

In this weird time, Tom and I have been purchasing mystery bags from the Eugene Friends of the Library. We receive ten books for $10. One can pick the genre but not the author. We have been exposed to authors whose books would not have been our first choice, and truth be told, never will be. We have resumed going to the YMCA for our workout class three times a week. One of my service clubs has resumed meeting, but my work for Habitat for Humanity has halted for the time being. I've been gardening in this beautiful weather, with the thought that winter rains and cold will arrive soon enough. I've been happily roasting tomatoes, onion, basil, garlic to use as sauces in the coming winter months. I have even dusted the house a few times, cleaned the bathrooms some, and tried to sweep every day, maybe— we have a twenty-month-old Lab/German shepherd mix who sheds mightily. She also requires daily visits to the dog park and a walk in the early morning hours.

Once shops started to reopen, I got my first haircut in four months. My next step was to locate some presentable clothes in my woebegone closet. Tom and I then went out to dinner! In celebration, I even purchased a new face mask to wear. It was such a treat to eat someone else's cooking. Yesterday, we prepared for our first social gathering at home—six friends were invited over to our yard with chairs placed six feet apart. We spent the day cleaning the backyard, the patio, the furniture, etc. The party ended when the smoke got too bad, totally hiding the nearby hills less than a mile away. Strong winds from the east to the coast were predicted—a rarity that happens maybe four to five times a century. The winds happened. The ash fell. As my grandmother used to say, "If it ain't one damn thing, it's another!"

CHAPTER ELEVEN

David Iovino

DAVID
IOVINO

Chapters of Our Lives

by
David Michael Iovino

I was born in Providence, Rhode Island, on June 21, 1949. When I was nine and a half years old, my parents and I moved to Southern California. When we first arrived, we stayed with my mother's brother and his family in North Hollywood in the San Fernando Valley, one of the hottest places on earth. We arrived on my mom's birthday, October 18. September and October were the hottest months in Southern California.

After a week, my father got a job at a Chevy dealer in Los Angeles, near Santa Monica Beach and Pier. It was so nice there. After five years, my dad got a job at Dick Daily Chevrolet in an idyllic little beach town named Carpinteria, California, just south of Santa Barbara. When the Spanish discovered a band of Chumash Indians on the beach, sealing canoes they were making with pitch that was plentiful at the beach, they named it Carpinteria or "little carpenter shop" in Spanish. I still have a soft spot for that little town. I was in the eighth grade at the time.

I have many performing talents I have honed over the years: dancing, singing, acting, and art, to name a few. These talents I acquired at Paul Revere Junior High School in the Pacific Palisades and at Carpinteria junior and senior high schools.

This next section is about my father, whom I'm very proud of. He was born north of Boston in 1903, and while in his early twenties, he had an act with a partner in vaudeville. I am very proud of his accomplishment to this day. The name of their act was Irving and Pet, after their real names Iovino and Petrocelli. They both were very talented. They sang, danced, were into comedy. My dad played the organ, the piano, and the mandolin. When I was four years old, my dad performed in a musical. He was dressed in a gray Confederate soldier costume, complete with sword and cap. He sang "The Girl That I Marry" out on stage. My mom, my brother, and I were in the wings. All of a sudden, this powerful resonant voice filled the hall. I couldn't get over that that was my father's voice. I was never as proud of him as I was at that moment. My whole family is very talented. My mom had a beautiful voice and played the piano by ear. My brother plays guitar and has a fabulous voice, and I still am a soloist at my church here in Coventry, Rhode Island.

My father used to tell us that we were related to Austrian land barons; however, when my brother had our father's DNA tested, they found us to be Italian, Basque, and Irish. When my cousin had our mom's DNA done, we were all Italian. My great-grandfather was tall, with red hair and green eyes. My grandfather had light brown hair and blue eyes. My brother also had blue eyes. My mom's and my eyes are hazel. My dad was the only one with brown eyes.

Enough about my family. I want to mention one of the most thrilling things ever to happen to me: in 1977, I took an awful job in a wood-staining factory in Santa Monica, California in order to save up enough money to fulfill my lifelong dream of taking a trip to Europe. My mom contributed over half the funds necessary to make the trip. She was an angel and my best friend. I set foot on Irish soil in the airport when we landed to refuel. I also went to Italy, Greece, and a two-week folk dance in Yugoslavia. It was the most awesome thing ever to happen to me, and I'll never forget it.

I would like to close by mentioning my wonderful friends I have from my church here in Coventry, RI. They are the best brothers in Christ another man could ever have. They give me rides to go grocery shopping and to church (my eyesight had deteriorated so much I can no longer see well enough). Their names are Dave and Erik, and in my opinion, they are the most wonderful friends anyone could ever have. I lost my thirty-one-year-old great-nephew on the 21st of July. This, I believe, caused me to have a heart attack on July 25. I still can scarcely believe he's gone.

Lastly, I wouldn't be able to close without mentioning my love of animals. I love both dogs and cats. When I moved back to Rhode

Island in 2012, I had all three cats and my beautiful white German shepherd Wolfie. I only have my black cat Jet left. At seventy-one, it's getting harder and harder. Thanks for taking the time to read my chapter. —David Iovino

P.S. One last thing about myself I'd like to mention is my fierce patriotism. My Uncle Bill was a naval commander. I'm very proud of my nephew Michael who is a retired Navy SEAL of twenty-five years. His son Chad is in the Army Rangers. Four of my mom's brothers were army, and three of my cousins were Marines. God bless the USA.

CHAPTER TWELVE

David Baldwin

DAVID BALDWIN

Defining a Generation: The Carpinteria High School Class of 1967

Ours was a decade that will be remembered in history as one of the most turbulent, influential, confusing, life-changing, and provocative of any in the twentieth century. Ironically, as we exited the field at Memorial Stadium, following our graduation ceremony, there seemed to be more questions than answers as to where our futures would take us. For most of us, it was a final farewell that we did not comprehend fully. We had grown up together and traveled through the halls of the Carpinteria Unified School District with familiar faces and strong community support. Tragically, graduation would end that status for most of us. We were not destined to see one another until a possible reunion surfaced. We did not realize the severity of this "divorce" until the years revealed its finality and its everlasting effects. It was a step toward maturity, and one of the many lessons that would be learned along the way for the class of 1967.

We were blessed to live in the sleepy seaside town of Carpinteria. It was quiet in the winter and bustled with campers in the summer. The ocean and the beach were welcome playgrounds for all of us. The surfing, diving, swimming, sunbathing, volleyball, and socializing were among the many advantages of living in this town. During the off-season months, the streets were empty by 6:00 p.m. Trips to Santa Barbara and Ventura were major events. We were isolated and, in many ways, protected from outside influences. Yet in the summer, the town came alive with tourists that filled the state parks. This provided new perspective and many life lessons that would never be learned in the winter. This strange seasonal way of life influenced all of us greatly as we navigated the path toward adulthood. However, Carpinteria did an excellent job of isolating us from what was happening in the rest of the world, in the United States, and even in California.

We ventured forth, with cap and gown, and set off to conquer the world. However, I often wonder how truly prepared we were for what was coming our way! I soon discovered that I was ill-prepared for college and the rigors of maturing. Initially, I blamed this lack of preparation on my high school, the teachers, the town, even my parents. This convenient approach avoided placing blame on me! However, as the years passed, I realized that I needed to take full responsibility for my life, its actions, and how things worked out. This was a long, arduous journey, with many realizations, awakenings, and insights. As I grew more confident with my world, my career, and my life, I started to see clearly the many people that were so influential in forming my current life. Rather than place erroneous blame on these individuals, I celebrated their influence in my life. First and foremost were my parents, Dale and Doris Baldwin. They taught me about a strong work ethic, the importance of completing the task at hand, the morals and values that are critical to navigating life, the importance of an education, the strength of a handshake, the bond in your word, and the importance of valuing everyone. My first mentor, Dr. William Carty, retired superintendent of the Carpinteria Unified School District, stressed the importance of listening before you speak, the importance of offering words of encouragement to others, always working hard at your craft, having a plan that has the end in mind, remembering your roots as a teacher and valuing each student each day, and refraining from saying anything negative about another individual. Doc also showed me the importance of recreation. Sunday afternoon was made for beach volleyball, surfing, bodysurfing, and ice-cold A&W root beer. If the ocean water was clear and we could go diving, our catch always resulted in a fish fry in the Cartys' backyard. Sometimes a simple event puts the biggest smile on your face. He was always available to talk about education, or just life. He and his wife Daphne, and their entire family, were present for all the major events in my life and the lives of my two children. My parents and the Carty family are missed each day. I was truly blessed to have each in my life.

As a student, I was not gifted or a natural scholar. I worked hard to achieve acceptable grades. I enjoyed writing and English, and made these pursuits my profession. I attended Westmont College in Santa Barbara, where I earned a bachelor's degree in English and physical education, and a teaching credential. I also played varsity volleyball for two years. I started my teaching career as a middle school English teacher at Anacapa Junior High in Ventura, California, in the fall of 1972. I taught English, journalism, and yearbook. While working at Anacapa, I coached girls' volleyball at Ventura High School. This experience lasted eleven years. In 1983, I transferred to Ventura High School as an English teacher. I taught college prep and honors sophomore English. I continued to coach the girls' volleyball team, and coached girls' softball, boys' basketball, boys' football, and started the boys' volleyball program. I was also a school counselor. Outside of school, for over thirty years I was active as a sports official, refereeing football and basketball. Officiating allowed me to stay involved in the athletic programs throughout Santa Barbara and Ventura county.

In 1998, I was hired as an assistant principal at Moorpark High School in Moorpark, California. This school grew from 1,600 to nearly 2,800 over the ten years that I worked there. I supervised the athletic program, ASB, counseling, and the master schedule. I was also the principal of the district's summer program for eight years and was the director of the district's adult education for eight years. In 2008, I accepted a job as the principal of Rio Vista Middle School in Oxnard, California. I was brought in to turn things around at this school. I retired in the summer of 2009, leaving Rio Vista in great shape. In retirement, I taught masters-level education classes at several colleges and universities. After a few years, I bowed out as a professor of education. These days, I make custom outdoor patio furniture for my customers, and try to keep up with my five grandchildren.

My career as a teacher, counselor, and administrator on the middle and high school levels lasted thirty-seven years, and it will always be one of my finer accomplishments. In 1998, I won the prestigious Golden Bell Award for the State of California for language arts. The California State School Board Association honored me for my efforts in creating a program called the Readers' Faire. It validated my teaching career and made me proud of the many students who contributed to this event's success over the twenty-two years that I produced it. I was also proud of two extracurricular programs that I developed for my students. For many years, I chaperoned students to off-Broadway plays in Los Angeles. We always went out to dinner to get the full experience. Most students were mesmerized as they witnessed their first live play. To this day, when I see these students, they remind me of the impact this experience had on their lives. These reactions are humbling and rewarding.

The other programs of note were taking students to Europe during spring break. For over twenty years, I supervised groups ranging in size from fifteen and forty-five students. We were scholars of these classical societies that would forever change our lives. So many stories evolved from these experiences, and so many lives were changed. My classroom instruction was always important, but these outside activities enriched my students' lives, enriched my life, and made all of us better citizens of this global world.

In my personal life, I consider my family as a major contributor to any of my successes. My wife and children have always inspired me to reach higher. Both my son and daughter attended high schools in Ventura. They were active in athletics, with my daughter playing volleyball, basketball, and running track. She was an outstanding setter in volleyball, having played on the collegiate level, and played on a state-ranked high school basketball team. My son played basketball and volleyball against top-ranked teams in southern California. My daughter currently works for the United States Department of Agriculture as a program coordinator for the NCRS division, and my son pursued a career in education, teaching AP US history, coaching basketball, and working as an assistant principal and principal on the middle and high school levels. He is currently the director of secondary education for the Santa Clara Unified School District. Long ago, both children surpassed any of my achievements in academics, athletics, and career goals.

My five grandchildren continue to keep me young and amaze me with their individual lives. My daughter's children are Moorea (the oldest grandchild, who attends Montana State, majoring in education), her brother Connor (who attends Humboldt State, majoring in engineering), and his younger brother Ben (who is an eighth grader at Aptos Middle School in Aptos, California). My son's children are Isabella, a sixth grader at Fisher Middle School in Los Gatos, California, and Siena, who is a fourth grader at Louise van Meter elementary school also in Los Gatos. All are unique, pursue different interests, are inspired academically, and each day make me proud to be their grandfather. My son's wife, Risela, is a middle-school science teacher in the Los Gatos area. My wife, Nikki, has endured, supported, and encouraged me daily. She has been instrumental in my personal and professional lives, while working as a travel agent in Camarillo. Her occupation has allowed us to travel extensively around the world. This experience has given us a true appreciation for the global society. Her support has been part of all my success. For that, I am profoundly grateful.

As I compared my career as an educator to my time as a high school student, I found certain shortcomings. Some teachers did an excellent job in their classrooms, but I hope they would encourage students more to go to college or even pursue the career of their dreams. I applied to college on my own, and I was accepted. Ironically, our school had no idea how many of us were going away to four-year college or universities. I always remember a rather revealing conversation during my senior year. I was asked about my future plans, and I mentioned going out of state to college the following year. I got an unusual response, but this negative exchange had me motivated to prove them wrong! I often wonder how many members of our class had a similar story to tell.

The class of 1967 was a special one. We were the last class to graduate from the old high school facility. With that special commencement under our belt, we entered that turbulent world that I referred to in my introduction. The old school was becoming a middle school. The old buildings were being repurposed, the walls and the fields were tired, and the new school was awaiting its first classes. Our decade was winding down, and we all faced a variety of challenges. As a member of the fiftieth reunion committee, I discovered that many of the male students in our class had died at a rather young age. This was unfortunate news. However, I also heard many classmates share a variety of stories about their successes and achievements that had transpired in their lives. They had all met the challenge, some had faced more adversities than others, and some had sad stories mixed with tales of joy. Most had children and grandchildren, and there were many proud stories to exchange. However, the most uplifting aspect of our reunion was the smiles and the handshakes that were given freely at our event. In some respects, it seemed like we had just seen other the day before, not fifty years ago. We told stories, laughed, and enjoyed one another, longing for that simpler, less-complicated time called high school. Those high school times seemed devoid of the woes of the world. We focused on friends, teachers, activities, sports, dances, dating, Fosters Freeze, cruising, the beach, surfing, jobs, and simply being teenagers. It was not that hard to define this class. We were all trying to figure out who we were, what we wanted to be, where we wanted to go, and with whom. The times were trying, the decisions difficult, but the journey was one that all high school students face. Our class of 1967 had journeyed down the road of life, had weathered the challenges, and now enjoyed the spoils of retirement. Congratulations on each of your journeys!

CHAPTER THIRTEEN

Rick Gesswein

RICK
GESSWEIN

Richard Gesswein

Class of 1967

Growing up in Carpinteria was a great experience. One of the best things was that everybody knew everybody. One of the worst things was that everybody knew everybody! Most of the time, everyone was friendly, which made Carpinteria a good place to grow up in. I was ten years and six years younger than my two brothers, and I had no sisters. A lot of the other kids I was friends with had older siblings, so it made for a lot of lengthy tradition, which carried over to the town and the high school. Carpinteria High School carried a rich tradition in sports, especially their football teams. We would have downtown pep rallies for homecoming where most of the shops would close at noon and most everyone in town would gather at the busiest intersection to support the team. The captains would give inspirational speeches while the rest of the players were displayed on a long flatbed trailer and they waved to hundreds of students, parents, and business owners. All games at Carpinteria were on Friday nights. The Memorial Field had been dedicated to all the servicemen from Carpinteria who had served and/or given their lives for our country. As players, we always gave all we had for our fallen, our school, and our town. It was a great tradition and a great honor.

Carpinteria High School had a student body of approximately 500 students. The solid classes that were offered were math, English, science, history, government, and language, which kept us all busy with homework, but the electives were informative and fun. I took art class, woodshop, and printing. The woodshop class actually was two periods, 2 1/2 hours, where we built two small houses, which were auctioned off at the end of the year. This experience was great and led me into the building trades as a sheet metal/heating and air conditioning journeyman and later an HVAC contractor. There were about twenty kids in the class, which led to about two to three thousand bent nails. Some splinters and smashed fingers happened also. Printing was another class I took. We actually learned how to set type and print out programs for sports and business cards. Some kids tried to print fake IDs and even money, which we found out was a big no-no! One of the duties I and a classmate had was to empty two garbage cans full of paper toward the end of class. We would take it out to an incinerator. The paper was used to clean the press roller plate that had ink on it. White gas was used as the cleaning agent, so it was highly flammable. After we dumped the cans, we took the long way back so we could watch the girls in gym class do calisthenics. It was a good laugh! The teacher busted us and wouldn't let us take the cans out anymore. He appointed two other boys to do the job. My buddy decided he would liven up their day and poured the can of white gas, about a quart, into one of the cans full of paper. Now when white gas and fumes hit live coals, there is a large reaction. When the two guys returned, one had a red face and almost no eyebrows. We got our job back, but we were put on a timer.

During the summer, we had two choices: go to the beach or get a job. The beach didn't pay much, so I decided a job would give me good experience. My first summer job was picking lemons. Several of my friends and I got a job at the local Bracero Camp to pick lemons at 52 cents per field crate. It looked easy. Just work your way around the tree and pull off all the yellow ones. The first morning we showed up, they issued us a bag that hung on our back, a ring that fit on my middle finger but had a larger ring welded to the finger ring, and a set of clippers. We got in the back of the truck with all the other workers and headed to the orchards. When we got to the orchard, we were given a row of trees that we would pick. We were shown how to clip, not pull, all yellow lemons. All the green lemons were cut if the ring didn't slide over. If the ring slid over the green lemon, it was left for the next picking. All this, of course, slowed you down as to the number of boxes you could pick in a day. The other thing that slowed you down was when you picked the bottom of the tree up to head height, the rest required a three-legged ladder. Some of the trees were very tall. Once, I left two lemons that I couldn't reach without damaging the tree. The rancher came up to me and told me to pick them or else. I put the ladder into the thorn-heavy tree, climbed up to the top step, bent the limb down carefully and pulled the lemons off the tree. I vowed not to get mad but to get even! My friends and I would pick about fifteen to twenty boxes per day, depending on the amount of fruit on the trees. Some of the Mexican workers would pick sixty to seventy boxes a day. I think the most I ever picked was twenty-five boxes. I found a great respect for the Mexican workers. We worked about two months and used the last month of our summer vacation at the beach.

We were always pulling pranks on fellow students, parents and teachers, but we needed one for our farmer friend. We came up with an M-80 firecracker and the farmer had a mailbox that was set out on the road, a good place for his firecracker! One foggy night, we went out to the box in my buddy's stick-shift woody station wagon. What a cool car. The idea was to pull up to the box, light the firecracker, throw it into the box, close the lid and get out of there before it went off (about five seconds). The plan worked great right up to the time I yelled, "Go!" The one thing that we didn't plan on was that the car stalled. Five seconds went by fast as he tried to start the car. I tried though to roll up the window. Well, neither happened. When the M-80 went off, the mailbox flew open, and all the debris shot through the whole car and the sound was deafening. It took a week for our hearing to come back and to get the powder smell out of the car. The mailbox, not a scratch. Lesson learned about pranks.

Before my senior year of school, I decided to get a job at a commercial laundry business. My first chore was to wash five big delivery vans and clean them out. The job was on Saturdays. I applied for a different job and got it. I was on the sorting table and, on Fridays, would work until 6:00 p.m. with the manager running the last loads through the washer and dryers.

My senior year was by far the most productive and fun. I got to spend some time with the vice principal of the school. Usually that's not a good thing, but in this case, it was. I was a member of a Catholic Church youth club called the Royal Jesters. I was not Catholic, but the kids I was good friends with asked me to join. We would make money with car washes, bake sales, and Saturday night dances. We would use the money to take some of the younger kids to the snow, bowling, pro sports games and donate to the church. I was elected to be president of the club in my junior year of school. The vice principal called me into his office. Waiting in his office to find out what I did wrong was painful. He actually was very nice. He wanted to let me know that no outside club jackets could be worn to school. He also reminded me that the school had dances every other week, so he would appreciate it if we did not have dances on the nights that the school had them. We complied.

Toward the end of my junior year, I was the campaign manager for the eventual class president candidate. So I had to talk to the vice principal about what was allowed for campaign literature. The only time I had to see him about a violation was for being late to my wood shop class. Our shop teacher wouldn't let us take our books into the shop area. I had a class off campus, which was a block away from the main campus. We had five minutes between classes, and it was not enough time to go all the way into my locker and then out to where shop was. The third time I was late, I was sent to the vice principal's office. I explained there was not enough time between classes. He said that he would walk with me tomorrow. The class off campus was my math class. Toward the end of the class, the vice principal showed up and sat down next to me. The kids were all shocked. The bell rang. As we walked along, I thought he was taking big steps. He was fairly tall but just walked at a steady pace. We walked across the street, across the football field, and into the main building to the lockers. I opened my locker on the first try. I closed the door, and we headed out the end of the building toward the shop. All the time, I was hoping the bell would ring. Usually it would ring about the time I reached the door into the shop. As we got closer, the anticipation grew immensely. Just as the vice principal put his hand on the door handle, the bell rang. He opened the door and let me go in first. My teacher looked at me in disbelief and told me I was late again. I said, "Yes, but I have my get-out-of-jail card." The vice principal walked in and said that it was all right and they would fix the problem in a few days. He ended up extending the time between classes to seven minutes instead of five, which worked out great.

Personally, I had a great season on the football team, making all-league at defensive tackle and setting a new record for tackles. The old record was 73, and I was at 70 going into the last games. I ended up with 13 tackles in the last game of the season, to give me 83 on the year. Unfortunately, we tied for second with two other teams in the league. The league decided to take only one team to the playoffs, which ended our season. It was tough to take because we all thought we were the best team at the end of the season.

When I first started high school, I was fortunate to have some of the older kids show me the ropes of the school. I remembered this and wanted to do the same. Most of the freshmen coming into school, I knew because of older brothers and sisters. I tried to get to know some of the freshmen to help them acclimate to the school and other functions. One of the girls that I got to know, I would marry in about six years. We had a lot in common. We both loved the outdoors and sports.

The other big thing that happened to me was that I was offered a job in the sheet metal and HVAC trade. My brother was working for this company. My dad was a carpenter for twenty years, so all this seemed like a good fit. I passed the test at the union, and I would report to work on the Monday after graduation. I served a four-year apprenticeship and became a journeyman. My boss also sponsored a female softball team that my girlfriend then wife played on, as well as my boss's secretary. I was the coach of this all-girl team and would remain so for about ten years.

One of the things I love the most is the great outdoors—hiking, hunting, and fishing. My then-boss and my brothers all loved to fish and hunt. So we did it for a lot of years. One of the fishing trips we had was in the Sierra Nevada Mountains. We didn't have a boat with us that we would usually put in Crowley Lake. This time, we decided to stream-fish. We were fishing in a creek, Hot Creek. Most of the stream is for artificial lure and flies only. We began fly-fishing, and we fished for a while, with a few bites. We decided we would cross the stream, as the water looked better on the side. The stream was about twenty feet wide and two feet deep. My brother had no boots and decided that I could carry him across on my back while he held the rods and gear. Being a good brother, I agreed. He grabbed all the gear. I stepped into the water and found the water was almost as deep as my boots. Nevertheless, we proceeded. He jumped on my back and put his legs around my waist. The first couple of steps went well. When I got about to the center of the stream, my feet sank in the bottom mud to above my ankles. I couldn't get my feet out of the mud. Of course, my brother was having a fit as he knew where he was probably going to end up. All I could do was laugh, and the more I laughed, the madder he became. I thought if I could get my foot out of the mud, we could get across. If I tried to step and couldn't, we would both be in the stream. I told him to hold on as I gathered my strength and made the step from the mud, freeing my feet. I knew I had to keep going to get to the other side. By now, my arms were almost numb from holding on to my brother. After one, two, three, or four steps, all I could do when I got to the bank on the other side was to turn sideways and throw him off my back. He didn't bounce too well, but all the tackle and rods flew all over the place. As he lay there, complaining about how I almost killed him, I noticed there was a snake right next to him. I said, "Well, brother, if I didn't kill you, that snake might." I've never seen him jump that high so quick.

One of my most favorite pastimes is hunting. It's not just the hunt itself but the beautiful country I have seen, the people I have met, and the companionship of friends and family. I have hunted in most of the western states of the United States and Alaska, British Columbia, Mexico, New Zealand, and Africa. A couple of the hunts also included my wife, Pam, accompanying me. She enjoys the outdoors and the adventure of being in the wilderness. Pam accompanied me on my grizzly bear hunt to the Arctic Circle in Alaska. My outfitter told me that there had been only two other women that had gone on this trip, but neither of them lasted more than a couple of days before he had to fly them back to civilization. The accommodations were our own four-man tent with two cots and a two-burner stove to boil water and heat the tent. When we got to Kotzebue, the outfitter met us at the airport and immediately loaded my gear on his bush plane, as there was a storm coming in and he wanted to get me out to camp so I could hunt the next day. You cannot fly and hunt on the same day. It was about a forty-five-minute flight one way. We unloaded my gear, and he took off back to Kotzebue to get Pam. The storm was almost on us, so he said he probably might not get her out to camp until the following day. Pam spent that night in a bed and breakfast and was able to get out to camp the next afternoon. I wondered how she would handle the plane flight as it was a two-person plane and the passenger seat was a small seat behind the pilot. The only place for some of the gear to travel was in your lap. There was no runway, just the rocky riverbank, so the landing was kind of rough, but they made it in safe. It took a couple of days to get acclimated to the weather. We were 100 miles above the Arctic Circle. There were small trees and large bushes along the river, but you could look over the tundra for fifty miles to the mountain ranges packed with snow. The rivers were glacier blue. The tundra was a rustic red with a touch of dark blue from the blueberries that were ripening. Pam and I ate our share when we were looking for bears. The total amount of grizzly bears we saw or visited our camp in the eleven days we were there was over thirty. I had harvested my bear on the fourth day of the hunt, but I also had a tag for a moose or a caribou. We saw three moose but only one small bull and no caribou. We also saw a small herd of musk ox, which we enjoyed watching. One of the funniest things that happened was on one day we hiked up onto a mesa that was about 100 feet higher than the tundra. We spent a lot of time with binoculars and spotting scopes looking over the large countryside. We noticed a bear making his way along the shoreline. He was about 1/4 mile off. He crossed the river at a bend but started diving for fish. It didn't look like he was having much luck. He came out of the water on our side of the river. Our camp was on the same side, and he was heading toward it. We watched him find his way through the brush until he came out where we could see him. He was about 50 yards from us and about 200 yards from camp. Knowing what a bear can do to a camp, the guide decided to fire a warning shot a few yards in front of him. When the guide put a shell in the camper, the bear stopped and didn't move a muscle. You could see his nostrils moving. He was trying to find out what the noise was, but he couldn't locate us, as we were above him. The guide raised his rifle and fired a shot into the ground about five feet in front of him. The bear jumped straight up and turned around while in the air and hit the ground running. He ran all the way back to the bend of the river where he had crossed. There was a log on the bank of the river where he sat down on his butt, put his paws on his knees, and looked all around to see what had happened. After spending eleven days on the tundra, we gained more respect and appreciation for Alaska. I was especially proud of my wife. I know our guide and outfitter were proud of her also. She loved the experience. We have been to Alaska several times and never get tired of it.

One of the other things I've done that I am most proud of is coaching kids' sports. Working with all the kids on the teams I coached and watching them develop and improve their skills and watching them develop into adulthood was great. I have adults come up to me and say, "Hi, Coach. Do you remember me? You were my coach when I was younger." I have coached boys' and girls' basketball, girls' softball, boys' baseball, and youth football. Several of the kids I have coached in baseball went on to division 1 schools and played baseball, and one I coached made it to the Colorado Rockies pro team. He sent me a picture of the team and signed it for me. It hangs on my wall!

Looking back on all the years that have expired, the experiences I have gained and the things I have learned have laid the foundation for helping shape the lives of my children and grandchildren. I'm so proud of my three children: Jennifer, Dennis, and Meredith. We are also proud of our nine grandchildren, of whom seven are boys and two are girls. This would all not be possible without the matriarch of the family, my wife and the love of my life, Pam. All this came about because of the little town of Carpinteria. Our family biography for Pam and me isn't ending but is just beginning!

CHAPTER FOURTEEN

Chris Blakeslee

CHRIS BLAKESLEE

Christopher Blakeslee aka El Sharko (class of '67)

Swimming the English Channel to Get to the Other Side

Prelude (and how I got the name El Sharko)

Mary Giannotti and Chris Blakeslee met at Carpinteria High School and were married in October 1972. Mary was from the class of 1968. She was the cheerleader and I was the ASB jock president. We moved to beautiful Sonoma County in 1979, near the waters of Tomales Bay, which became my swimming grounds as an aquatic sort of creature.

Many of my friends soon began calling me El Sharko (I know El Tiburón is mas correcto), but this is how that all started: I convinced a group of pool swimmers to join me for open-water swims in Tomales Bay. I would often go down to Nick's Cove with my black Lab to swim out to Hog Island and back (about 1 1/2 miles round trip). One particular windy afternoon I was swimming out from Nick's Cove, after having a few beers, and as I was passing the small pier jutting out into the bay, I vaguely heard a woman's voice yelling and pointing to me. I pulled my cap up and took an earplug out to hear her say, "Don't swim out there. It is the breeding grounds of the great white shark." I irreverently said, "I am not planning on breeding any sharks today." (There used to be a bronze plaque on the shore at Nick's Cove, which erroneously said that Tomales Bay was in fact a breeding ground for the great white shark. There are white sharks feeding near the seal haul-out area at the mouth of Tomales Bay, which is a couple of miles west of Hog Island. The area is part of what is known as the Red Triangle, an area noted for large numbers of very large great white sharks. This area extends north and south of Tomales Bay and out to the Farallon Islands.) She was not too happy with my response and marched back to the café. I am not particularly proud of my boozy irreverent response to this concerned lady. I have not used any mind-altering substances for many years now. My swimmer friends heard the story from the locals and started calling me El Sharko, which, for some strange reason, stuck after all these years.

This swimming ultimately led me to the South End Rowing and Swimming Club at Aquatic Park in San Francisco, where I became a Polar Bear marathon swimmer, and in 2004, at the age of fifty-four (two weeks shy of my fifty-fifth birthday), swam the English Channel in fourteen hours and forty-four minutes. A marathon channel swim turns out to be a transforming experience by swimming from one shore and emerging on another shore. I will discuss more about this and other swims later.

Mary and I have lived in beautiful Sonoma County, on a small acreage, since moving here in 1979.

Early Years (childhood and move to Sonoma County)

I spent my early years growing up in Southern California, at the beach mainly, surfing and diving since my father was the co-originator of *Skin Diver* magazine. When he sold the magazine, we moved in 1965 to Carpinteria, where he became an avocado grower. My brother, sister, and I were stoked to be less than a mile from one of the best surfing spots in the world, Rincon. I attended Carpinteria High School my junior and senior years. Carpinteria was a great place for the continuation of surfing and diving with not all of the Southern California crowds. I became a surf bum, for a while going to Hawaii in the winters. I had a great time during those years. After high school, I got a summer job as a state lifeguard at Carpinteria State Beach.

After high school, I went to Cal Poly and studied agriculture science and obtained my bachelor of science degree. I started managing agricultural properties in the Camarillo area and eventually managed a 24,000-acre ranch near Bakersfield. It was hard being away from the ocean, so in 1978, I took a job at a large bank's trust department in San Francisco and I commuted from Petaluma to the San Francisco office or to the trust ranch properties. In 1986, I formed a vineyard and winery consulting business for local, national, and international clients. I am now semi-retired, still swimming and gardening mostly.

Marathon Swimming (and what I learned about myself)

I was about forty-five years old when I became an avid Polar Bear open-water swimmer. At the South End, most of the swimmers skinned it year-round, with water temperatures dropping below 50°F in January and February. At the South End, we have a tradition of swimming from Alcatraz to our club on New Year's morning (about 1 1/2 miles). The club puts on regular swims throughout the bay for swimming members (the club also supports rowing shells and wooden boats for rowers, and there are championship-level handball courts for the handball contingent).

Swimmers training for marathon channel swims such as the English Channel and the Catalina Channel are mentored and supported by veteran swimmers and pilots. Training swims are conducted throughout the Bay and beyond. There are various achievement plaques and vintage photographs on the club walls, of those that have achieved greatness by their swimming successes as club members. (If you are ever in San Francisco, ring the doorbell, and someone will likely open the door and give you a tour of the club. Tell them El Sharko sent you. Their website is serc.com.)

Open-water and marathon swimming is a passion and an obsession to many club members. I have observed within me and others a swimmer's need to work through their demons that get in the way of a more peaceful life. A marathon swim is defined differently by different organizations, but there is some consensus that a ten-kilometer swim or more is considered a marathon. (My English Channel swim wound up being about thirty-one miles due to the currents or about twenty-one miles in a straight line.)

Some people will invariably ask marathon swimmers, what do you think about for hours and hours on end and don't you get bored? Actually in my experience, the first hour or so, my mind is running on the issues of life and then I go into a very calm state of awareness and sometimes extreme compassion for others. In my write-up right after my English Channel swim, shown below, you will note my mental and physiological take during the swim.

Below is a write-up of my September 4, 2004, English Channel swim (David Frantzeskou was our host and cheerleader in England):

David, someone told me there are no sharks in the English Channel. And David replied, "But there was one today, September 4, 2004. You were there, and you did it, Sharko!" And so I did, with the support of a lot of people and sharks everywhere! For fourteen hours and forty-four minutes, I was carried by your support, and in return, I gave my heart to you. One week after my swim, I was back at the South End Club, after a Crissy Field Club Swim, my Dover Strait swim chart stretched out, trying to explain all the zigging and zagging on the nautical chart, when one of our members said, "Why did you do it?" And I believe I said, "Aahhh, that is the question, isn't it? There is something very big about this swim, some deeper meaning . . ."

I met Carol Sing at Chapels in Dover after my swim, and she looked into my eyes and said (as closely as I can remember), "The large feelings you now have from your swim will last a long while." Why is that? I don't think the swim is a totally selfish endeavor; however, it does take long-term focused training to accomplish the swim. During this swim, I recalled all of us who have suffered, and are suffering, and I decided to dedicate the swim to all of them and us, some with cancer, many dealing with issues of life that appear too large to handle to handle. We all need help.

Final preparations for the swim began at 7:30 p.m. when Reg Brickell confirmed the swim was on. "Meet me at the Folkestone Harbor at 2:30 a.m.," he said. (I didn't think I was that nervous, but I probably only slept an hour or two.) I calculated that I would need to get up at 1:00 a.m. to get feeding supplies and warm clothes together, do some stretching and breathing, get the closest shave of my life, and carry all of the gear out to the taxi driver.

My wife, Mary, who flew in the night before, was there to encourage and feed me, with no real sleep for twenty-four hours or so. At about 3:00 a.m., we motored north in the darkness, with only boat lights leading the way, to Shakespeare Beach. On the way, Mary coated me with sunscreen and greased my shoulders, armpits, and between my legs. I continued to breathe using the alternate nose-breathing technique I had been using to help saturate my muscles with oxygen and to stretch. A light stick was attached to the back of my cap and one pinned to the back of my Speedo. At about 3:20, we began to back up to the beach, and at 3:25, Reg said to swim to the beach. I jumped over the stern of the *Viking Princess* into the dark and cool English Channel water and stroked easily to the beach. I felt good. The time had finally come. I told myself to relax and swim easily for the first hour until my first feeding. Reg had his boat lights and a beamed flashlight pointed to the pebbly beach. I touched bottom and walked to above the water line. I guess a horn was blown, but I didn't hear it because of the tight silicon earplugs. The lights were flashed, and I dove back into the cool and dark Channel waters.

I guess I swam for about three hours in the dark. I started feeding at one hour and every thirty minutes after. The feedings were very quick as I had my liquefied food in large-mouth plastic containers that were tossed over in front of me. The containers had one-twist screw caps, and with a quick twist to the mouth and throwing my head back, down went the Cytomax and sixteen ounces of water . . . ten seconds, maybe fifteen. A second bottle contained liquefied GU and Cytomax if I needed it. At four hours, I was to receive Cytomax and a whey protein mix.

After three hours, it was a welcome sight to see the beginning of light and some pink in the clouds. What had I been thinking about all this time? I get that question all the time from non-swimmers: What do you think about? Don't you get bored? Sometimes it's such a relief to have no other distractions than my own rhythmic stroking and breathing, but I guess if you are not a marathon swimmer, you wouldn't know what I am talking about.

As it got lighter and the sun came up, I realized I would need to change my clear goggles for a pair of tinted ones. I was a little worried that a new pair might leak, but I wasn't about to stare into the sun for the next ten hours. The switch was made with a pole with a cup on the end. The new pair sealed in a minute or two, and the glare was gone. I began to see large passenger and container ships streaming by. There is a lot of boat traffic in the Channel. At this point between 4 and 6 hours into the swim, my stroke was strong and consistent at about fifty-four strokes per minute. And I was stretching and rotating well. At 6 1/2 hours, Reg indicated that I was at the halfway point, and shortly after, I could see the coast of France. Feeding from 6 1/2 hours to 10 hours was with Cytomax and whey or Cytomax only with an occasional Cytomax and GU mix. I wanted to be hydrated but not saturated with sugar. I was taking 200 mg of ibuprofen every two hours to keep muscle inflammation down. Somewhere between 10 and 12 hours, my speed began dropping. My stroke rate was still over fifty, but my right shoulder had lost power. Fortunately, my left shoulder was still in good shape and was compensating, but my back was starting to seize up because the natural rolling of my body had been disrupted by my shoulder.

I was watching the Cape Gris-Nez lighthouse drift by. "How much farther, Reg?"

"Three to four hours," said Reg.

Oh shit! I said. The period from 12 hours to 14 hours and 44 minutes became the mental struggle to overcome the fatigue of the body and persevere mentally, to push on beyond what I thought I could.

This time, then, became the swim. This, then, is what I came here to find out about myself. And I did persevere and felt the sand under my feet, and I stood up. My leg cramped, and I fell down and crawled over a small reef, cutting my hands and snatching some French beach pebbles, then finally up onto a beautiful sandy beach near Wissant, France, at 6:10 p.m. It was a hell of a good day and the culmination and release of something of grand proportion. There was a Shark in the English Channel today!

Chris Blakeslee, El Capitan

CHAPTER FIFTEEN

Terry Galvez

Terry Galvez

Hello there, my name is Terry Galvez, and we need to ask ourselves how did seventy years of our life pass us by? I never left Carpinteria! This place is the most beautiful place and I have traveled many places: Hawaii, the Caribbean, Italy, China, and many states in the USA. My parents were living in Carpinteria. My mom was born in Santa Barbara, and my dad was born in Carpinteria; both were born at home. We lived in a very tiny house on Cramer Circle before the 101 freeway was put in. My dad had a sister that passed at a young age and left behind two little girls that my dad and mom raised as their own. I came along later, and all I knew is, I had two sisters and that's who they are to me. We later moved to a ranch where my dad was the foreman, on Casitas Pass Road right behind the Lions Park.

I started kindergarten at Canalino school and was there until junior high, which was called the main school, then to Carpinteria High School, which is now the junior high. My memories growing up out on a ranch are my most memorable. My siblings and I had so many outside activities: playing in the orchards, building a tree house, riding our bikes, and of course, our chores. They consisted of cleaning our room, doing laundry, helping to cook, and cleaning up after meals. We all learned at a young age to clean house, thanks to my mom. Holidays were always a fun time for us; one Easter Sunday, we were all dressed up with our Easter baskets, ready to go to church. It had been raining for some days, and we were unable to cross the creek that led out to Casitas Pass Road. My parents had to use the back way to drive out, which was a long ride into town to St. Joseph's chapel. I had great friendships with the other kids that lived on Casitas Pass Road. Some of these friends still live in Carpinteria: Ester Cerda, Emily Brown, Wendy Bliss. We all rode the bus to school every day, and at the time, it seemed like a really long ride. We would go to each other's houses and hang out, riding bikes, horses, and homemade go-carts, having sleepovers. Summertime was the best, riding your bike to the beach and going to the foot of Linden to the boardwalk. There were pinball machines, other games to play and food to buy. Reggie's Bate shop was on Palm Avenue where we would stop and buy candy before going to the beach. There were summer dances that were held at the Canalino school cafeteria with real live bands. My friends and I joined the Brownies and then Girls Scouts; it was such a great experience learning about all sorts of things in life. Going on trips and camping. Back then, the clubhouse where we would have our meetings is where Lions Park is located. During my junior high school days, I was a cheerleader and, in high school, was a song leader. I graduated and went on to find a job, wanted to attend a trade school but my parents couldn't afford the expense. So off I went to an electronic firm in Santa Barbara. I didn't have a car, so I got a ride from a dear friend that worked there. In the meantime, I got married, and my husband at the time was drafted to the Vietnam War. We weren't married very long before he was drafted, and I moved back to my parents' house. My dad had gotten a job with the University of California as an equipment operator so they have moved from the ranch to a home they had bought before moving to the ranch. I had my daughter Lisa while my husband was in Vietnam. Lisa is fifty years old and lives here in Carpinteria. When my daughter was two years old, I needed to go to work to help out my husband as we were struggling with the everyday life expenses, raising a family. So at the time, a new manufacturing company had moved into the old lemon-packing house on Linden Avenue right next to the railroad tracks. The name of the company was Kilovac, founded by Mr. Foster Campbell. I applied with no experience and was hired in 1972 and worked there until I retired in 2011. I took two years off when I had my son Marc, who is forty-five years old. He lives in Carpinteria also; I am fortunate that my two adult children live here in Carpinteria.

I wasn't sure if I would be hired back at my job since I was gone for two years, but my boss did! It was such an experience for me all those years and all that I learned. I started out as an assembler, then I became a lead and a supervisor of a department, which consisted of twenty-two people. There were many challenges in managing people of different nationalities and ages, but I enjoyed it. The company had been bought out twice in my years working there, Tyco being the last one when I retired. It has now moved to North Carolina, and there are a few employees still working in the far end of the building where you can see the Tyco name if you drive down Linden toward the beach. My husband and I divorced after fifteen years of marriage. I met my second husband at my job, and we were together for twenty-five years; he passed away in 2009. It was very devastating, but with my family and good friends in my life, I got through it. When I retired, I purchased a mobile home here in Carpinteria and I am very happy. I have four grandchildren whom I am very involved with, and my mom, who will be ninety-two in July, keeps me very busy. I enjoy cooking, reading, going to the gym, riding my bike, and going to the beach. I have a group of eight girlfriends; we play Bunco every third Friday of the month, each of us taking turns hosting at our homes once a month to catch up on what's going on in our lives.

I want to end by thanking Joe Lovett for his idea of writing this book.

CHAPTER SIXTEEN

Colleen Olszewski

The Dog Days

by Colleen Wolski

One of the first things we did when we moved to our house in Oregon was to get our four-year-old Kelly a dog. Mike and I both had dogs as kids and knew that it's a kid's right to grow up with a dog. Kids need that unquestioning acceptance and ultimate affection from a dog to give them a sense of security, right? Mike had Shaggy, Shorty, and Big Rick running around the California desert with him as a kid. My sister and I had our guy Dukie in Illinois, a black-and-white border collie mix. We loved him desperately the four years we had him. When our mom "gave him to a farmer" when she married our stepdad, our hearts were completely broken. I never did forgive my mother.

Anyway, Kelly picked out a fluffy cream-colored cocker/golden mix, a male, from the litter of four remaining we'd found from a personal ad. He'd run to her at the house, so she chose him and then held him in the back seat of the car all the way home. "Jesse." She loved him. He was gentle and sweet with all the neighborhood kids. He grew up mid-sized with a beautiful, long, silky coat. He was so smart; I think he was house trained in a week. All I had to tell him was "Go pee!" He'd comply, and I'd shout in a high-pitched, singsong voice, "Such a *good* dog!" He'd squint his eyes, glare, and then raise his head in a superior manner as he walked back into the house, clearly insulted and trying to regain his dog dignity. Soon, he would test my patience, my resolve, and my intellect.

He didn't like being alone. If we left him outside when Kelly and I went to get groceries or went to a park or had lunch with Mike downtown, between nonstop barks, he'd lick the sliding glass door. I mean icky, viscous dog spit. Thick, gooey slime all over the window as far up as he could reach. So every single time we'd go somewhere, I'd have a disgusting mess to clean off the windows.

His other habit was to chase kids on bikes or cars going through our cul-de-sac, but inside our fenced yard. Mike had spent hours and hours putting up the fence to keep Kelly and Jesse safe inside, and landscaping and planting the backyard to perfection, only to watch Jesse run muddy (Oregon!) paths through the yard and all along the fence.

Remember the long, silky coat! From running the fence line, his underbelly would be *caked* in mud. And he did *not* like baths. The whole time in the tub, he'd be growling at me, baring his teeth. He knew (like dogs do) that I was intimidated by him, and he reminded me during the entire bath that *he* was *my* boss, and at *any time* of his choosing, he could easily bite. And cutting his dog nails? That bath time growl/warning was nothing compared to the snarling and gnashing of teeth he did during that.

Why didn't I use a groomer, you say? Well. Do I *look* like a foofy poodle (no offense to poodle lovers) person? Oh, no. And I take care of my own kids, furry or not. In fact, that's why Mike and I moved to Oregon. We'd hit a financial roadblock trying to buy a California house. Determined that our daughter not be raised by a daycare system, our plan was for me to be a stay-at-home mom until Kelly went to school, kind of a fantasy dream in high-priced California. So we bought a 1,500-square-foot three-bedroom house in Salem for two-thirds the price of an 800-square-foot "house" in Morro Bay, even though Mike had to take a career and pay cut. You pick your priorities, right?

But back to Jesse. All the long silky hair, he shed all over the brown carpets, the brown couch. I had to vacuum every other day. I admit that some days, I wished for a smaller house. Or better, just no dog. Once, when Mike and Kelly and I went out to dinner, we came home to the dining room's woven wood shades (remember those?) ripped down from the windows and scattered in chewed-up pieces all over the floor. Why? Did someone come to the front door? Maybe. All I know is, I was at the end of my rope, and these are just a few of the stories of what I determined to be Jesse's destructive nature. To me, he really was the worst dog I ever knew.

Four years and a lot of cleaning up later, Jesse and I had settled into an uneasy understanding—I knew he could bite me and he knew I was physically able (barely) to pick him up. While I was thoroughly tempted, I never resorted to violence; it's just never been my way. But it was definitely a war of wills. I spent a lot of time trying to outthink and outmaneuver his antics. And we did a lot of glaring at each other.

Kelly was in school by then, and I was working part-time a couple days a week and volunteering at her school during her school hours. I'd had to figure out a way to keep the house in one piece while I was away. If he was loose in the house, despite our giving him plenty of dog toys and chewy bones, Jesse might put giant gouges in the doors or chew up anything he could reach, including the wood trim around the doors. So he spent time, by my hand, chained to Mike's workbench in the garage. When I was a kid, I'd always hated seeing dogs chained up, believing the owner must be some bullying prison warden. Here I was, thoroughly guilty of being that mean guy.

One Saturday, Mike was on his way out to do yard work at his mom's, or maybe my mom's (he's done a *lot* of yard work in Oregon), and said to a query I couldn't hear from Kelly, "It's OK with me, honey, but you have to ask Mom." When she ran to me, she begged in the way only hysterical little girls can, "*Mom!* Can I have that puppy? We *have* to keep him! If we don't, they'll make a *coat* out of him!" These were the *Pound Puppies* kid TV cartoon days. Out on our front lawn was the cutest, funniest-looking little black puppy with a white stripe down his face, doing that "play with me" butt-in-the-air, tail-wagging puppy pose. Meanwhile, I'm thinking, shhhhhhh . . . great, just what I need, *another* dog. Apparently, the teenage girls across the street got this pup from a girl whose mother wouldn't let *her* keep it, and these girls' mom said no way—she was taking it to the pound. At least that's the story *my* daughter told me, pleading. Well, I never could turn down my daughter in distress, and I sure couldn't resist the goofy little ball of fur on my front lawn. Go ahead, call me a sucker. I said, "Well, we know lots of people, maybe we can find someone who wants another dog." You know what happens.

Petie (a la Our Gang) Wolski was the best dog I ever knew. He was sweet and loving and playful and fun. He was that dog who sensed your moods and would lie by you in sympathetic support. And he was obedient. Once, when we were out front, he took off running after a cat going down the sidewalk. Fearing he would run out into the street (though we seldom had cars in our cul-de-sac, I was in high-alert protective mom mode), I yelled, "Petie, *stop!*" He came to a screeching halt, like the proverbial stomping on the brakes of a car. Was it the fear he picked up in my voice? Maybe. All I know is, that dog literally slid. I was happy to be *his* mom.

Meanwhile, Jesse tried to teach Petie a few things. Like how to eat. Jesse would take a mouth full of dog kibbles, walk over and spit them out on the floor and *then* eat them. Maybe he was counting the nuggets to make sure Petie didn't have more. Thankfully, Petie didn't completely agree with that lesson. Instead he'd just flood the kitchen floor when he drank out of the water bowl. Was Petie thinking, "We're doing a mess on the floor, right, Jesse?" Maybe. But Jesse did teach Petie, because he learned first that there was no begging at the dinner table. They were both perfect gentlemen, politely lying on the floor, not even paying attention, while people ate. Jesse also taught Petie, though, that the couches and people beds were *much* better places to sleep on while the people were away than the dog beds. Jesse was such a dichotomy of good and evil!

Then one day, Jesse trapped Petie out in the doghouse Mike had made them (that they never really used) and wouldn't let him out. Jesse snarled and charged at me when I came near, trying to rescue Petie. Apparently, according to our vet, whom we'd called in a panic, Jesse was teaching us all, especially Petie, that *he* was the alpha dog. Knowing from experience that my daughter would never, ever forgive me if I "gave him to a farmer," though I really, really wanted to, Jesse (and then later Petie, when he was old enough) was neutered. Thankfully, that solved *that* dog problem.

But having two dogs changes your life. We were tent campers. So we took the dogs with us over the mountains to eastern Oregon. It rained one weekend—hard. A kid and two very, very wet dogs in a tent with a moat around it—oh boy. Needless to say, we had to problem solve *again*. So we became trailer campers. And that was fun. But you find that you confine yourself to certain types of family entertainment when you add furry members to your family. We did take a few fabulous people-only vacations and even were able to drive across the country for a month once, seeing the highlights of the USA. Thankfully, for those events over the years, my mom stayed at our house to take care of our dogs though she absolutely was *not* a dog lover. "Animals belong outside," my mom always said. Was my asking her to stay with our dogs my revenge for Dukie? Maybe.

According to my mom, dogs were very germy. When we'd return from our trips, the whole house would smell like bleach. And I could tell the dogs had spent most of their time outdoors; they seemed bedraggled and sad. Trust me, we'd tried kennels, and Petie, my big, sweet baby, wouldn't eat there while we were away. So the dogs and Kelly and the neighborhood kids played in the yard and in the playhouse (that Mike built for Kelly which was very, *very* much used), and we mostly camped in our trailer or rented dog-friendly vacation houses at the beach for entertainment. And we took a lot of family hikes. Did our dogs change my mom? Maybe. Or maybe because she had to live with them if she dog sat or when she went on some of our trips with us, she became somewhat of an animal person. Later in life, she actually allowed a cat to live *in* her house. Dog miracles!

Speaking of miracles, remember that gross licking-the-door stuff Jesse did? Petie, according to the vet, was pit bull mix, though he had really long legs—Mike's mom called him an Imperial Walker—and he would body block Jesse away from the sliding glass door and cured him of that horrible habit! And the chaining up in the garage? Over. Now that Jesse had a pack, thanks to Petie, he was no longer destructive. He'd happily and calmly sleep on his dog bed (well, you know, the couch) in the house until we got home. Did he stop making paths in the yard? No. Did I get to stop cleaning so much? No. In fact, I wore out two vacuum cleaners. But we later moved to a slightly bigger house with a bit more property, and while it was a lot more landscaping for Mike and more vacuuming for me, at least there were no more muddy paths.

I mentioned that Petie was sweet and fun-loving. But two big dogs can also make you feel very well protected. Whenever Mike had to go on business trips (he'd gone on to have pretty high-profile jobs with both the City of Salem as the environmental compliance manager, for which his group won state and national acclaim, and later for the City of Albany as the assistant director of public works) or got called in the middle of the night because of a dramatic environmental incident/ disaster, I believed Kelly and I were completely safe. Petie was seventy pounds fully grown and had a very low-pitched, rumbling growl, a deep-throated bark and a very feral, unblinking stare. He'd scare me if I didn't know that in reality, he'd probably wag his tail and show the robber where Mike's grandma's silver was kept.

Well, we all grew up together and had busy lives in work and school. Mike and I were supportive spectators for Kelly's dance recitals, play and choir performances, volleyball games, etc., and played host to an array of her friends through the years. During one such event, some gathering of the cheerleaders, I think, all the girls ate some of the pizzas we'd ordered before Mike and I went out to some more adult event, and went upstairs to do hair or change clothes or some teenage-girl thing. Remember my praise about our dogs being such gentlemen? Suspend that thought; there was a notable lapse. This time, when the girls returned downstairs, they found empty pizza boxes lying on the floor. But our two guys were looking innocently back at them on their dog beds. There no was furniture near enough for one (or both) of them to climb onto the counter. Kelly said there wasn't even a mess on the floor. So how the heck did they get those boxes down? Was Jesse able to jump that high and drag them down? Maybe. However that smart guy accomplished *that* feat, it forever remains a family mystery.

Did I just say Jesse was a smart dog? Oh yeah. He went on to a long life of fourteen years, though in the last few he was completely blind. He knew where every piece of furniture was in that house (and I was careful never to move anything in those days) and he never faltered, even going up and down the stairs. See? I *knew* count! In the yard, if he lost his bearings, he would walk in circles, ever widening, head down so he wouldn't hit his nose, until he found a bush he recognized and then would turn correctly and walk directly to the back door of the house. Genius is the better word.

Fast-forward to 2001, almost five years after Jesse passed, Kelly graduated from the University of Oregon, I was working full-time in the administrative offices of the school district, and Mike was winning a national award for his group's work to reclaim and restore a wetland near the wastewater treatment plant in Albany. I think Petie held on waiting for his girl to come home from college, but Mike and I knew he was getting frail. After all, he was almost sixteen years old, pretty old for such a big guy. We took him on a last trip to Yellowstone late that summer. And our still very alert boy saved us, warning us with a growl and a bark that there was a rattlesnake curled up around a bush we were about step over while on a hike.

He slept a lot when we got him home, on my lap—he always did think he was a small lap dog. He'd wake me in the night when he had to go pee by gently touching my face with his big nose. He really was the sweetest boy.

I have to acknowledge the horrific 9/11 that ushered in that devastatingly sad fall season. On October 2, always the saddest day of the year for us because Mike's dad had died that very day in 1985, Petie began having seizures. They came closer and closer together as the morning wore on, and he was terrified. We couldn't help him or calm him, so we had to take him to the vet. He died in our arms. Only the passing of Mike's dad and then his mom eleven years later were sadder days in my life.

Kelly went on to get married a few years later. Perhaps carrying on our family dog tradition, she and our son-in-law Dave adopted two rescue dogs, first Hunter and then Cooper. Big dogs. Cooper was 110 pounds, Hunter about 85. Good dogs, fun dogs, smart dogs, they were great and sweet, and we were happy to dog sit them when Kel and Dave would travel. Our granddogs.

How we behave when we have furry friends in our life can disclose our true characters. According to the choices we make regarding the issues that come up, we can reveal traits like understanding, kindness, and forgiveness. Our shortcomings will also rear their ugly heads if we react with meanness, pettiness, stubbornness, or cruelty. Do these self-revelations, if we take them to heart, raise our consciousness? Maybe. All I know is, regardless of our actions, dogs continue to grace us with their loyalty, trust, and unconditional love. I think they're better people than we are. Throughout my trials and tribulations of caring for Jesse, I had to confront my own principles as he challenged my sanity and my psyche. But I learned to respect, admire, and yes, even love him. Maybe what I've personally realized as I write this is that all the time with our dogs is simply tangled up with the wonderful, fulfilling, sometimes hectic, extremely happy, though occasionally profoundly sad, memories I have of our young family life. And setting aside any lessons, I do know, because the heart *never* forgets, that there's a piece of my heart that belongs only to the best dog.

Colleen and Mike Wolski pet dogs Petie and Jesse

CHAPTER SEVENTEEN

Linda Fryer

LINDA
FRYER

When I was born at Santa Barbara Cottage Hospital in the winter of 1949, it had snowed in Carpinteria the week before—a weather phenomenon for this sleepy coastal town. I grew up on Seventh Street with my recently divorced mother, brother, and grandparents. The house is still there and sits behind The Palms. When I was four years old, my mother remarried and we were uprooted and moved to Oklahoma, and then to Texas because my new father was a geophysicist and worked for an oil exploration company.

After three years, my mother convinced our father to return to Carpinteria. We lived in a red house on the corner of Maple and Seventh Street (the original house no longer exists but there is still the same jacaranda tree in the front yard). By this time, we had three more siblings added to the family, and two more to come later. Ricky G. and Janice B. lived next door. One block away lived my first best friend Clare, and interestingly, our lives crossed paths later on in Germany.

When I entered Aliso School in the third grade, I arrived with a Texan drawl (and still have remnants of it now). Looking at my report cards (yes, my mother saved everything from kindergarten through high school), I appeared to be a good student, albeit a bit shy in the third grade (probably because I was the new kid). I finally came out of my shell in the fourth grade, and my teacher Ms. Jamieson wrote, "Linda does very good work in school but she is still too talkative." Later she wrote, "Linda is a perky little girl and has a well-developed sense of humor." By the fifth grade, Mrs. Clawson wrote, "Linda has been careless about handing in social studies assignments. She needs to improve in self-control in the classroom." I forgot to mention that my favorite class-time activity was show-and-tell. I just loved listening to the adventures of Kevin S. Also, I remember a new student from Delaware who came to class on his first day dressed in a suit and tie (that's how they dressed on the East Coast), but the next day, he arrived in slacks and a striped T-shirt. I sure wished I could remember his name.

In 1960, my family moved to my grandfather's lemon and avocado ranch on Gobernador Canyon Road. It was also the year that I transferred to Canalino School and attended sixth grade. Academically, I did well and didn't have any behavioral issues. I attribute my relatively good behavior to being a bit shy with meeting so many new kids (I can't remember if there were any former Aliso School classmates in my class). I guess I acted out when I was in my comfort zone and I wasn't there yet at Canalino.

Junior high school is a blur except for the Bay of Pigs crisis. I'm not sure why I still remember it, but a lot of us thought that the USSR was going to drop the A-bomb on us. Now this brings back memories of the A-bomb drills since grade school when everyone would hide under their desks. Of note, in junior high I started to spindle downhill scholastically. Oh, I managed to keep my head above water, but my body was going through hormonal changes that all teens experience and my focus was not on doing any homework. Since we had so many children in our family, my parents were too busy to ask me if I had any homework. So there was zero pressure, and I shrugged it all off.

During my high school years, we moved back into town and lived on Linhere Drive and Vallecito Road. My social life expanded to different groups because I didn't feel comfortable constrained to one particular group. I was not a social butterfly, brainy, or athletic. If anything, I wanted to be cool. I never dated until I was a senior, and my boyfriend was going to the Brooks Photography Institute. I did not go to the senior prom. The most infamous day was when JFK was shot on November 22, 1963. I was sitting in Mr. Burke's science class when the announcement came blaring over the PA system.

Graduation day was the happiest day of my life at that point in time. No more typing and shorthand classes from Mrs. Shenkmann, which is ironic in a way because the office and secretarial skills that I got from her classes helped me to enter the workforce with no work experience.

On further reflection, high school does bring back some good memories of going to Fosters Freeze for lunch (hamburger and Coke for thirty-five cents). Gas was cheap at twenty-five cents a gallon. I was also a Girl Scout Mariner, and the highlight was sailing to Catalina Island with a hodgepodge of classmates (Pam C., Lola A., Irene O., and others whom I can't remember right now). Sue M. taught me to smoke cigarettes, and she used to scare us with spooky stories. I also took my first try at alcohol (OJ and vodka) and got pretty tipsy right away prior to going to a school dance. Someone wrote in my yearbook, "To Linda the Lush." Wow, my mother went ballistic over that one.

There was one ugly incident that I remember that stays with me to this day. One of our classmates was sexually attacked by some of our students. It was a hush-hush cover-up. I think the boys got off, but she was tarnished—very sad. I didn't want to mention this here in my chapter, but I think it is important to note that in those days, a lot of stuff was swept under the rug. Pregnant girls were sent away and some hastily married.

After graduation, we moved to Santa Barbara. Needless to say, after high school, I finally blossomed. I enrolled full-time at SBCC and started working at Cottage Hospital as a ward clerk. It took me about three months to feel comfortable working in a serious setting. When I started, I didn't even know what an IV was. Several of the RNs I worked with were married to Brooks students, so I ended up meeting more Brooks students, who were always so fascinating to me. Oh, I almost forgot to mention that I failed miserably at SBCC and had to drop out. My attention was work and making money—and not cracking the books. My mother was disappointed in my carefree life and nudged me to visit my brother Roger in Germany. In other words, she kicked me out of the family nest at the age of twenty.

So in March of 1969, I flew to Munich, Germany, to live with my brother and his wife. However, after three days I declared that I was going back home. But my brother told me that I should give it three months, not three days. I will always appreciate his advice because I soon landed at job with the US Army in Munich, which provided benefits: housing, medical, commissary, and PX privileges. I ended up living in an apartment of sorts with five other roommates. That summer, my childhood friend Clare came to visit me with my mother. Clare ended up staying and married a German. I also met my future husband there, who was in the US Army stationed in Bad Toelz. The biggest news of this time was the moon landing in 1969.

After returning to the United States in 1970, I married and the next year we had our son. In 1972, we returned to Munich, Germany, and stayed there two years working for the US Army. In 1974, my husband joined the US Department of State Foreign Service and we moved to Ankara, Turkey; later, Jakarta, Indonesia; then Frankfurt, Germany; then Cairo, Egypt; then Vienna, Austria. In 1987, we returned to the United States, but things weren't quite right and we ended up getting a divorce.

In 1989, I joined the US Department of State Foreign Service and traveled around the world. Again, I found myself back in Cairo, Egypt, just before the Gulf War broke out. While in Cairo, I was sent to the US Embassy in Addis Ababa, Ethiopia, to assist in a search-and-recovery mission involving an airplane crash with a congressional delegation and embassy personnel. Next, I was assigned to Bogota, Colombia, during the time of Pablo Escobar and civil unrest from guerilla warfare. My next tour was in Panama when the US Embassy was deeply involved in returning the Panama Canal to the Panamanians. After Panama, I was transferred to Lima, Peru where I visited Cuzco and Machu Picchu. It was also in Lima where leftist rebels held several US Embassy colleagues as hostage inside the Japanese embassy. Fortunately, the US Embassy staff were released a few days afterward. Following Peru, I was sent to Bucharest, Romania, to work for our US ambassador. At that time, it seemed like going back twenty years in time when Romania was a communist country because stores were lacking goods in comparison to Western Europe and there were a lot of poor people, children living in the streets, and wild dogs running in packs. I remember buying extra loaves of bread at the bakery to hand out to the elderly waiting outside. However, one highlight of my time in Bucharest was meeting

President Clinton and Secretary of State Madeline Albright. After Romania, I was transferred to El Salvador, one of my favorite tours. While there, I was sent to Santiago, Chile, to support US presidential and Secretary of State visits. When my tour ended, I was transferred to Helsinki, Finland, another favorite place to serve. In Helsinki, I learned to sea kayak during the short summer months and managed to survive the brutally cold winters. While there, I was also sent to Rome, Italy, to support the US delegation at a NATO summit. As it seemed to be a normal pattern of crisscrossing the Atlantic, my next tour was in Tegucigalpa, Honduras, where I worked for the US ambassador, and it was also my fourth and last tour in Central America. After three years, I was sent to Berlin, Germany, and lastly Reykjavik, Iceland.

People often ask me which was my favorite country, and all that I can say is that I always left a piece of my heart when I departed because of meeting and making new friends. It was always bittersweet to say farewell, but for the most part, I keep in contact with them.

When I finally retired in 2009, I returned to Santa Barbara. After getting settled in my new home and the dust had settled from my life overseas, I found out that I needed a hip replacement. Very bad news, but I recovered quickly and was back to leading a normal life to the point that I volunteered to go back into the Foreign Service as a contractor. I was sent to Islamabad, Pakistan. After arriving there, I discovered that I had made a big mistake in going backward in my life. I needed to do something new with my life, so that was my last overseas assignment.

In 2010, I decided to go back to SBCC part-time to pursue a degree. One elective class was photography, and suddenly, I found a new passion. In 2015, I graduated with an AA in applied photography and became adept at digital processing and started my own photography business. After several years, I discovered that everyone is a photographer with smartphones, so I ended up closing my business. However, I still shoot pictures and spend time restoring old photographs and creating digital images.

Since retiring, I traveled to Ireland to walk the Dingle Way Walking Trail. I went on an ocean cruise to Alaska and had a reunion with former colleagues in Paros, Greece. In the United States, I've traveled to Hawaii and camped throughout the Southwest.

In January of 2015, my older brother Roger unexpectedly passed away, and a few months later, Mother followed him. It was a difficult time for me to deal with them not being in my life. Then my father died two years later. I will always have a sense of loss, but sometimes I can feel their presence; that brings me a sense of peace. But damn, I miss them!

In 2017, I moved back to Carpinteria, where I plan to stay put in the most beautiful place on earth, and where I still maintain contact with old pals from school. We all grew up in the golden years, and we were blessed to live in paradise: looking east is the mountains and west is the Pacific. What more could one want? I have been blessed with my son and three grandchildren and a great-grandson, along with many friends and memories. Now that I'm seventy-one, life can't get any better. I just pray that the COVID-19 stays far away from my loved ones and me. But when my ashes are put into a little box at the Carpinteria Cemetery, you can rest assured that I am at peace being in God's country.

Thank you, Joe, for giving me the chance to share my life that started in Carpinteria.

1959 Linda Fryer & Clare Colson
(She's in our family 1959 pic to the right)

1959 Linda Fryer's Family Pic
(still 1 more baby to arrive in 1961)

Machu Picchu, Peru

Giza Pyramids, Egypt

CHAPTER EIGHTEEN

Jack Moyer

JACK
MOYER

Carpinteria

Ah yes, Carpinteria, not just an ordinary town, but an extraordinary town! One of the special rural small towns spiced throughout America, spotted between Ventura and Santa Barbara on the California coast. A town that has the mountains on the east and the ocean on the west, giving the feeling that one lived in the country and at the beach at the same time, with clear skies and salty fresh air. A town with a constant temperature, where it doesn't get too hot or too cold because of the great Pacific Ocean. This sleepy little town provided a safe haven for most people and had a feeling of belonging to a family community. As many graduating classes before us and after us, the class of 1967 can also proudly say, "We grew up in Carpinteria."

Carpinteria is one of the towns that people visualize as a place to either raise a family or grow up in. We as youngsters, no matter what age we were when we arrived in Carp (as we called it), probably didn't know how lucky we were to be there, because that was just the way it was. Some of us arrived in junior high or high school, but we all knew that we lived living in Carp. Most of us could look back with life's experience under our belts, and we could put the pieces of the puzzle together to see the whole picture of what a wonderful place Carp was to grow up in. Until that point, we just lived our lives in Carp style, with the many splendors that Carpinteria provided for people of all ages to enjoy. What Carp is probably best known for is its great beaches, with avocados coming in a close second.

How many people can say that when they grew up, they enjoyed the World's Safest Beach at their doorstep? We can! Main Beach, straight down from town is still called that today. Google it! It is called that because of the gradual sloping sandy beaches into the water and mild surf as it is protected by the Channel Islands. At the Main Beach, when we were young, there were summer craft and game programs for us to participate in. There were swings, rings, and monkey bars to have some fun. We could lie on the beach, swim, ride waves on our rafts, bodysurf, skim board, and dive for sand dollars and clams. We could tell Mom we were going to have fish for dinner, before we went fishing or spear fishing, because fish were plentiful. As we got older, we could walk on the miles of beaches, water ski, play volleyball or just spend time with our friends there. In the early days, we could also grab a bite to eat at the Snack Shack at the Main Beach and enjoy the infamous pinball room there. In Carp, there were good surfing places like the Tar Pits, jelly bowl, the pier (when it used to exist), and the famous Rincon Point. Surfing was big in Carp! Many people were either surfer jocks or jock surfers. What a life we were living!

There were many other things to do when growing up in Carp. We could ride our bikes in town and in the foothills, as the streets and roads were safe because they were not crowded most of the time. We could also hike in the mountains, skateboard in our neighborhoods, and play Little League. As we got older, we cruised the same streets in our cars, and we could hang out at Fosters Freeze or the Spot, which were our semi-fast-food places, as there were no large franchises in Carpinteria at that time. We also had our small theater called the Tradewinds, where many of us stole our first kiss. If we wanted to shop beyond our nice little stores and shops in Carp, we could go to beautiful Santa Barbara ten miles away. In Santa Barbara, there was expanded entertainment: large theaters, drive-in movies, restaurants, bowling alleys, and concerts. We also had Santa Barbara City College and University of California at Santa Barbara, which had beautiful campuses that overlooked the ocean, where we could go to concerts and sporting events.

Carpinteria was a real *Leave It to Beaver* town. In a small town, everyone knows or thinks they know everyone's business. Most everyone in town knew each other. We grew up in small neighborhoods, each with their own personality. Parents in their neighborhood knew each other. I would come home and sometimes Mom would ask me, "Are you going to tell me what happened, or am I going to tell you what happened?" We knew every kid in our neighborhood of all ages. Because schools were small, we knew almost everyone in our class grade, as well as the classes below us or above us because of brothers and sisters in other grades. Almost everyone in town knew who you were. That was good for the most part, but it did have its drawbacks. Some people were real busybodies, and if you didn't do something their way, you were not perceived well.

Being a small high school, Carpinteria (about 500 students) gave students a better chance to participate in school activities, student council, clubs, yearbook, cheerleading, homecoming activities, rallies, dances, assemblies, and sports. Because most students took part in several of these activities, they felt connected and really part of the school. It was their school because they were involved. They also got to know other students better during these activities to feel further connected. During this time period, sports brought the school and community together. There was lots of student participation at the games: players, cheerleaders, band, and clubs working the concessions, and the whole town watching the game. In sports, one really got the feeling that it was our town versus your town, as that was the way it was, with only one high school in most towns. Our closest competition was a twenty-minute bus ride. Football games, because of the town's support, were *Friday Night Lights*. Carpinteria had a great winning tradition in football that was respected throughout our area. With that came pressure for the players to work hard to live up to and carry on this tradition. Playing football in high school created lifelong friendships. Playing football created trust and respect among players. You need to pull together mentally and emotionally, as it was our physicality versus theirs. It's hard to explain, but if you played football, you understand.

Speaking of schooling, being in a small beautiful area had its benefits. First of all, we had the influence of SBCC, UCSB, and Westmont College (private), as well as Brooks Institute of Photography, near us. Also, we had great teachers in Carpinteria, for the most part, because of the competition for these jobs. These teachers wanted to live in the area for the many reasons we know now; therefore, we could bet on a good education at CHS, if we wanted to. One didn't know how good one's education was until one had to use it in educational experiences, through travel, working, going to trade schools, technical schools, fire and police academies, college, and armed services (especially during this Vietnam War time period). In college, when you come from a small high school and you are competing both academically and athletically with students who went to larger schools, you think that the larger schools are better, just for the fact that people think bigger is better. Not necessarily! Athletically, many students from CHS competed with the students from the larger Santa Barbara schools and played at SBCC. In our English classes at SBCC, we were taught an expanded version of what we were taught at CHS English classes, during our junior and senior years. Our high school teachers must have known that and prepared for that task ahead. The college professors were interconnected in Santa Barbara. I asked my English professor at SBCC, "What is the difference between the same class you teach at UCSB and the one you teach here?" He said, "About $400."

Carpinteria provided great opportunities for students to get a job in town as they were going to school. Students worked in gas stations, retail stores, grocery stores, restaurants, semi-fast-food places, nurseries, picking lemons and avocados, and many other odd jobs working around other people's homes as they were finishing their high school years. Pretty much every business we went to in town, we knew someone working there, which made it more comfortable. These jobs enabled us to buy clothes, go out on a date, buy car insurance, and buy a car to fix up and or repair. Working was also a good experience for us, as we had to learn how to juggle and balance between school, work, co-curricular activities, school social activities, sports, cheerleading, free time, friends, and family life. Who said that life was easy for a teenager? Well, for most of us, because we lived in a small community, our lives were made much easier through cooperation. We were lucky as our parents, employers, teachers, coaches, and activity directors worked to help adjust our and their schedules to make them compatible so that we could participate in as many activities as possible.

When our class graduated from CHS in 1967, most men were going to have to make life-affecting decisions, knowing a draft into the armed services was coming. In December of 1969, the draft lottery was established. We were all going to be eligible for the draft. Most men drafted, went into the army and a quick ticket to fight in the war in Vietnam. We had choices. We could join the army, go to college full-time as a student and receive a deferment temporarily from the draft, try to get a deferment from some sort of medical ailment, injury, or psychology disorder, join the armed service of your choice and have a better chance of not having boots on the ground, fighting in Vietnam for effect to Canada. Some people got out of the draft system with a high number. I was not so lucky; my number was 35. The war in Vietnam brought sadness to all towns and cities in the United States. In Carpinteria, friends that we went to school with died in that war. The Vietnam War brought rallies, protests, and riots across the nation, just like Black Lives Matter. That war was brought to an end; hopefully, racism will be brought down.

Going to college was my choice. Not really knowing what direction I wanted to go, I chose Santa Barbara City College. There I could get a general education, decide on my career path, possibly play football, then transfer to a four-year school and get a degree in something. The football part ended quickly that year, as I was hit by a car in May of my senior year. It was my own car that rolled down a hill and pinned me between another friend's car. I had surgery in late August and started college on crutches at the hilly campus of SBCC—not what I had pictured as my first college experience! Life goes on, and I did play football at SBCC. Things worked out better than I thought. I got a football scholarship to play at San Fernando Valley State, which is now known as Cal State Northridge, and continued my education. I had a few other scholarships to other schools, but I decided to stay close to Carpinteria so my family could come watch me play. I blew out my knee, returning a kickoff against Fresno State. After two major surgeries, the draft physical said I was no-go. I healed up well enough to play football my senior year as well as rugby. I also decided to coach a year of JV football at Culver City

High to see if I liked doing that. At that point my life, I was pondering becoming a teacher and a coach.

After graduating from college, I was tired of going to school. I decided to take some time off. I figured I could go back later and get my teaching credential. I went to live with a roommate for a while, in a small town called Mendocino, which is hallway between San Francisco and the Oregon border on the California coast. It is a beautiful area, with a lot of personality. After being in Mendocino, I realized that there were things there that were very similar to Carpinteria. In fact, the similarities were spooky. The names Carpinteria and Mendocino have a nice ring to them. Santa Barbara and Fort Bragg are two words. Both have the ocean on one side and the mountains on the other side. Fort Bragg is ten miles north of Mendocino, as Santa Barbara is ten miles north of Carpinteria. Mendocino's population in proportion to Fort Bragg's is about the same as Carpinteria's is to Santa Barbara's. The phone numbers began with 964 in Santa Barbara as well as Fort Bragg. There were no stoplights in Mendo (as they called it), like it was in the early years in Carp. There were people surfing. And yes, I could go fishing or diving for dinner. Hmm, this feels a bit like Carpinteria!

When I found out that they were changing the teaching requirements to get one's credential, I made the quick decision to scramble back to school mid-semester. While I was finishing my credential, I did my student teaching back at Culver City High School and coached two more seasons of varsity football. I really learned a lot about coaching from the head coach there, Warren Flannagan, my mentor and friend. His coaching style was much like our head coach, Lloyd Earhard, when we were playing football at Carpinteria High School. In the meantime, I played two more seasons of rugby, reacquainted with a friend, traveled to see Mendocino with her, and got married a little bit later. My wife thought Mendo was wonderful too! We both had interviews for teaching jobs in Mendocino and Fort Bragg that we didn't get. We decided that the most important thing for our lives was where we lived, not our occupations. We thought about living in Carpinteria, but I thought that Carpinteria was going to get much larger and lose its quaintness and feeling of a small town. As when we grew up, housing developments were continuing to take out lemon and avocado orchards, and tomato and strawberry fields. We did not know at the time that local officials were putting a stop to this practice, and Carpinteria is still today a really unique beach town that we love to visit.

We decided to move to Mendocino, buy property, and build a house. We didn't have jobs or a place to live. We substituted, and got jobs in restaurants. I got a job as full-time aide at Mendocino High School. I coached football there for three years with two years being head coach, with a promise by the principal of the next teaching job that opened up. Mendocino hired a new superintendent, the principal quit, and no job for me—typical small-town politics. Oh well, life goes on! My wife (Laura) worked at a center for the developmentally disabled. We had bought property and already started building our house, thinking we were not going to get teaching jobs. I was going to become a carpenter. As we were building our house, we lived in an 8' × 13' trailer in the woods on our property, with no running water for a year and half, but we did have a really nice open-air outhouse with an umbrella. We could shower at work. One night, I came home to our trailer, from scouting a football game on a Friday night in Saint Helena, at 2:00 a.m. (a three-hour drive) to find the our golden retriever was having puppies on our bed, not her box that we made for her. Needless to say, with ten puppies, we didn't get much sleep that night. No room, but lots of puppies. I still had to be at the school at 10:00 a.m. (no lights yet) to coach our Saturday games. Life was good! We were enjoying living there! Well, we both landed teaching jobs. Laura got one a few years later in Fort Bragg, teaching elementary school. I was in Carpinteria at Mom's house, when Fort Bragg High School called me and offered me a teaching/coaching job over the phone! At first, I wasn't sure if I wanted to take it, as I had kind of got teaching out of my mind, and I wanted to finish our house with a little help from our friends. I decided that if I didn't take the job, I wouldn't know if I liked teaching. After declining a full-time driver's training job (can you imagine doing that job for seven hours a day?), they called back and offered me a job teaching US history, government, and physical education, coaching football and track. I took it. Thirty-three years later, I retired. I stayed; it reminded me of Carpinteria!

Fort Bragg? Knowing the history, I could never understand how a Confederate general and slaveholder could have two forts named after him, when he fought against the United States. The fort was only a small building about 12′ × 12′, like the one in the movie *Dances with Wolves*, but made out of wood. The fort was going to be built to have US Cavalry protect the people from the Indians, but they had to protect the Indians from the people. Well, the name of the town and school are now very controversial, and a possible name change could happen. We will see how it all plays out. Carpinteria High School's nickname, Warriors, might be in the same boat.

Fort Bragg was very much like Carpinteria. The towns are about the same size, as well as the school's enrollment. There are two elementary schools, one junior high school and one high school (with 500-plus students) in both towns. If I was going to teach and coach, I wanted to be in an environment like Carpinteria, Fort Bragg turned out to be that place. My roommates in college were college coaches, but I never wanted to coach at the college level because of our town and community support. Like Carpinteria, Fort Bragg was known for its tradition of playing good football. At Fort Bragg, it was town versus town, with our closest game an hour away. The Fort Bragg community built a new stadium (with lights) at the same time that Carpinteria built their new stadium. Teaching and coaching at Fort Bragg High School was stimulating and rewarding. The friends, teachers, coaches, and ex-players that I have been associated with have been invaluable. The experiences there were numerous and memorable. One experience will always be special to me. I had the opportunity to coach my own son and his close friends as they won the CIF North Coast Division IV Championship, their senior year. Coaching doesn't get any better than that. I think that he enjoyed many of the same things that we did, by growing up with that small-town feeling.

So what did I learn from Carpinteria? That it is a special place that I was fortunate to have experienced. It enabled me to pick out a beautiful area to live, raise a family that would live in a safe place, that could participate in many activities socially, intellectually, recreationally, and be part of a community. I learned that there is a lot of Carpinteria in Mendocino and Fort Bragg!

1966 Football Awards Dinner (L to R: Ken Williams, Jack Moyer, Bob Walsh, Robert Perez, Bob Coster, Joe Lovett, Mike Barbari, Rick Gesswein)

CHAPTER NINETEEN

Emily Brown

#19

Chapters of Our Lives

Some people might say I'm accident-prone. I don't really believe that. It's just that I happen to do things that can put me in harm's way. Not on purpose but my lifestyle is such that something is bound to happen, no matter what precautions are taken.

We have always lived in the country, the outskirts of Carpinteria. We have horses and mules, and one of my greatest joys each year is when summer comes around and the snow has melted enough for us to load up our truck and horse trailer and head to the trailhead in the High Sierra. We (my husband and I and sometimes others, as in family and friends) pack up our mules and ride our stock to our camp in the Sequoia National Forest. This is a tradition that I have been following since I was eight years old, when my father deemed us old enough to manage on our own in the mountains with mostly minimal oversight from my dad. My four brothers and I looked forward to this coming-of-age event in our lives, and the tradition has continued since my husband and I married ourselves in late November 1971 on the Golden Trout Creek near the mouth of the Kern River, Sequoia National Forest. We had gone in on a spur-of-the-moment trip to try to help my father find a horse and mule that he had lost sometime in October. He started one of his many infamous control-burn fires, which had scared the stock off (of course). Anyway, we decided to get married (what the heck) after just five months of off-and-on dating as he was in graduate school down south and I was going to SBCC and working.

So we were on a long weekend break. We returned home about a week or more later, after an eventful trip with my dad. No stock was found, and it had already snowed once. Of course, the mountains were deserted of other travelers. My father made us a wonderful and unique marriage certificate about how we plighted our troth, etc., declaring himself the bishop of Kern River and mayor of Kern Canyon with a great 1900s-era historical photo of a mule train on switchbacks in the High Sierra. I made the three of us clam chowder for our wedding dinner. But before we returned home to Carpinteria, Bradley insisted we go tell his grandfather what we had done, which meant traveling by car from the western side of the Sierra to the eastern side, where his grandparents lived in Big Pine, just south of Bishop. Well, Granddad, who was a Methodist minister, and Cleo, his wife, thought our marriage was sweet, but they felt we should be married legally, not totally buying in on my dad's version of legal. They took us to Goldfield, Nevada, several hours' drive on a windy mountain road through the spectacular White Mountains. Now, in Esmeralda County at the County Seat, we met up with the justice of the peace who was a friend of Granddad's who had just returned from deer hunting, accompanied by the county clerk. The two of them opened the courthouse in this all-but-deserted town to make Granddad and Cleo happy and marry us legally. I was definitely reluctant to make this next step as I wanted to be able to get out of this marriage easily and I was sure this would complicate things far beyond my immediate plans. My long-term plan was to stay single until at least thirty, and I was just twenty-two! Anyway, I was lured into the sudden excitement of it all, not to mention the huge garbage bag of loot given to me by the county clerk! It had everything in it from instant coffee to sanitary pads and more—everything except diapers. So the JP married us in our still very dirty mountain clothes, said a Native American prayer, had to skip the part about exchanging rings as we didn't have any, and off we went to the bigger town of Tonopah for our second wedding dinner. Granddad and Cleo drove us back to Big Pine in their big Bonneville station wagon with us asleep from exhaustion in the back seat.

Back at home, we went back to our usual lives, me in Carpinteria and he in Los Angeles, finishing up his semester. After a month or so, we set up camp on one of our properties. We bought a little travel trailer from Nick Razo for $50 and hooked up water but did not have electricity for five years. I had a regular ritual of cleaning and filling kerosene lanterns for light. We added a front room on to the trailer right away to double the space.

All that changed about five years later when I got pregnant and declared that I was not going to raise my child as "used-trailer trash," and we needed a house now! Well, it just so happened that Bradley's former neighbors in Hope Ranch were razing their horse stables to put in a tennis court. After three days of hard work, Bradley and some friends jacked up the stables and loaded the building on John Sheaffer's big boat-moving trailer. That was when there were still four sets of lights on the 101 freeway, and with a $3 moving permit, off they went with our future "house," rolling down the freeway. John said, "I'm not stopping for anything." The first light was green, the second light was green, the third light was yellow, and the fourth light was *red*! He was right. He didn't stop for anything. The building barely cleared the overpasses by just inches. Because of an oncoming car on Casitas Pass Road, John did clip an oak tree just 1/4 mile before our property, which did some damage to a corner of the roof, but amazingly, he delivered it to the building site in one piece. Bradley had envisioned this whole building to be his new shop but in the end, 2/3 of it became our house and 1/3 his shop. A few years later, we built a new shop for Bradley and expanded on our house, even building a second story, which doubled our square footage. Good thing since I had a second child ten years after the first.

Well, this is a very long way of getting around of talking about being accident-prone, but life went on as we continued to build our lives in Carpinteria.

So I have experienced at least five major accidents that have all happened in the Sierra or here in the foothills. It has never dampened my desire to continue doing what I love, although I feel as though I have used up at least half of my nine lives.

The first big one, many years ago, was caused by my dog Beau, a Queensland/Aussie/Kelpie mix. He was about eighty pounds of pure muscle, and one of my dearest dogs ever. I was at our cow camp in the Sequoia National Forest by myself when I heard on the radio that there had been a terrible accident at the Santa Monica Farmers

Market. An elderly driver had run over and killed at least ten people and injured many more. My friends and neighbors, the Colemans, sold produce at that market, and I was so worried and had no way of finding out if they were all right. I decided I would make the three-hour ride out to the pack station to be able to make a phone call. Well, my arrogant Arabian mare decided that she was not going to be caught and had the run of a forty-acre pasture. After spending an hour trying to catch her with no luck, I decided just to walk out with my dog, leaving the horse and mule behind. I packed a sandwich, water, napkins, a lighter, and paper towels along with a notepad and a pen, and a toothbrush, all in the feed bag slung over my shoulder. I packed light as I thought I would just spend the night at the pack station and return to camp the next morning.

The weather was changing rapidly the last hour of my hike up the mountain, going from 5,000 feet to 8,000 feet. We started to get thunder and lightning, which was scaring Beau. I found some hay string on the trail and made a leash for Beau so he wouldn't run away from me out of fear. We all have things that scare us, and this was his big bug-a-boo. It started to rain, and soon I was drenched since I was only wearing a thin shirt. I was also wearing a pair of leather gloves, as is my usual custom in the mountains. I had made a loop on my end of the leash, and just as we reached the trailhead, I slipped it over my wrist so I could stand under a tree and eat a few bites of my sandwich, hoping the rain, thunder, and lightning would let up a little. All of a sudden, there was a very loud crack of thunder, and Beau took off in a dear und with me running behind, unable to stop him. The loop had caught on my glove, and after a few moments, I tripped on a tree root, and hit the ground hard, still being dragged by my dog. He finally stopped, and I was in a bad shape. I could not get up, not even on my hands and knees. The rain kept coming, and I knew I had to get under cover. I dragged myself with my arms to get under a big pine tree where it was drier. It was late in the day, no cars or people around, and I was still a mile from the pack station. I got a long branch and gathered other branches and pine needles toward me. Although they were wet, I knew I had to get a fire going to get me through the night. I had the lighter but could not get the fire going. I finally decided to use some of my paper towels and was able to get the fire going. Pretty soon, I had quite a large fire, which was saving me. I wrote a note and attached it to Beau's collar and sent him off toward the pack station. I was furious with him but hoped he would come through for me. I took a Vicodin and aspirin that I carry in case of an emergency.

After about an hour or so, I saw this image of a packer with a string of mules coming over the rise. It was Luis from the pack station. I called out to him. He was so bundled from the rain he had not noticed me as he was passing by. He didn't speak English, so I told him in Spanish that I was hurt and needed help. Pack animals always come first, so he said he would get his boss. About forty-five minutes later, Dan and his brother visiting from Tennessee drove up to save me. Dan was shocked when he realized what bad shape I was in and my circumstances. I had known him for at least twenty years. They lifted me into the truck and took me to the cabin. They wanted to take me down the mountain to the hospital, but I declined. His wife Kelley and her sister-in-law stripped my muddy clothes off and put me in a hot bath. They brought me a hot dinner and took such good care of me. I was so lucky but still could not walk at all.

I was starting to worry about Beau as he had not turned up. About an hour after my bath and warming in front of the huge fireplace, Beau did bark at the door. I was so happy to see him after I had punched him with what little strength I had left before sending him off, and he was so happy to see me.

Back at home, Dan called Bradley, who was in the middle of having a writer's party. He told him he had to come help me out. The next afternoon, Bradley and my daughter Rebekah came to get me. It was a six-hour drive from Carpinteria to the pack station. Rebekah drove me back and made arrangements for me to see an orthopedist in Santa Barbara, where she took me the next day. Bradley borrowed a horse from the pack station and rode to our camp to close it up properly until the next trip. I had not done the usual close-up, thinking

I would be returning the next day. He could not catch my horse either, but he did get our mule.

I didn't have any broken bones, but I had internal injuries, which made me unable to walk. I spend the next three weeks on crutches. My horse was finally caught a month later. She had gone wild, as was her way.

The sad part for me was that I had to put her down last September, along with that same mule. Luna was over thirty-six and Chabela was thirty-three, both excellent animals, and they are buried here on our property.

About twenty-two years ago, I was back at our family camp, fourteen miles farther from our present cow camp in the Sierra on the Kern River. Some friends and neighbors had come in for a visit with their daughter and one-year-old grandson. Their daughter had pushed a stroller in twenty-three miles over narrow trails and rough terrain and over five mountain passes. Amazing! I'm sure no one else has ever done that. Anyway, after a week or so, they were headed out with all their gear, one riding mule, and two pack mules. I decided to walk a short way with them just to make sure they got across the bridge and down the trail. After forty-five minutes of traveling, Skip decided he had to do a repack on the mules and asked me to hold the lead rope of his riding mule. Well, he was a big strong mule and rather mean and unruly. He ended up knocking me to the ground and jumped on my rib cage. He was headed for another jump when I quickly rolled to the side against a log and Skip got him away from me just in time before the second strike. Skip felt terrible about it and wanted to help me back to camp, but I told him to go on because his wife, daughter, and grandson were at that point well ahead on the trail. He couldn't leave them, and I just wanted to get back to camp. I walked very slowly as I had at least three cracked ribs and could hardly breathe. I stopped by the ranger station, which was across the river and about 1/2 mile from our camp just to let her know I had been hurt and that I would be in camp for a few days by myself. She checked on me that evening and every day until more arrivals came to join me. Sleeping and reclining was the hardest and I don't think

I had any pain medicine but I survived. It takes about six weeks for ribs to heal.

So a few years back, I was in the Sierra at our cow camp with my cousin Mary Louise and high school friend Sara. We had all gone in with our riding mules and pack mules for about ten days. After a few days in camp, we decided to take an extended ride to an amazing place called Painters Camp. It was supposed to be a one-day ride to get there, probably about five hours. On the way out of camp, we had a chain reaction of bumping and banging with my two pack mules running into my riding mule. She started bucking and threw me so hard that my whole right side was completely banged up then she took off running and joined up with some horses from the pack station that were in our pasture. I had only had this mule for a few months, so she was still new to me. I had to walk quite a distance but finally got her back. We continued on our journey.

There had been a major fire a few years before, and we were within an hour of getting to Painters but could not find the trail because of so many fallen trees from the fire. We finally quit for the evening and set up camp. The next day, we started out again, but after a few hours, we gave up and went back to Kern Flats, which is on the Kern River and has nice camping spots and feed for stock. We high-lined and staked the stock for the night and next morning. My mule Bella was very anxious, and since I was banged up, I decided to just go back to the comfort of Cow Camp, my home base. Sara and Mary Louise offered to come back with me, but they were having a good time and I said that they should stay. It is only a two-hour ride back to camp.

Bella was extremely stressed and basically raced up the mountain with the two pack mules in tow. She stepped right over a coiled rattlesnake, as did the others. When we were halfway up the mountain, we got to an area called Doe Springs. There were at least fifty free-range cattle there and we were going right past them when Bella looked over and saw a black one in the distance and just bolted. She thought it was a bear! She took off running full speed, and I quickly dropped the lead rope of the pack mules so as not to drag them along. After a minute of that, she started bucking hard and threw me off. I landed headfirst. I just lay there awhile and slowly checked my head and neck to make sure it wasn't broken. Luckily, it all still worked, although I was weak and shaken by the whole event. I looked for Bella, and she was running full speed in a circle around the meadow. I called her, and she came running back to me. She was scared to death! At that point, I was furious with her. Now my left side was all banged up. We walked back to the pack mules, who were standing right where I had dropped the lead rope with cattle milling around them. They were calmly grazing and nonchalant about the happenings. At this point, I was afraid to get back on the mule, fearing that she might truly kill me, so I led her for the next two hours with the mules dallied to her and we headed back to Cow Camp. Every time I thought of getting, I reconsidered and kept on walking. We made it back to camp, and I unpacked the mules and unsaddled Bella and put everything away.

It was 7:00 p.m. by that point, and I needed to take care of myself. I took off my hat and looked in the mirror. My whole head was covered in blood, which was dripping off my blood-soaked braids. I wasn't even aware of that before, because my hat was on. There was a big split on top of my head from the fall. I called my husband in Carpinteria on the satellite phone and let him know what had happened and that if he didn't hear from me by nine the next morning, he should be concerned. At that point, I walked down the hill to build a fire for the shower, came back up the hill, and poured myself a glass of wine, had a few hits off the pipe and then took a nice hot shower, washing my hair. I couldn't go to bed with a bloody head (this was way before selfies). I then had some dinner at nine and went to bed. I did call Bradley at nine the next morning. My head was still bleeding a little, but it was healing up OK. Sara and Mary Louise came back the next afternoon, and I told them what happened and then cried for the first time. It finally hit me as a close call.

The next accident happened when we were crossing the bridge at the Little Kern. It was a very long suspension bridge, about six feet wide. It is also very high, and if for some reason you fall over the side, well, you would be dead, no doubt about it. It can be a little scary for animals as the bridge moves and sways while they are crossing. I made the mistake of trying to walk my riding mule Bella across. I had the lead rope of my pack mules, Tule dallied on the horn of my saddle. I was pushed to the side as Bella raced to get across the bride. Then I was knocked down by the metal pack boxes from behind. As I was laid out on the bridge, I was trampled by my pack mule. Bradley was in the lead and had just finished crossing the bridge when he looked back in horror to see me being trampled.

Nothing was broken, although I was seriously bruised and my back was injured, to say the least. We were headed to camp, and as usual, we had all the food and a camp full of people waiting for dinner. Bradley had to help me back on, and we rode another hour to get to camp. I was in real pain and having a hard time breathing, but of course, I had to get there. I had my Vicodin and aspirin in my saddlebags, and again, that saved me. I had a few cracked ribs but still managed to get dinner on the table, all cooked on a wood burning stove. Again, sleeping and or being reclined is the hardest part of having cracked ribs, which reminds me of another accident.

The last accident that I will tell you about happened five years ago, on the 22nd of September. I was hiking in the local mountains here in Carpinteria, up the Rincon Canyon. It was a hike I went on usually every day. It would take me an hour to go up and back on the route. I was taking pictures of bear scat, thinking I would make a bear scat calendar as a joke for the California Avocado Festival since I have been very involved with the festival for several years and the bears at that time of year in our area eat ripe avocados all day so they have scat that looks like green guacamole!

I always walked with my dogs, and we were near the end of the hike on our return. There was very fresh scat in the area, so I knew there were also bears nearby but wasn't too concerned until my dog Callie, a Queensland heeler, flushed a bear out from under the first avocado tree. The bear chased Callie, who ran right past me. When the bear saw me, she turned on me instead of Callie. It turned into an immediate fight with the bear. She was then standing on her hind legs, batting me, and I was hitting back. I was yelling at her from the top of my lungs to get away. At one point, there was an opening, and I took off running as fast as I could. I looked back as I ran down the dirt road and could see she was coming after me. You can't outrun a bear. The next thing I felt was her sinking her teeth into my thigh and taking me down. I landed on a rocky downhill slope with her facing me and standing above me. Even though I knew I had injured my back, I was able to do a bicycle kick and continued yelling for her to get out. I figured you are not supposed to look them in the eye, but I couldn't look away. I really thought this could be my last few seconds to live. She finally came down on all fours, looked at me awhile longer, and slowly started walking off. I figured she was tired of hearing me scream at her to get out. Every once in a while, she would stop and look back. I became very quiet once she started walking away. When she was a distance down the road, I rolled over, got on my hands and knees and slowly got up, and started moving a couple of hundred yards toward a gate. I kept thinking she could come at any time and finish me off, but she didn't. I went through the gate, which was a joke because there was no side fence, down a hill, across a creek, and up the hill to my girlfriend's house. I said, "Alice, I need help. I have been attacked by a bear." Well, Alice was used to bears in the area as her house was at the end of the canyon, and it was bear season.

She put a towel around my leg, which I didn't want to look at. I was in pretty intense pain all the way around. We found the dogs and took them to my house to drop them off and get my medical information. On the way, I noticed that her gas tank was almost on empty and encouraged her to get gas because I wanted to make it to the emergency without another stop. It took an hour to get admitted because of the sick people and scary-looking drug addicts in line ahead of me. When they finally did admit me, I was suddenly a hospital celebrity with doctors, nurses, and Fish and Wildlife wardens surrounding my bed. They had never had a bear attack patient before, so I was a novelty. My back was technically broken, I had deep claw scratches on my back, and luckily, the bear had not torn my thigh off. She had just sunk her four incisors in and then let go. So I had these very deep holes, but I was still intact. They used a machine with saline solution for flushing the holes for several minutes on each one but decided not to stitch them as they wanted the holes to keep draining. After many hours, they released me to the care of my daughter, who drove me home. Bradley and my son Wesley were in the Sierra and came home to all the hoopla.

I was immediately barraged with requests for interviews. After four interviews, the Fish and Wildlife representatives recommended that I refer all calls to them. I needed the rest, and I was in pretty serious pain.

Within a week, we were setting up for the Avocado Festival. I am a board member and am in charge of the big expo tent, which we decorate with historical and current data about avocados and it is also occupied by various representatives of the avocado business. I was just starting to get around after being laid up for a week, and by the end of the first day of the festival, my body completely seized up. The pain meds had worn off, and I couldn't move. My son had to come get me and take me home. I also had to have a series of rabies shots. They are horrible like days of the past. It took time, but my body healed up and I was left with a lumpy deformed thigh. After a couple of years of that, I had plastic surgery to smooth it out. I was done with wearing that scar.

I have constantly had people ask me about the attack although not so much these days. I get teased about it too. I just thank God that I had Medicare. It was an expensive accident and not work related, so everything was paid for in the end.

The moral of the story is, watch out for fresh bear scat!

CHAPTER TWENTY

Linda Pino

LINDA
PINO

Somewhere Over

When I was asked to do this, so many things went through my head: nothing exciting or earth-shaking, some very happy times, some not so happy, but all growing experiences.

When I look back, it is almost like I had two lives so totally different from each other, and it even seems as though they were in two different eras.

My early years were starting up on my grandparents' farm and the other growing up in Carpinteria, California. They both had a very strong deciding factor in making the person I am today.

My grandparents' farm was very similar to *Little House on the Prairie*. Their farmhouse was totally void of any modern conveniences except for electricity.

My grandmother's kitchen had a wood-burning stove, which we used to heat the house and, of course, cook on. It was also used to heat up the irons, which had removable handles. We would keep about two or three on at a time because they would cool down pretty quickly. The stove had a tank on the side that we could put water in so we would have hot water available. There was no indoor plumbing, so the toilet was an outhouse that, when you are a little kid, seemed a mile away from the house. It was scary for me because Grandpa would only make a big hole on the seat. When I had to use it, I hung on for dear life because I just knew if the devil lived anywhere, he was down there. I couldn't get out fast enough.

Grandma would make my clothes, and my favorite thing she made me was a coat made from my father's old peacoat. It had two rows of black buttons down the front and a faux leopard collar that wrapped around my neck.

Grandma was Apache and Grandpa was from Spain. Grandpa came from a wealthy family, but they disowned him for marrying an Indian (not called Native Americans yet). They had fifteen children. Grandma was an awesome cook, and Grandpa made all their shoes, built their house out of adobe, raised the meat they ate, built their furniture, and grew the food they ate.

When it came to dinnertime, I was the youngest person at the table, and many times, I got passed over when they were passing the food around. When the meal was over, Grandma would notice I hadn't eaten, so she would serve me. I was shy and quiet, so I didn't speak up for myself.

I remember watching my grandpa go underneath the cow and pull on the things that hung under the cow, and white stuff came out. I would carry it in to Grandma, and she said it was milk. I told her I wasn't going to drink that stuff that came out of the cow. Grandma got me to drink it finally when she told me that the milk from the store was made when they would scrape dead people's bones and add water to it—not true but it worked.

My favorite thing Grandpa made me was a small table and chairs just my size that looked like Grandma's.

I loved being on the farm, collecting eggs in the morning, pumping water from Grandma's kitchen, bringing wood in for her stove. My favorite thing on the farm was lying on the haystacks on a warm day and watching the clouds float by. There were times when I could feel like I was on the clouds, floating with them. When I would lie there, I would sing "Somewhere Over the Rainbow." That was my favorite song and movie. Even though I loved being on the farm, I missed being with my parents. I just knew if I could get over the rainbow or the clouds, my parents would be there, and they would love me.

I got my first Hula-Hoop when my uncle made me one from black plumbing hose. It was very heavy, but I would Hula-Hoop from one end of the farm to the other. I loved it!

My school I went to was a four-classroom building with multiple grades in each class. Mine was first grade to third grade. The school went from first grade to twelfth grade. The cafeteria was amazing. I can still smell the wonderful aromas that came from there. My teacher was the same teacher that taught my mother and her brothers and sisters. Our principal was the one who would give us our vaccines. I remember getting my smallpox vaccine; my shoulder swelled up and was bright red and hurt really bad. I couldn't imagine getting those all over my body, which would happen to some without the vaccine. When my vaccine dried up and scabbed over, I lost the scab down a hole in my grandma's living room floor.

By other people's standards, they may have said I was poor. If I was, I didn't know it. The only thing I ever felt I was missing out on was parents, but I knew they were "somewhere over." I really feel that being raised on my grandparents' farm gave me a strong foundation for life and gave me the tools I would need for the future.

On My Way to California

My stepfather went looking for his own rainbow, for a better life for us, so he hitchhiked to California. His road took him to Goleta, California. When he got a place to live, he sent for my mother to join him. They both got a job at Santa Claus Kitchen. He was a cook and she was a waitress.

They would send us postcards with beautiful pictures of the ocean and beautiful homes that we could dream about living in Somewhere Over.

My parents eventually sent us three kids' tickets to go out to California on a Greyhound bus. I remember being so excited to see the ocean, but the ride getting there was horrible. We were in the back of the bus, and I was stuck by the bathroom and an extra-large woman that was taking up part of my seat.

Well, Somewhere Over wasn't as glamorous as it had been presented to us kids. We lived in a tiny one-room house with a tiny porch, which my brother used to sleep in. My sister, I, and our parents slept on the same mattress on the floor by the stove. Thank goodness we weren't there too long, just long enough to be eaten by fleas. Never knew about fleas—they were horrible. Why would God make fleas? We eventually moved to another home or apartment, which was at the end of the Goleta Airport runway. It wasn't like LA Airport; at the time, they only had small planes and some military planes that flew out of there.

It's funny; we only lived about a mile from the beach, but I don't remember going to the beach in Goleta. We always spent time at the beach behind Santa Claus Kitchen. I do have nice memories of that beach and riding the train at Santa Claus Lane and the wonderful date shop that had marvelous milkshakes and candy. Of course, I can't forget the high delicious cinnamon rolls and pies my dad made. Pretty much, we lived there.

My Somewhere Over still wasn't happening; my parents worked so much that I don't remember them being around much unless we were at the restaurant.

I went to Goleta Union School for half of my fourth grade, which was in 1958. I really loved the cafeteria in that school too. The aromas that came out of there were awesome, and I can still remember the ice-cold milk that came out of the milk machine and it would froth. *Yum!* I also got to be a safety guard and got to wear a white belt that went around my waist and across my shoulder, with a badge on it. My job was to keep other kids from doing things they shouldn't be doing. If we caught them the second time, we gave them a ticket, and they had to go to the office. I felt very important. I wasn't. I had a wonderful sweet friend in this school; her name was Allison. We were very close, and at times, we even dressed alike, but not on purpose. I was very sad when I got transferred to Aliso School because Allison didn't.

Just a little side note: The husband I have now said he remembers me from fourth grade in that school. I don't remember him.

I got transferred to Aliso School, which was at the north end of Carpinteria. Canalino School was being built at that time.

When I went to Aliso, there were a lot of Hispanic kids that went there, but none of them spoke Spanish. I thought that was weird; Spanish was my first language. Yes, Joe, I'm Hispanic, so funny that you never knew that, but that's another page. The plus side of Aliso School was there was a very cute guy there. I had a crush on him, but he probably never noticed me.

We moved to Carpinteria but not to a house on the beach that looked like any of the postcard pictures they sent us. It was an old gas station that was converted into a house, and it was right across from the old Carpinteria High School.

I remember my first time at the beach. I couldn't believe all that water. The largest body of water I had ever seen was the ditch my grandfather would use to irrigate his fields. I didn't know how to swim, still don't, but that didn't stop me from jumping in.

The ocean at that time was crystal clear. I could walk out up to the neck and could see clear to my feet and see seashells and fish swimming around me. It was awesome! I pretty much spent all my free time at the beach, and I got as dark as a copper penny, an old one, not a new one. The beach at that time looked nothing like it looks now. There was a snack shack there, and it had pinball machines, which I loved playing. It had beach shacks along the beach, one level and very rustic. Miss that old beach!

Now I started fifth grade and Canalino School finally was finished, so goodbye, Aliso School and cute guy.

Mrs. Lamb was my teacher, and I just thought she was so beautiful and very kind. She had snow-white hair and always had it up in a Gibson hairdo. Much to my surprise, that cute guy also got transferred to Canalino. He was tall, at least to me, had black wavy hair and hazel-green eyes. I loved the way he walked like he had purpose and was important. I was a tomboy, and this guy (I'll call him JOHNDOE7) was into sports. And I loved all sports. I would always wear shorts under my skirts or dresses in case I would get into a game. JOHNDOE7 had a special sparkle in his eyes when he smiled. You know who you are, so don't let it go to your head, just keep the sparkle and smile.

One of my memories in fifth grade was when we were at recess. Because it was a new school, we had more dirt than grass at the time. I was going to play a game with friends, but before we could play, there was a rock in the way, so I grabbed it and threw it between my legs. I did say I was a tomboy. Anyway, as I threw the rock, this delicate blonde girl walked by at the same time, and the rock hit her in the head and split open her head. Of course, she had to go to the doctor and got some stitches, and of course, I was in trouble. My mom had to leave work, and we had to have a teacher-parent conference with both sets of parents and me and Vicki. I apologized, but I certainly didn't do it on purpose. After that, I always thought that all blondes must be very fragile. I've grown out of that idea, and I apologize to all blondes.

In sixth grade, JOHNDOE7 decided to like me back, and we started going steady. He bought me a black-and-white Saint Christopher medal, and I bought him a matching one. I used to think that JOHNDOE7 and I were going steady from fourth grade until tenth grade, but I'm not too sure of that. Anyway, during this period, we had fun going to the beach and going to the different carnivals they had in town. JOHNDOE7 was very good at the different games at the carnival and would win me stuffed animals. I had all those stuffed animals pinned to my bedroom walls. I must have had over thirty of them. One Christmas, JOHNDOE7 bought me a present; it was a turquoise-blue dress that had a watch necklace attached to the neck. I think he had TG help him pick it out. I got him a watch.

I had a really good teacher in sixth grade. I just can't remember his name right now. I do remember he made science and history enjoyable and I didn't much like those subjects.

One funny thing I remember, not funny then, is apparently some of my classmates were experimenting with their sexuality. There was this one girl who was always outgoing and funny, but she ended up getting a bad reputation and I always felt sad for her because I never thought she was a bad girl. Who knows if the rumors were true, but I chose not to believe them. Another rumor going around was that JANEDOE1 had a venereal disease, and we were told that we could get it off the toilet seats. So true or not, that was the end of me ever using a public toilet until a couple of years ago. Age changes a lot of things!

At the end of sixth grade, we moved to a nice house on Church Lane. It was right behind the Community Church and behind BW's house. I'll get back to him when I get in the eighth grade.

Big times began, now in seventh grade at Carpinteria Junior High. Today, they call it middle school.

My sister was in high school at this time and she ran with a pretty tough crowd at time. She and I were so different. She only hung out with a certain group, and I just liked everyone. Well, her group thought that I should follow in her footsteps, but that wasn't me. They wanted to beat me up, but my sister put a stop to that so I could just continue being Lil Pino.

My memory isn't real clear on this memory, but I apparently made JANEDOE2 very mad, so she wanted to fight me so she told me to meet her in the front of the school, which at that time had a low brick wall. I told my sister, so she came with me, I guess, to make sure I didn't get hurt. Maybe she was going to fight her, I don't know. I just know I didn't want to fight. JANEDOE2 was a tough girl, and I would have no chance to beat her. Well, I'm not clear, but something happened and she came at me and I just tried to protect myself and I don't know how it happened but I ended up pulling her blouse and bra off and that was the end of that. SM and I became close friends down the road, which was great. I ended up living around the corner from her when we lived on Camino Trillado.

Humiliated

In seventh grade, there was a group of young ladies, or at least they should have been. My mother loved going to rummage sales, today called yard sales. Rummage sales were all the yard sales gathered together under one roof, usually the Community Center. One day, Mom came home with these two really cute matching skirts and vests for me. One was shades of olive green and the other shades of gray. I wore one outfit to school one day feeling pretty sharp, which soon turned to humiliation. The outfit belonged to one of those young ladies who felt they were all that. She went around school telling her friends that I was poor and that outfit used to be hers. I was so embarrassed I went home crying. Her mother was the principal or secretary for the school and had heard what her daughter had done to me so she made her call me that night and apologize, but it didn't make me feel any better. The damage had been done. After that, I never wore anything from a rummage sale again, silly me. I love garage sales now. Had I known . . .

I mentioned before that I was a tomboy, so I played sports in school. We weren't allowed to wear pants or shorts to school yet. At recess, I was playing baseball one day and I hit a pretty good one, so I ran the bases but I had to slide into third. I was wearing a really cute tan dress with dark brown cording trim. Had been wearing—as I slid into third, I also tore off half the bottom of my dress from the waist.

That same year there was a new girl in school, and she and my friend JANEDOE3 got into an argument. The new girl JANEDOE4 was a very big girl, and I don't mean fat; she was just unusually large. Anyway, she and JANEDOE3 were at the top of the stairs yelling at each other so I went up there to stop them, wrong idea. I don't know how it happened but JOHNDOE4 went falling down the stairs. It wasn't my fight, but SS and I got kicked out of school for two weeks and nothing happened to JANEDOE4—oh well, lesson learned.

Eighth Grade

This is a coming-of-age year. Interesting teachers this year. One was Mr. JOHNDOE5. I think he must have been a military man. I remember when Mr. JOHNDOE5 was upset at a couple of boys and pinned them up against the wall and was yelling at them with his hands grabbing their shirts around their chests. It was an upsetting scene. You just never messed around that teacher. I didn't have him, thank goodness.

I did have Mr. JOHNDOE6, who was very attractive and he knew it. I didn't learn much in his class because I spent more time out of his class. Mr. JOHNDOE6 would turn off the lights in class to show a film, but I learned that when the lights went out, so did I. Mr. JOHNDOE6 had a problem with his hands if a girl had boobies and I did, so I walked out. I didn't know what else to do about that. Years later, I did, but too late.

This is where BW comes in, my Knight in Shining Armor. Well, maybe not but this young man was a class act, especially for an eighth grader. Most of the boys at that age are usually very immature.

BW and I had Mrs. C for English; we were in the same class. Well my changing of life came whiles I was sitting in Mrs. C class one morning. The bell rang for us to go to our next class. I knew very little about girls having their period. Remember, I was a tomboy and no real direction from mom. Anyway, I got up from my desk, and what happened to me was very noticeable. BW came up right behind me and said "Pino, you'd better go check yourself in the bathroom." Mrs. C's class was way at one end of the hall and the bathrooms at the opposite end. BW walked right behind me so no one else could see, and he walked me all the way to the bathroom. I got in there and didn't know what to do. I couldn't go anywhere. I didn't know at the time that BW went to the office, had them call my mom, and she came with a change of clothes. That has to be one of my sweetest memories of that young man, one class act. This was a young man that had no sisters, but his mom and dad taught him well. Thank you with all my heart, BW. Ran into BW a couple of years ago, and he still seems like a class act. BW and are a day apart in age.

Somewhere Over Lost

Ninth Grade

This was a year of many changes in my life. Going to high school was a big change for me, going from a small campus to a much larger one, at least for those days and for a girl who was never sure of herself.

PE was a big change for me. I never liked undressing in front of anyone, not even my sister, and I shared a bedroom with her for several years. I knew going to high school, I would have to take showers with the other girls, and I was terrified. It became a very uncomfortable experience especially when we got a PE teacher who liked looking at us change and shower. I started changing in the toilet stalls so I could have some privacy. I ran out of Song leader because you could take PE last period and didn't have to shower there.

One day, we had a fire drill when I was in the middle of changing my clothes. Thank goodness I was wearing pantaloons under my skirt because I had to run out in the field with them and a shirt on. Pantaloons were non-see-through, at least the ones I wore. They looked more like short leggings like we wear today. I was probably the only girl that wore them, and that was just because I could join a game and not worry about falling down with a skirt on.

I think JOHNDOE7 and I were still going steady at this time. I thought at least for a while I thought JOHNDOE7 was going to by my Somewhere Over. JOHNDOE7 was always a gentleman and never tried anything funny or unacceptable. Well, except for this one time he caught me off guard at the movie theater. I think we were only in sixth grade and he went to kiss me and I totally didn't expect it and I think I hit him out of reaction. There were many times after that were acceptable and pleasant and quite enjoyable.

If I am clear on the facts here, I think JOHNDOE7 only went to ninth grade with us. I remember him taking me to Santa Barbara to a Rexall drugstore on Milpas St. I think he had someone drive us there, if I'm correct. He bought me a huge pink stuffed dog that was about three feet tall. I think it was a going-away present. I don't remember us talking about him going away, or if we did, I don't remember. His parents sent him to a private school or a different school out of the area. His friends would tease me and say he got sent back to Mexico. One of JOHNDOE7's best friends was GL, who would always tell me about JOHNDOE7 having a girlfriend in his new school. JOHNDOE7 never wrote me so I really had no clue and eventually GL's stories got to me so I just gave up on the idea that JOHNDOE7 was coming back, at least to me.

Tenth Grade

There were a lot of people leaving me that year. JOHNDOE7 went away, and my mother and little sister moved to Hong Kong. My older sister had gotten pregnant when she was fifteen, and about a year after having her baby, she met a guy that was going to college in Santa Barbara, and they moved to Hong Kong. When my sister got pregnant with their first child, she sent for my mom and, of course, my little sister. I always wondered why I didn't get to go; after all, I was only fifteen but I didn't, so there! My sister's husband was very wealthy; he was number one son from number one mother, and that was a very important position in their culture. My dad didn't go with them right away but eventually in a couple of months. Even though he was still home, I hardly saw him since he worked all day and night. Eventually my Somewhere Over went overseas.

Now I was mostly alone for the rest of my school years. I say mostly because for the first year, my dad would come back every other month for about a week. Looking back, I am grateful that I at least had a house to live in; they eventually lost that when I graduated.

The only ones who knew I didn't have parents around were Mr. Mac and Mr. Coats. Mr. Coats lived on my street, and he would knock on my bedroom window to wake me up for school. I took driver training from Mr. Mac, and he would drive over to my house with the other kids in the car and bang on my window and get me up for driving. I think we had four kids, me included, in the car at one time. There was one guy in the car that was a very scary driver; even Mr. Mac was scared. We would drive all the way out to Refugio Beach. I loved having Mr. Mac as a teacher, and Mr. Coats was pretty cool.

Somehow, living alone didn't seem so weird to me at that time, except I didn't like the nights, still don't like being alone at night. I was able to get food by going to the beach and finding money in the sand, and on the way down to the beach, I would stop at the laundromat, and with a stick, I could find money between the machines. I existed on bear claws and suicide sodas from Fosters Freeze, which was next to our school and is still there today. There were also school lunches; that helped for the afternoons, and they weren't bad. My favorite was when they had mashed potatoes with a meat gravy on top with green beans on the side. I did a little shoplifting on the side for other things I needed, or maybe a lot. I owe the Mills Drugstore money for those days. Actually, I did go back as an adult to give them some money, but the store was gone.

One really stupid thing I did then, now that I look back on it, involved driving without a license or training. I had a business class, and about four of us were to go to Santa Barbara to Brooks Institute to have interviews. Well, no one had their driver's license or a car. I had the keys to my mother's car she left behind, so I drove all of us to our interviews. Looking back, it could have turned out so bad, but thank goodness nothing happened; we all got back safely.

Somewhere toward the end of tenth grade, a Black Irish boy and I started dating. He was tall, again to my standards of tall. I was 5'2". He had dark brown hair and green eyes, and he was an athlete, something about that combination I loved. His mother and mine were best friends and worked together at The Palms. I guess it was just natural we go together since our mothers were friends and we did things like camping together. He was a sweet kid and had a good sense of humor, and his body wasn't not bad to look at, either. Oh yes, he had good-looking teeth and a nice smile. Teeth are the first thing I notice on anyone; his passed. I'll call him JOHNDOE8 for reference's sake. JOHNDOE8 and I went steady from the end of tenth grade to the end of eleventh grade. He was a fun guy to be around, but each summer, he would dump me so he could be available for the beach bunnies that came into town for the summer. We would go back together when school started up again. How dumb was I? I must have really been desperate or really liked the guy. I'll go with the latter. There was only one incident where we got a little too close and almost made a big mistake for the both of us. Nothing happened; someone came home unexpectedly, and he bolted out the window.

Eleventh Grade

JOHNDOE8 and I went to junior-senior prom together. I must say we were a good-looking couple. I still have the picture up on my wall—just kidding. That would be very weird, but I do have it.

The prom almost didn't happen for me because I didn't have money for the dress, and my mom wouldn't give me any. She didn't like me having boyfriends; maybe because of what happened to my sister. I only had two, but I really cared for them both. Back to the dress: there was a boy, MV, who was about four years older than me that lived across the street from me. He liked me, but I made it clear that we were never going to be together. But we were still good friends. MV took me to Santa Barbara and took me shopping for my dress and shoes, and he bought them for me. Thank you, MV, I think of you often and wonder what happened to you. Dinning for those days. After dinner, we drove back to Carp for the prom.

JOHNDOE8 took photography in school, and he would use me as his model sometimes. I wasn't a very good model. He took a picture of me for FFA Princess that year to put in the case in the hallway of the school with the other contestants. I have to say, JOHNDOE8, it was not your best work, or maybe it was just me. Anyway, another Linda got the win; she was a senior and was very pretty. There were too many Lindas in that school, so we usually got called by our last names.

Sometime in eleventh grade, JOHNDOE8 gave me a very pretty opal ring, but again, summer came along and so did the beach bunnies. JOHNDOE8 and I had an argument right in front of the art class about getting together but I was done. I took the ring off and threw it at him, but it went flying into the hedge that was there and I walked away. I went back to look for it but never did find it; maybe he did. I always have loved opals, and I think JOHNDOE7 gave me a necklace and matching earrings. I think that was the first time I had ever seen opals. The necklace and earrings had a teardrop pendant that had some kind of fluid in it with tiny opal stones in it. I loved that set.

Senior Year

JOHNDOE7 came back to town, and I have to say that I still had a crush on him but he was totally over me. I didn't get back with JOHNDOE8 either that year; he was different and was experimenting with drugs, and they really changed him.

Well, a new kid, RG, came into town. He was a totally different guy compared to the ones in Carpinteria. He didn't have any of the looks that the other two had. I don't mean he was ugly; he just had big brown eyes with great eyelashes and dark hair. He was a pretty boy that actually went to salons to get his hair done and wore tight pants with Beatle boots and mostly white shirts with a tie. He was a surfer but didn't look like the surfers I grew up with. He was from Huntington Beach. It was not love or even like at first sight. I thought he was gay. He was a playboy and very good dancer, and all the girls loved dancing with him. He also was a good singer. He and another girl entered a talent contest, and they sang a Sonny and Cher song and won. He still is a good singer, and so are his sons; they all do a very good imitation of Elvis Presley. He didn't graduate. I think he took the GED and got out of school; he didn't like that school.

My brother took me to the Kingdom Hall toward the end of my junior year. Apparently, he was one of Jehovah's Witnesses, I had never heard of them before that. I was very impressed with how they actually used the Bible to teach from. I always had an interest in the Bible. My grandmother raised me Catholic and I was baptized Catholic, then I tried Church of Christ and went to the Mormon Church with JOHNDOE8 for a little while. I remet RRG at the Kingdom Hall. It was a gradual relationship. By the end of my senior year, we got engaged.

In the meantime, I was also getting ready to graduate and trying to get my parents back in the country for my graduation. Needless to say, no one from my family, not even my fiancé, came to my graduation, which I thought was a big deal since I was the first in my family to graduate. Well, my parents did come back for my wedding, which was the weekend after I graduated then they went back to Asia that month.

I think back on it now, and I probably got married so I could make my own Somewhere Over.

We had three beautiful children, and I loved being married and a mother.

I didn't find my Somewhere Over with RG either, but I did find it in the brotherhood of Jehovah's Witnesses and it will be even better in the near future.

Me,
Linda

Teachers Give Their Personal Opinions of Carpinteria's 1967 Graduating Class

The various persons working in the CHS classrooms and administrative offices have formed personal opinions concerning this past year's senior class. The following question was posed to several persons: "Does this year's class of graduating seniors (as a group) have any distinguishing characteristics (honesty, purity, wit, etc.)?"

Their answers are as follows:

Mr. El Ruiz: "This class has displayed the traditional high standards which are characteristic of Carpinteria High School graduates."

Mrs. Geraldine Blakeslee: "They seem rather serious compared to last year's class."

Mrs. Dorothy Tripp: "They are a very tightly knit group. I don't know how they're going to unravel."

Mr. Allan Coates: "This class seems to be very casual in most respects. They also, as a group, give the impression of being rather secretive about their activities. I would say that they are generally pretty capable, but not overly ambitious."

Mr. Christopher Nicholas: "They display a good sense of humor."

Mr. Burdett Shearer: "This year's senior class is industrious. They have worked hard at the things they have attempted. For example, the successful events they have undertaken are Ditch Day (Senior Education Day), the senior reception, and graduation. Most seniors have worked hard toward June 16, while others have worked just as hard and steadily to get out of working hard. Therefore, all seniors have been industrious."

Mr. King Feicock: "They display independence with recklessness."

Mrs. Pamela Thayer: "The group is very close; everyone gets along with one another. They are enthusiastic and well-mannered."

Mrs. Helen Rocky: "To me there is a very important distinction: my son is one of the graduates. But additionally, each succeeding class seems to become dearer to those of us who have the privilege of working with the students."

Ms. Barbara Callahan: "At this point, the old rhyme 'What can't be cured must be endured' seems appropriate. But I'd like to state that given the right incentive, such as June 16, this class seems to be able to work toward a common goal."

—Marcia Lesher

Teachers Give Their Personal Opinions Of Carpinteria's 1967 Graduating Class

The various persons working in the CHS classrooms and administrative offices have formed personal opinions concerning this past year's senior class. The following question was posed to several persons: "Does this year's class of graduating seniors (as a group) have any distinguishing characteristics (honesty, purity, wit, etc.)?"

Their answers are as follows:

Mr. El Ruiz: "This class has displayed the traditional high standards which are characteristic of Carpinteria High School graduates."

Mrs. Geraldine Blakeslee: "They seem rather serious compared to last year's class."

Mrs. Dorothy Tripp. "They are a very tightly knit group. I don't know how they're going to unravel."

Mr. Allan Coates: "This class seems to be very casual in most respects. They also, as a group, give the impression of being rather secretive about their activities. I would say that they are generally pretty capable, but not overly ambitious."

Mr. Christopher Nicholas: "They display a good sense of humor."

Mr. Burdett Shearer: "This year's senior class is industrious. They have worked hard at the things they have attempted. For example, the successful events they have undertaken are Ditch Day (Senior Education Day), the senior reception, and graduation. Most seniors have worked hard toward June 16, while others have worked just as hard and steadily to get out of working hard. Therefore, all seniors have been industrious."

Mr. King Feicock: "They display independence with recklessness."

Mrs. Pamela Thayer: "The group is very close; everyone gets along with one another. They are enthusiastic and well-mannered."

Mrs. Helen Rocky: "To me there is a very important distinction; my son is one of the graduates. But additionally, each succeeding class seems to become dearer to those of us who have the privilege of working with the students."

Miss Barbara Callahan: "At this point, the old rhyme, 'What can't be cured, must be endured,' seems apropriate. But I'd like to state that, given the right incentive, such as June 16, this class seems to be able to work toward a common goal."

—Marcia Lesher

Courtesy of Jack Moyer from the Carpinteria Herald, June 16, 1967

Courtesy of Jack Moyer from the
Carpinteria Herald, June 18, 1967

10/24/2020 Class members meet at Carpinteria
Beach to go over *Chapters of Our Lives* book.

Front row (R to L): Emily Brown, Linda Fryer,
Esther Cerda, Cori Deaderick, Linda Pino
Back row (R to L): Joe Lovett, Terry Galvez, Dianne Darcy,
Linda Kohnke, Thais Meyer, Steve Wright, Robert Perez,
Rick Gesswein, Richard Morris, Mark Campbell

Pictures courtesy of Barbara Swing.

Pictures courtesy of Barbara Swing

The boat ramp at the end of Ash Avenue

Courtesy CHS Yearbook

Courtesy CHS Yearbook

Courtesy of Jim Campos, Coastal View News

Greetings from SANTA CLAUS, CALIF.

Courtesy of Sy Kinsell

Courtesy of Tom Moore

Courtesy of Tom Moore

Kevin Sears RIP.

Robert Perez

Robert Perez

#21

Robert H. Perez – Carpinteria High School – Class of 1967

I was born January 9, 1949, the week it snowed in Carpinteria for the first and only time so far! I guess you say I arrived in a storm! I lived with my parents, Leo and Christina Perez, and my older brother Raymond (CHS class of 1964) on Seventh Street.

My first decade in Carp circled around two major places in my life: a creek that ran alongside our house and Aliso School, which was across the street. That humble creek gave me the thrills and adventures of Tom Sawyer growing up. It had everything a kid could want—a giant weeping willow tree with a rope swing attached, and perfect branches to make the best bow and arrows from. The Amazon River can't compare to all the fantastic wildlife I found there: frogs and more frogs, slithery snakes, tons of tiny tadpoles, creepy crawdads, and freaky fish. Daring dragonflies swarmed overhead.

The water in the creek flowed all year long; sometimes it even overflowed its banks in winter and flooded our neighborhood. A few years ago, I had the opportunity to visit my beloved childhood creek, only to discover it had become a cold concrete basin with a sad finger of water running through it—devoid of all wildlife. So much for progress—at least there are no more floods to contend with.

In a strange way, I see this humble creek as a metaphor for life: all things must change and all things run to the Sea of Life.

As I mentioned, Aliso School was across the street. I thought of it as my personal playground as a child. Maybe this was because my dad, Leo, was the school custodian there for over thirty years. Aliso School was an amazing adventure as well for me. It had long straight hallways where I roller-skated on the weekends all day long. I can't forget the dangerous but oh-so-fun playground equipment! For instance, nothing beats the infamous teeter-totter, which could catapult you a mile high if you let go. Then there was the "ladder of death" next to the fire pole that seemed to be ten stories high with no safety mat at the bottom! You only had one chance to come down the right way—a thrill every time!

Next stop: Carpinteria Junior High School! It was great time as a pre-teen and an awkward transition to high school. Talk about education limbo land. I think about this time in my life in Carp as a line in a Simon and Garfunkel song: "My Little Town," especially the part that says, "I was my father's son in my little town."

Carpinteria High School, here I come! Ready or not! My years in high school reminded me of the film *American Graffiti* with better music and prettier girls! That was the *fun* part. My academic scene was another story. Let's just say I wouldn't have won any Nobel Prize for my grades. However, the sensational social life was a blast, and the treasured friendships I made I wouldn't trade for the world!

When I consider the good times versus the bad times, it was one of the highlights of my life! The bad times included the Vietnam War draft hanging over our heads during the last year. I still remember hanging out in the quad with the cool kids showing off their fashion and getting up my Friday night football games—Go Warriors! I still have my letterman's jacket and guess what? It still fits. It's fun to wear at pep rallies and even Halloween!

My passion for art was celebrated in a special way during sophomore year when my design was selected by the City Council to be the design for the city seal of our new city of Carpinteria! Was my art teacher shocked!

After graduation, I was drafted by the US Army and served two years in Germany, which was really the luck of the draw. Upon returning to Carpinteria, my town, I worked at infrared industries for a year before moving to San Francisco to attend Academy of Art University to follow my passion for art and received a degree in fine arts from the University of San Francisco. It was there that I reconnected with the love of my life—Kathy Donovan. I first met Kathy in 1965 at a Y dance in Santa Barbara. That was the same year I designed the city seal of Carpinteria—two events that would forever change my life!

I am delighted to share that we have been happily married for forty-six years and still going strong. We have two amazing sons—Hart and Devon Perez, who are following their bliss as independent filmmakers—living in Hollywood. Check them out at PerezBros. com. My wife Kathy just retired as professor emerita from Saint Mary's College of California in the Bay Area.

My five passions in life are family first, art, teaching, traveling, and magic! Let's explore those now. I have been very fortunate to have blended all of my passions in my lifestyle.

1. Family—After getting married, Kathy and I settled down in Oakland, California, and raised our sons for about twenty years until we moved to Alameda, an island community in the San Francisco Bay Area. We have also kept Kathy's childhood home in Santa Barbara, so we are lucky to split our time between both properties. When I am down in Santa Barbara, I always make time to visit my mom, Christina, in Carpinteria and enjoy a feast at The Palms. In many ways, it is like I never left Carp. It is hard to break old habits, and why should I?

2. Art—I continue to enjoy painting and drawing in my retirement years because art allows me to see the world in a new way every day. I have been fortunate to win some contests over the years (including Carpinteria's Avocado Festival contest), and this allows me the time to celebrate my talents artistically.

3. Teaching—My passion for art led me into my teaching career, where I could ignite the creative spirit of preschool children as their teacher for over thirty-two years. Going back to school for an advanced degree in early childhood was a win-win for me—because I could still be a freelance artist and combine my career as a teacher. An added bonus was having my own sons as students—a life-changing experience to have them in my class at that age!

4. Magic—This world has always seemed magical to me—seeing a tadpole turn into a frog at the creek or a rabbit coming out of a hat! Magic is alive when I see my own sons' faces

light up with a simple "Abracadabra." This led me to my stage persona: Roberto the Magnificent, a proud member of the Hollywood Magic Castle. Although I don't perform for kids' parties anymore, I still delight in Vegas Magic extravaganzas.

5. Travel—Kathy and I made travelling the plant a priority from the very beginning. During our first year of marriage in the 1970s, we put our dreams in our backpacks and explored the world. Since then our planetary adventures have taken us to over eighty countries and counting, including living a year abroad in Wales, Great Britain. Some of our memorable stops include the heights in Machu Picchu, the marketplace of Casablanca, Morocco, the fiords of Norway, the treasures of the Taj Mahal, going on safari in Africa, the white sands of Tahiti, and so much more! Next stop: after the pandemic, we will pack our bags to Antarctica. However, home sweet home will always be Carpinteria!

To the Class of 1967, *thanks* for all of the great memories. I will never forget all of you and all of the good times we shared. *Go Warriors!*

By Robert Perez

Robert Perez was in
Miss Tripp's Art Class
and won the contest
to create the first seal
of the City of Carpinteria
when it was incorporated
in 1965.

Original seal

Robert Perez with modified seal at 2015 50th Anniversary
of the City of Carpinteria.

CHAPTER TWENTY-TWO

Jackie Niccum

JACKIE NICCUM

#22

My name is Jackie Niccum Yantis, and I am a graduate of the Carpinteria High School class of '67. My high school memories are pleasant ones. I am grateful for the small schools and class sizes of Mt. Carmel and Carpinteria High School. It allowed us to get to know each other and form friendships. The respect and kindness I received has accompanied me throughout my life.

The experience formed my life decisions. Following graduation, I worked in several office-secretarial/assistant type positions. My career choice was to join a small start-up company, King Radio. King Radio was a company that designed and manufactured avionics, electric and electronic equipment for aircraft and spacecraft.

King Radio was founded in 1959 by Ed King Jr., who had the vision to design units for general aviation. At that time, avionics companies concentrated on where the money is—commercial and transport avionics. In general aviation, products are sized to fit the smaller personal airplane and business jet instrument panels. Someone once said that the greatest inventions come from creative, free thinkers who haven't been told by experts that it couldn't be done. In a way, this is how King Radio Corporation was born. King Radio was a manufacturer of general aviation avionics and aviation gauges and indicators. It was a major avionics supplier for Cessna, Piper, and Beechcraft.

General aviation was and remains popular in North America. Commercial airports number around 560 in the United States while there are over 5,200 airports available for public use by general aviation aircraft. King Radio was at the forefront of the industry because many of the employees were pilots who may or may not have owned an aircraft and/or were flight instructors. Ed King himself was a pilot and owned several planes. The pilots knew what they wanted in convenience and performance, thus the excitement of innovation was all around. New ideas and projects were always in development.

Being a small company and centered around a core market, decisions were made quickly. There was no reason to form a committee, talk over proposals, and sometime later come to a decision. Employees could bring their ideas forward, and they were listened to. Product innovations and new products were daily occurrences.

In 1973, I interviewed for an office position, but the company was growing so fast that I was hired on the spot and began training in instrument manufacturing and engineering. Mechanical engineering wasn't as interesting for me, thus I joined the electrical group. By that time, the company had outgrown the farmhouse where it began. King Radio had a hangar and planes at a local airport along with engineering headquarters in Olathe, Kansas, and several satellite manufacturing and repair and overhaul plants in other cities.

Design headquarters consisted of mechanical and electrical engineers along with sales/marketing, prototyping, human resources, financial department, and of course, pilots. The company was so small that the headquarters' phone book was a single sheet of paper. Everyone knew each other, and many of the employees were related in some way or another. King Radio developed an actual profit-sharing plan. If an employee joined the plan, their contribution was matched 1:1, but if the company did well during the year, the company's contribution was increased. It was a very generous plan. Another benefit offered employees was learning how to fly without a large investment. I did not take advantage of the opportunity. The money was a detriment, but I also lacked a strong desire to pilot aircraft.

Ed King periodically strolled through the headquarters, airport hangar, and satellite plants. He would engage with people and ask questions in regards to whatever a person was working on. Everyone had to be on their toes as although he personally was interested, he also expected every employee knew and understood what they were doing and the importance of their contribution to the product and company.

The '70s and '80s ushered in awesome changes and inventions. Aviation buffs were building airplanes at home. Several employees had their own aircraft. At that time, most units were primarily manual, thus the performance was codependent on gears, resolvers, and other components. Some individual components were purchases from other companies, but design, manufacturing, testing, and shipping were all done locally. The integrity and quality of the instruments were paramount. Even if an employee pilot purchased a unit for his personal plane, all instruments had to meet the Federal Aviation Association requirements, documentation, and certification. New products could take six months to a year to meet all the required records and testing.

FAA safety requirements are to protect the public. As King Radio designed and manufactured equipment and instruments for flight, bench testing was not adequate. The instruments have to be used in real situations, extreme temperatures, and validate airworthiness. Engineers involved in some instrument designs were required to ride with the pilot as the aircraft was put through various aerobatic maneuvers. On your next flight, pay attention to the airsickness bags as the flight attendants go through the preflight prep. Some engineers returned to the facility a little green, and the airsickness bags had to be replenished.

It was exciting working with so much innovation all around and going to the various facilities, exploring the planes, taking jaunts, etc.

The late '70s and '80s ushered in computers to aid in design. For initial design instead of manual drawing/blueprints/schematics were now being captured on computers. Personal computers were yet to become available. We worked with mainframes and proprietary systems. VAX, UNIX-based Scicards, Mentor, Cadnetix, ProE, and other systems were used. Arrangements were made for a professor to come in a couple of days a week, and most of the team signed up to learn coding. All participants passed the course and everyone began writing code to simplify processes. It was exciting to see and use codes written by the team. One software supplier was so impressed with the improvements made to the program, the company offered to purchase the scripts.

Temporary employees were hired by the technical publications group (something like a hard-copy library of the product manuals and design documentation) to enter data from the engineering manuals into a master database. The engineers were not informed that it was happening. Several weeks into the effort, engineers began to notice that non-typeface essential graphs, charts, drawings, etc., were missing from the manuals and records. The temps were not informed that the images must be included. Some engineers maintained personal copies for quick reference, for those it expedited correcting the documentation. It took the good part of a year to clean up and replace all the missing documents.

In 1983, Ed King Jr. sold King Radio to the Allied Corporation. Around that time, Allied also purchased Bendix Aviation. Ed retired and, with his son Ed King III and other family members, founded King Estate Winery in 1991. The winery is located southwest of Eugene, Oregon.

Upon the sale, the King Radio profit-sharing plan was designated to be dissolved and the net proceeds to be dispensed to employees. Lawyers for Allied changed the plan to roll the money into Allied's savings plan. Through rewriting the plan, it now read that if the employees sued to overturn the change, all legal fees would come from the employees' share of the plan. Needless to say, there were a lot of unhappy people. Some people left the company, but many employees had invested time and were proud of their jobs and remained.

The King brand name was changed by Allied to Bendix/King, and the King crown logo was retired. In 1985, Allied Corporation merged with the Signal Companies and formed Allied Signal. The combined company was less efficient, and upper management began bringing in new people in key positions. There were pilots, and thus the company moved further from the end consumer.

Sometime in 1986, Burt Rutan's Aircraft Company met with King Radio regarding using King equipment in a plane designed by Burt, the *Voyager*. King Radio equipment was donated for the flight. In December 1986, flying the *Voyager*, Dick Rutan (Burt's older brother) and Jeana Yeager were the first to navigate an aircraft around the world without stopping or refueling during the 25,000-mile nonstop flight. Following the flight endurance record, both Dick and Jeana returned to thank the employees and distribute mementos.

In the late '80s, employees still presented their concepts to the company. The company though had lost the dynamics. No immediate decisions were made. The guess was since the company was so spread out, assessments were made by committee. Eventually, the employee was notified of the outcome, but in some instances, the moment was lost. Olathe site vice president of engineering Gary Burrell proposed to upper management to enter the GPS (global positioning system) market. Allied Signal ultimately declined. Gary Burrell and engineer Min Kao left the company, and by 1989, founded Garmin. The US Army became Garmin's first customer. There was an exodus of engineers and other personnel to Garmin. I remained with Allied. At that time, only two of my team of printed circuit designers left to join Garmin. Sometime early in the 2000s, the company branched out and entered the avionics field. Garmin headquarters remain in Olathe.

The next engineering VP's office was close to mine. As he was new to the company and avionics, he would invite me into his office, lay out a problem, and ask me to think about a solution and get back to him. His secretary and my team would give me advance notice that the VP was looking for me. He was there about a year or so until he was let go because of upper management politics.

Restructuring brought in outside managers lacking experience in avionics. We would sit through meetings while the group would be put down for taking so long to get a product to market. The manager denigrating the assembly had experience at a factory that made electric golf carts. He was informed there is a difference between flight and golf carts on safety requirements and FAA testing and certification. The company also began slowing down on research and development. Previously, King's engineers routinely applied and held many patents on their inventions. Now they were being reduced to supporting existing units while the R&D support went overseas. Again, there was an outflow of engineers to Garmin. Garmin had entered the general aviation market. Management was concerned about competition and sent out directives that employees were not to fraternize with Garmin employees or even mention Garmin. They might have been unaware that family members of employees were working at Garmin.

Honeywell merged with Allied 1999. Allied Signal adopted the name Honeywell. Today, cell phones and other items become obsolete. There comes a time when parts/components are no longer available, and thus, you must purchase a new one. King Radio equipment had to be maintained as long as original product was in flight. Finding parts to service a decades-old unit is a challenge. Some of the unusual components were stocked through a lifetime buy. Of course, that doesn't look good for inventory. Allied would transfer employees into Olathe's facility without any knowledge of the requirement. To make the numbers, they would auction off the lifetime buy components only to have to repurchase them with a price increase.

Outsourcing is the business practice of hiring a party outside a company to perform services and create goods that traditionally were performed in-house by the company's own employees and staff. As a cost-cutting measure, internal departments and satellite plants were shut down. The original King headquarters lost their camera and printed circuit board fabrication departments. There was a RIF (reduction in force/layoff). I traveled to various sites coordinating facility shutdowns. Entering the plants, I saw the employees knew what I was there for, but personally, they graciously accommodated my requests. Obtaining and filing electronic design and manufacturing date was paramount to continue supplying our customers.

The development of a global free market has benefited large corporations based in the Western world. Globalization opened up many countries around the globe. India and China have greatly advanced economically and technically. Allied Signal continued with takeovers and mergers. Small companies such as Skyforce in the United Kingdom and others were acquired. The influx of green card holders from around the world required US employees to mentor and train them. It was determined to be more cost-effective to purchase a company or even just products and place the company name on them.

The company was now so massive that your manager could be far away only to visit one's site once a year. Managers were certainly not familiar with one's day-to-day performance. Once if there was a mistake on your pay, you could walk up front, talk to finance, and have a corrected check before the end of the day. Now one would contact their out-of-state manager, who in turn would contact financial headquarters in another state. Several weeks later, it might be resolved.

Human resource personnel were now directing hiring. It was frustrating to interview for an electrical technician or engineering position but could not ask questions on the individual's experience. Questions were limited to whether or not they were familiar with Microsoft Project or they could create a chart or some other non-applicable proficiency. The push was to concentrate on hiring from Ivy League colleges. Engineers would come in knowing formulas but not how to apply them. Experienced site engineers were tasked with mentoring them.

Globalization allowed me to work from home. Team members were in Singapore, the Czech Republic, Canada, India, Puerto Rico, and the United Kingdom. Working from home allowed me to connect with them during their working hours. I would transfer work to and from their site computers, handle issues, and generally keep the work flowing. There were times I was on four separate computers simultaneously. IP addresses and security logins swarm in my head. Today there are days where I don't log in to my personal computer.

Five years ago, I retired and am enjoying it. I volunteer at the election office three or four weeks before each election. I am active in several clubs and have several hobbies.

Lessons I Learned

> Bigger isn't always better.
> Know your customer and end consumer.
> Ask the worker for their input. Those that do the job
> probably know it better than you do.
> Code can be manipulated to determine the output. As
> it is said, garbage in, garbage out.
> Give credit where credit due.
> Teaching others your profession will eventually turn
> into assigning them to perform your job.

Over the years, Honeywell attempted to divest the general aviation segment and focus on the commercial market. In 2019, the Olathe facility cut the remaining engineering staff. The primary focus now will be on repair and overhaul of units.

My life has been blessed. From Carpinteria until today, all my days have been excellent. I enjoyed my career. I led a fantastic team, troubleshooting, writing software code, designing/laying out printed circuit boards, implementing engineering change orders, assembling and staging units, documenting performance; it was all a tremendous experience. The best part though was working with and meeting fantastic people.

Jackie Niccum Yantis and George

CHAPTER TWENTY-THREE

Joanne Hinson

JOANNE
HINSON

#23

Joanne Gurely
From Miss Carpinteria to Living off the Grid

It was September 23, 1966. All week, Carpinteria had been gearing up for an amazing event. It was the celebration of Carpinteria's first birthday as a city! There were lots of events, and one in particular was the Miss Carpinteria contest. There were seventeen candidates, and I was the lucky one chosen! I was the first Miss Carpinteria. I was seventeen years old, surprised, happy, hopelessly in love!

Carpinteria celebrated with a BBQ at the beach, a parade, and a talent show. One of my prizes as Miss Carpinteria was to go to a modeling agency and learn all the fun things about makeup, pictures, being able to talk to the public, and of course, modeling. I modeled clothes in the old Spanish-style restaurants in Santa Barbara and had a really fun time.

After graduation, I went to a business college in Santa Barbara, learned a bunch of stuff I'll never use, finally got a really good job at the Santa Barbara School District in the administration offices, moved out of my parents' house and into an old house in Summerland with the girls I met at the business college, and my boyfriend, Joe. I was still hopelessly in love.

I loved my job at the school district. I worked in the vocational education and superintendent's office. We devised classes for students, which were held at different businesses. For example, a man who owns a gas station would take two or three students who wanted to learn about cars. They would work and learn to do the job, while earning credits for graduation. They were given uniforms, regular work hours, and most importantly, they learned a trade. With the Distributive Education students, we eventually had a restaurant at the high school, for students, teachers, and of course public, so it actually made money! We used students in the art programs to design menus, cooking students to come up with recipes, home-making students to make aprons. We had students building, painting, and decorating the restaurant. Our students cooked all the food, as well as seating and serving all the customers. It was a wonderful program. The kids felt so proud of their work. It made me feel so good to get the kids thinking ahead to their financial future, and having fun at the same time. I've seen so many times that kids always learn when they are enjoying it.

By the time I left the school district, after fourteen years, quite a few changes had occurred in my life. The love of my life got drafted and went to Panama. I thought my life was over. I couldn't see how I was going to even get out of the stupid air terminal when his plane took off. It was awful. So to me, the changes that occurred next felt natural, or maybe I was just depressed. I stopped wearing nylons and heels and started wearing A-line skirts, and flats, or sandals. I sold my Mustang and bought an International Harvester Jeep. I'm sure my parents thought I was going nuts!

The week Joe got home, I could tell things weren't going to be the same. He seemed different, but I was so stupid in love I didn't want to see anything wrong. Time passed, and as much as I wanted him to want to marry me, I could see it wasn't going to happen. He started seeing other girls, and I just couldn't trust him anymore. What good would it do to hang on to a love that isn't there for both people?

I had bought him a motorcycle for his birthday, and he decided to on a cross-county trip with his friend of his. Sounded like a much-needed break to me, so he went. He had a great time with his "friend," who turned out be a girl. I was crushed. I couldn't believe it until another friend showed me pictures Joe had sent him. So the next day, I found another place to live. I took all my stuff out of the house we had been living in. When he got home, there wasn't even a bed to sleep in. Darn. Too bad. He was very surprised, to say the least. He didn't think I'd ever find out. Well, that was it for me.

Time went by, and I met another man through some friends at work. His name was Ron. He wasn't someone I was attracted to, but he was nice. He also was interested in me, which by that time, was something nice, after the heartache I still felt. He was an abalone diver and he had a diving boat. We got to be better friends, and I started to feel more than just liking him, so our relationship grew. He wasn't making much money with the diving, because to make money being a commercial diver, you have to have nice equipment, and Ron didn't. I think he was ready for a change, and I was ready for a change. After all, I had a Jeep, for Pete's sake! I had to go somewhere!

Around this time, we had a friend who moved to Napa. He asked us to come and visit. He lived on few acres at the top of Mount Veeder. Mount Veeder is the mountain that sits between Napa on one side and Sonoma on the other. Ron and I had been to Weaverville when we eloped in 1973, and it was beautiful, but not this beautiful. There were so many trees and lots of little barns that people had converted into homes, and a rushing creek. It had a feeling of really living out in the country. We loved it and wanted to move there, but we had a cabinet/mirror business in Santa Barbara, so we had to figure out how to do it.

We decided if we made our cabinets and mirrors and took them to local fairs to sell, why not set up shop in Napa and do fairs from there? Sounded like a great plan. So we loaded up all our earthly goods and started off—like the Beverly Hillbillies! The pictures of that are funny! We finally got there and settled into the cutest, smallest cabin I ever saw. We had a part of a big barn for our wood and inventory, and started scanning the paper for fairs and other events. We had no water, no electricity, and no bathroom. We hauled seven gallons of water a week from town. We used kerosene for our lanterns. We insulated the walls with egg cartons and cardboard. We had a fifty-five-gallon barrel drum with a door cut out for putting wood in, and hole in the top for the smoke pipe. It was so warm in our barn. Ron welded a grate inside the door, so we could roast a chicken or steak. They always turned out great—OK, maybe not the first one! For refrigeration, we had one of the first iceboxes made. The walls were about six inches thick; there was space in the top for a block of ice, and it had a drain hose you could collect the water from the ice block for a vegetable plant! Perfect!

My first son was born in 1975. His name is Sun Ray. He was born two weeks early, on Thanksgiving Day! I was surprised! I hadn't even finished my Lamaze classes yet. Having a baby on a holiday means you don't have the same doctor you've had the whole nine months. What an experience. Living an hour from town means you have to give yourself plenty of time. The birth turned out just fine, and I was so happy to my little pumpkin.

Living on top of Mount Veeder was a wonderful way of life. Our landlord's name was Roland. He lived on the land, in another barn. He was a psychologist at Napa State Hospital. He was the nicest, craziest man I'd ever met. He had white long hair, kept in a bank in the back, white mustache and beard, and he had a big potbelly! He wore suspenders at all times, even if he only had on his shorts! Roland liked to meet us at some of the fairs we went to. He was our good-luck charm. He was so charming he could bring in a crown to our booth, and before we knew it, we'd sold a ton of mirrors. Our mirrors were on wooden backgrounds of different shapes. The frames had a small shelf on it, for a plant. We had different types of shelves. Some had holes to hold a pot or a plant; some were solid. Some of our frames were full of knots; some were not. People could choose which type of design they wanted. It was great customer service, they liked it, and we had fun while making a couple of dollars.

As all good things come to an end, so did the mirror business and us going to fairs. The land we were living on sold. We all were upset, even Roland. He had only owned 1/3 of the land, and his land partners wanted to sell. So we all had to move. We moved to the other side of the mountain, to Sonoma. Man, what a place that was. The town square wasn't big, but it had the best and yummiest places to eat there ever were! We moved to a big house. Roland came with us, as well as a couple of other people from the mountain. We all loved that place. There was a prune orchard across the street that sold honey the old-fashioned honesty-system way. You left five dollars when you took a jar. You bought the jar back; the next jar was only $4.50. Wow! It was so good!

By this time, I was pregnant with my second child. Ron as working as a carpenter, working on a house in Napa while we lived in Sonoma. We saw him on the weekends, and it was great fun walking the few blocks to the town square. We'd go to the Cheese Factory and get fresh cheese and a really good kind of triple cream cheese called St. Andres. If you have never tried it, you should if possible—it is really good. Next, we'd go to the fresh produce stand and get crispy apples, or pears, and then on to the bakery for French bread. Man, what a place.

Our second boy was born in 1977. He was born in a hospital that was just a few blocks from where we lived in Sonoma. His name is Forrest Lynn. Now I had my Sun and my Forrest. My life was complete. I felt that if you had your sun and your forest, what else could you want?

The only constant is change. Again, we needed to find another place to live. The thing with living with other people is that they get antsy, need a change, break up, all sorts of stuff. So our lives change too. I always liked Coos Bay, Oregon. I've always loved the coast, but I wanted a different coast from where I came. Once again, all our belongings were piled up and off we went! Now we had a van, a small Honda, an old (and I mean old) dump truck, and somehow it was all hooked together and we were driving it to Oregon! Man, what a journey. Now I had two babies and a whole ton of junk, and somehow we were getting there with only a small amount of smoke coming from the brakes! It was very steep at some places. I promised myself never again!

We finally got settled into our new house. It had three bedrooms, two bathrooms, a large living room, and the prettiest kitchen I had ever seen, with a ton of windows all along one side and a pantry big enough to rent out! The backyard was big and fenced, so I knew the boys would be safe to run around.

Ron had to go back to Napa to finish the job on which he'd been working, so the kids and I were getting to know the neighbors in town on our own. Everyone was so nice. They liked the kids, even though they thought they had strange names. They said, "That's OK, they're from California!"

Ron joined us when he finished his job in Napa. He soon found the same type job in Coos Bay. The town was really nice to live in. There was an all-you-can-eat buffet with the freshest fish of the day and crab and fresh salad, so I was happy! There was another treat in Coos Bay for food—Bandon cheese! Coos Bay is close to Bandon, where there was a cheese factory. Another local yummy was cranberry candy. There were a lot of cranberry bogs in the area and they made delicious candy—so good.

We had been keeping in touch with our friends we had in Sonoma. Their names were Nathan and Debra. We missed them since moving to Coos Bay. About a year after Forrest was born, they wrote a letter that said they moved to Humboldt County. They said they loved the area and wanted us to move there. They said they knew someone who had a cabin that would rent it to us if we wanted to move. I hated the idea of moving again, but it wouldn't be such a big move this time. We had gotten rid of the dump truck and van by this time. We could get rid of lots of other things as well. We hadn't made any real friends, and I wanted to get back to California. So we moved once again.

The strangest thing happened when we were driving to our new cabin. We were driving along this very narrow road. We realized we had driven on this road once before. We remembered looking at a map years ago and deciding to drive on this road in order to get to a place called Honeydew. We loved this drive along this particular road because of the foxgloves growing at least six feet tall on the one side of the road, and the tall locust trees on the other. We said at this time, "What a beautiful place to live!" and just sighed, because we knew that you only get to live in places like that when you know someone who lives there. Oh well . . .

This was *that* road! We couldn't believe it. Our cabin was just down the road. How often does a thing like that happen?

Our cabin was made of redwood. It was a loft cabin, owned by a wonderful lady named Peggy. We were her caretakers. We loved the cabin, the woods, and our boys had a wonderful place to live. I was determined never to have to move again. We were settled in. Again, we had no electricity, or bathroom. We had an outhouse. But there we at least had water! Sounds like something everyone has, but it's not, as I had found out, and I was so happy to have it.

I took a correspondence course with the Dominion Herbal College in British Columbia to learn about the healing qualities of herbs. It was a year in length, and it was a wonderful way to learn about everything from how your body works: its bones, disease and etiology, as well as growing and using herbs for health. The boys were growing up and again we lived an hour from town, so I wanted to know as much as I could about living healthy with what I could grow. Sun was three by now, and he and his friends were climbing all the trees and getting cuts and scrapes and having a grand time. Our friends all had kids, and we gathered quite often for dinners and get-togethers. Our kids went to school in the first public school in Ettersburg. We parents had to lobby the school board with our kids to show them we needed a school. We all lived at least an hour's drive from any town, and none of us were willing to put our kids on a bus for that amount of time, not to mention the condition of the road. The district gave us a one-room temporary school. It had a kitchen attached, and bathrooms. We had students K–6. Most of the kids had never been to school, so it was a challenge to bring everyone up to consistent school levels. We had a PTA of our 300, although we only had 29 students. Our students had lots of relatives who supported our school because it was such a good thing for the area. We had an orchard and taught the kids how to maintain and grow fruit, how to harvest and cook or preserve. We had a greenhouse for the same purpose, as well as having the kids participate and sell produce and seedlings for fundraisers. We taught the kids how to plan meals and cook. They learned dancing, singing, clothes making, natural dyeing, and a million other wonderful things. We had a teacher who made learning fun. One year we had a two-day fundraiser that the whole community and all the businesses were involved in. We had raffles for products from the businesses, a dime-a-dip dinner, horse riding, and lots of other fun events. The profits paid for the grading of the playground and building of the playground equipment.

It was during this time that I re-entered school for myself. I took classes at the College of the Redwoods in ornamental horticulture. It covered everything from identification, greenhouse practices, redesigning and drawing blueprints for landscaping, and writing a business plan. This was so educational for me. I wanted to build a greenhouse just for perennial hardwoods and sell them. That didn't happen, but it is still a good idea.

Ettersburg School was great school, and a great time for the kids. They have all grown up and gone on to other adventures. The district has sold the property. I was diagnosed with cancer in 1998 and was divorced in 1999. I continued to live on my property until it was sold. I hated that I had to move off my mountain. I moved to town, which at least had electricity, indoor plumbing, and all the water at a touch of the button you wanted, so I guess it wasn't too bad. Town was Redway, just twenty or so miles down the mountain, but it felt like a million miles to me. Now it would seem like a very dark time in my life, but as luck would have it, I met someone who would change my life. I thought I must be crazy to fall for this man. I was tired of getting hurt. I didn't want to love anyone right then. I had just been going through all the cancer stuff one can go through, plus a divorce. This man didn't have a job and he was an alcoholic, and I had cancer! What was I doing? Well, he was thinking the same thing! And yet somehow, as fate would have it, our paths kept crossing, and one thing led to another, and my single life was suddenly glowing again. I was happy. I hadn't been happy like this in a long time. We had many things to work on, but if we really want something, I feel we can do it. This man's name was David. He was my knight in shining armor. He showered me with attention and made me feel like a teenager again. He quit drinking and smoking. I got well from cancer. His two boys know my two boys. We loved each other.

We got married in the Redwoods. He was a Scot, so of course there were bagpipes, and he played the table with it. He wore a Tab're Mor that we had a little ole lady in Scotland knit for us. My family came and BBQ had a fantastic dinner, David's family was all there, and all our friends came. We had a wedding procession with flowers being strewn about. It was magic.

Now I live in the house David and I bought in the quaint little town of Miranda. This is absolutely my last move! Miranda is on the Avenue of the Giants, an hour's drive from Ettersburg and only ten minutes from Redway. It is a small town surrounded by redwoods. Both David and I loved birds. We both had birds as pets since we were both young. David was an avid bird watcher. When I first met him, he was nursing a raven with a broken wing. He loved birds. We helped with the yearly Audubon bird count. Watching their habits and trying to understand their needs became a goal for David. He had a lovebird named Kiwi, and I have a Hahn's macaw named Sweet Pea. I always loved birds too, but it was the horticultural aspect of attracting birds that I loved. It's a good match.

David died in 2014 from a long battle with cancer. His bird, Kiwi, died the same day. They rest together now. He will always be in my heart.

My oldest son, Sun Ray, lives close by in Myers Flat with his girlfriend, Isis. My other son, Forrest, lives in Nevada. I retired in March of 2020, after working twenty-five years for the local grocery store in Redway. I loved my job as bookkeeper. I had some really awesome people to work with, some of whom I consider my friends, not just people whom I worked with. It's a great community, but the community I like the best is the one I live in. Miranda is quiet and friendly. Everyone knows everyone, and it's beautiful with the giant trees.

As I sit on my back porch and look around at the different plants in my yard, I see the moss rose that I brought back from Oregon when the boys were just small, so it's about forty-five years old. It is beautiful. Then I see the pink rose called Laughter. That one was given to me from Ettersburg School when the boys grew too old for the school and I moved on to another PTA, and the Thompson seedless grape I brought down the hill from Ettersburg. All of these survived years of living in a pot until I could find a final spot for them. My yard is full of flowers and shrubs intended for the birds, as well as human pleasure. Their blooms fill the air with fragrance.

All of these remind me of special places I've lived and special people I've known, especially the mosaic sunflower picture I made in Mrs. Tripp's art class in Carpinteria. My mom and dad had it on their patio wall for years, and when I finally stopped moving and settled down, they gave it to me for my patio wall. As I look at it, I'm taken back full circle to a wonderful childhood. I feel truly blessed to have known so many wonderful people.

Joanne Hinson's beautiful surroundings

CHAPTER TWENTY-FOUR

Richard Morris

RICHARD
MORRIS

Untitled Story

I liked going to school in Carpinteria. I grew up in that town. Everybody knew each other. I remember one day my dad got a call from Bud Sanders; they knew each other. Bud told my dad that my older brother was laying a patch down at the stop sign. That is how close Carpinteria was.

By the time I was ten, my younger brother and I were allowed to ride our bikes to the beach. Had my first burrito at the beach. I didn't like it 'cause it was fried.

Carpinteria has a special place in my heart. When my kids were growing up, I would take them to Carpinteria beach.

I still live in Bakersfield, and every chance I get to, I go to Carpinteria just to go to the beach and lie in the sand, squishing the sand between my toes. Someone said going to Carpinteria was like going to memory land, and it is.

When we were old enough to drive, my buddies and I would go to the orchards and drink beer. We would drink beer at the drive-in. I guess we drank beer everywhere. We weren't big beer drinkers; one beer and you couldn't stand up.

When the time came to get into college, I didn't take the test, and after that, I guess I was just waiting to be drafted. I fooled them. I joined the army.

So I was out of high school and what was I going to do? I didn't take the junior college test, so no college and I was just waiting to get drafted and get sent to Vietnam. I decided to go into the army. I entered on April 16, 1968. I trained at Los Alamitos, CA for two months. There I made acting training sergeant for my platoon. I must make sure the barracks for my platoon were in order for the next morning's inspection. On one morning's inspection, the lieutenant stood in front of me and greeted my rifle. He asked me for my rifle serial number. I said one million two hundred and eighty-six thousand, four hundred twenty-six. He quickly looked at my rifle and said, "What did you just say?" I repeated the number very fast. He said, "You gotta be shitting me," and threw my rifle back at me then moved down the line. Funny I remember that his name was Lieutenant Dillion.

Two months didn't seem very long and then off to Fort Leonard Wood, Missouri, for combat engineer training. There we built a timber trail bright. Our training included explorers map, diagram holes, and long marches. I missed the explosives training because I was sick with pneumonia and chickenpox and in the hospital.

Well, I graduated engineer training, and back to California for thirty days' leave. I got some beer and went to the beach to watch the sunset. I was wondering what was to become of me; the war didn't scare me yet.

My dad and my mother drove me to Travis Air Force Base near San Francisco. There were airport signs directing us where to go. There was a six-foot chain-link fence with several hundred people standing behind, shouting and throwing bottles, holding up signs that read "don't be a baby killer," etc. I was ashamed my mother and father had to do that.

The plane ride to Vietnam was twenty-two hours long. We had to circle the airfield for a long time because of attacks against the airfield. We were low enough to see the mortar canister, and it was raining hard. When the plane finally landed, we were told to exit the plane quickly. When we arrived at Bien Hoa Air Force Base, we were ordered out of the plane, and when I got to the doorway, a blast of hot air hit me in the face along with the disgusting stink of Vietnam.

Outside, we lined up in ranks of twenty-five. Each twenty-five followed a sergeant to a row of corrugated steel tubing that was Camp Bagdad. Oh, and don't forget the tubes were full of water that passed your knees. So we stayed in those tubes for what seemed like hours. Finally, someone came for us and we were led to a two-story barracks, which only had bunks in it. We were told not to unpack, as we would not be there long. A few days later, about thirty of us were on C-130s to the central highlands. When we landed, it was raining like crazy. We formed up in formation of engineering on the left and infantry on the right. He walked to the left and said, "All of you people to the right of my hand are now infantry." Well, now I was infantry.

So off we went in a deuce-and-a-half to some camp that I don't even know the name of. They gave us some huts to stay in. They just have bunks in them, nothing else. So we settled in. I awoke and heard what I thought were tanks, but when I looked outside, there were two APCs (armored personnel carriers) coming up the road. They stopped in front of our hut. In the first APC, there were bodies on the front board, about seven or eight dead. I was told they were VC and they were caught in one of our ambushes. The American soldiers were taking off AK-47s and other weapons. I was feeling sick and had to go around the corner to throw up.

Next day was sandbag day. The pile of sand was in the sun, no shade. It was hot, hot. We filled about 100 bags and started again the next day. We filled bags around noon. A sergeant came and told us to stop and go to the mess hall and get lunch, then go to the supply sergeant and get our gear 'cause we were going out tomorrow. We went to supply and the sergeant gave me all M-14 rifles. They didn't have any M-16s, so we were stuck with the old M-14. Mine had full auto switch, or would you say it was like a machine gun? So we spent the rest of the afternoon cleaning our weapons and getting equipment ready for the field.

Sergeant woke us up at 5:30 a.m. We ate breakfast and went to briefing. There we find out there were sightings of NVA soldiers and we were going to investigate. If there was a problem, there was a company of men ready to choppers but to assist. There were thirty of us and we flew to about 3,000 meters from the sighting. We jumped off, and the choppers were gone and it was too quiet. So the eight newbies and I were in the middle of the column.

The first day, we just walked for hours. Before night, we had two ambush sites. I was told where I could shoot. Night set in and it was really hot. Mosquitoes were in the thousands, and the mosquito repellent was not 100 percent. During the night, we suffered from the heat, insects, and the fear of the night.

We woke up, and it would be C-rations for breakfast. After about an hour, we packed up and hit the trail. After several hours of walking, I heard a gun fire at the front of the column. A sergeant showed up and told us to follow him. We ran through the jungle for about fifty meters, and I could smell gun smoke to our right. The sergeant placed us in a straight line about fifteen meters apart. He stuck a stick in the ground and said not to fire to the right of that stick. I don't see anything but that smoke. Sergeant said to fire to the right of the smoke. So we opened up and shot into the jungle. After about a minute, I saw small branches were falling on us. Oh shit, the enemy was shooting back at us. We kept shooting; the sergeant came back and said, "Keep your head down—artillery is going to shoot some rounds." After a few minutes, I heard a round coming. It sounded like it was going to land on top of us, but it continued past us. There was a loud boom in the jungle somewhere. After five minutes, another round went over our heads; this time, it landed past the smoke into the jungle. That round looked like it landed on top of the enemy. I was shaking and my brain was somewhere else. More rounds went over our heads; there were four or five explosions in the jungle. Sergeant came back and got us all up and had us walk forward and fire. That was a part of our training. So we walked and fired into the jungle.

Somebody yelled, "Cease fire!" We continued to walk forward, and we finally came to some bodies, five in all. There was a lot of blood, and we could see drag marks and blood trails leading out into the jungle. People were following blood trails. Sergeant said for the newbies to stay put as we didn't have enough experience to go out there.

Sergeant told us to help bag up the dead enemy soldiers. I was getting ready to puke. I walked into the jungle and let it go. I felt better, and my brain was starting to recover.

A little "lock" copter flew over us and flew off. Five to ten minutes later, it flew back. I could see the door gunner had a 60' 60 machine gun. The chopper hovered above us, and over the loudspeakers, I heard, "Follow me." Everybody grabbed their gear and three dead bodies. We ran through some underbrush; we came to a narrow trail. We followed it to a clearing. Sergeant got us circled up and into Hueys. I was thinking to myself eight per chopper (or was it seven?) pointing our rifles down so we didn't shoot the engine. The Huey took off and circled, and I was looking straight at the ground. Couldn't fall out 'cause I was stuck to the floor.

My experience in the war spanned two and a half years. I make AJ (acting jack) or acting sergeant after eight months, and I was now assistant squad leader. There I learned to direct artillery without dropping it on my head. During my last seven months, I got a message from the colonel and I needed to report to him. So I got to his office, and of course, I had to give the hand salute. He returned the salute and welcomed as mousis. He said, "I have a job for you."

Great, a job, when a colonel tells you he has a job for you, it is big. He tells me he is going to give me sixty men, two motor teams, and two APCs (armored personnel carriers), one with a 50 cal and the other with a 4.2 motor. I must take this mess fifty miles south on QL 7B. There the engineers were building a hood extending QL 7B South. So we convoyed to a place called wercht Davis. When we got there, it was not very big. Living fighting bunkers, firing ports to the front, sandbags on the roofs on all sides so it was like living in a pile of sandbags. At least we didn't have to fill them. We settled in, which takes about a week. I find a bunker and set up a TOE (tackle operation center). A couple other sergeants and I were in a helicopter and we surveyed the area around the camp. At this point, we didn't have any idea about an area of operation. We flew out to about five thousand meters, which is a pretty good distance.

In two days, I was out with twenty-five guys to take a look around in the jungle. We crossed a river, and on the other side was a jungle. Walking into the jungle, you can feel the heat coming out of it then you are with the 100 percent humidity. It is nasty hot; you start to sweat right away. It isn't too long before sweat is running off your face, neck, and arms. It's running down your back, but after an hour or two, you sort of get used to it. I mean, it's still hot but like a walk in the park. Walking along behind the point man, I saw some people walking toward us, damn it was VC, maybe ten or more. They just ran into the jungle. I don't think they were even firing. I could see one of the VC was down. Point man and some others ran forward to the wounded VC. I screamed because some of my men were running into the jungle. I didn't want anybody running in there. I went back to the downed VC; it looked like a bullet went through his shin just below the knee. I could see bone pieces around the wound. That was why he wasn't going anywhere. We made a two-legged drag thing and dragged him back to the river and took him across. Medics fixed him enough to drive him back to a special forces camp about ten miles away and left him there to be interrogated.

The next day, Special Forces Captain came down to our camp to tell us the prisoner told them there was a big camp of NVA. He would like us to go out there and find it. He had a map, and it was all drawn out on the map. The next day, the captain came bright and early, and we took off across the river and followed the map. After about two hours of walking, we walked around a corner, and what the hell, there were three NVS just standing in the trail. I was seconds from the point man, and we both opened up; two fell and the third took off. We could see him running around a rice paddy, and he was an easy shot. The captain ran up and said not to shoot him 'cause he might be running to the rest of his guys. We saw him walking up the side of a hill then he was gone.

Captain said we needed to go toward the hill to see if we could find him. We got to the bottom of the hill. I could see the captain just standing there, talking to another sergeant. Out of nowhere, there was AK-47 fire; rounds were hitting everywhere. Then B-40 rockets were dropping all around. I saw two NVA running up the hill. I pointed them out to the machine gunner who was next to me and he opened up on them, and they went down. The firefight lasted for about twenty minutes, till two Cobra helicopters arrived. They opened up with those mini guns and rockets a bomb. That lasted for about three minutes later, when F-4 jets arrived. I had seen those jets operate before, and I knew there were going to be some big booms going off. It was about four hundred meters to the top of that hill, and those jets were dropping those bombs dangerously close. I could see the ground jumping at least inches. I was jumping off the ground; that ground was hitting me in the chest. I can't say how long that was going on, but by the time it was over, there was ringing in my ears.

I was sure those jets blew the top of that hill off, two guys wounded. I'm sure one of them died in Japan, shot five times.

After that, I only had three months and it would be over. I spent most of my time in TOE calling in fire missions and working the radio. It was over: two years, five months, and eleven days.

After Vietnam, it was easy. I didn't have anybody to worry about. I worked in a prison for five years; that was different. I couldn't stand it; being inside was hard.

I decided maybe being a cop and outside would be for me. So I started to take tests all over California and ended up third on the list for LAPD and second on the list for Bakersfield, CA. As for LA, there was nowhere to live that you didn't have to drive one and a half hours on the freeway. Bakersfield only had 89,000 people, less traffic and looked like a better deal. So I decided on Bakersfield.

As I found out later, Bakersfield had a higher homicide rate then LA; it was a tough town back then, but as the population grew, it started to slow down.

Went to call, two people who had been kissing told me to look out for a guy in red jacket. I saw what people do to each other because of hate, saw more dead bodies, some of them friends, again sitting with them until they died. Just like war, being shot by a charged suspect. The bullet was .38 plus hollow point entering my left shoulder, breaking my shoulder blade and continuing on through my heart and lung, only stopping at my spine's t9 and t10 parted on my left side. I could hardly move the rest but was able to get off four shots from my .45, only missing then putting my head down to die. A little later, I recovered, no one around, just me and the dark. Pain, unbearable pain—my whole body was beyond pain. Couldn't want anything more than for the pain to quit. I couldn't see the suspect. One small light near a large dark building. Radio, radio traffic, I could hear it, nothing about me on shootings.

I reached with my right hand to key the mike. I could only whisper. I knew my limb had a hole in it. Dispatcher asked for me to clarify. I tried again, but nothing was coming out. I don't know what I sounded like. Dispatch asked me to get off the radio, it was police. Then with all I had in strength, I turned the radio to channel 2. I whispered, "999, officer down." She asked me to say it again. I was getting dizzy; my thinking was going. I was able to say, "999, officer down." Channel 2 went dead.

I don't know how long, but I heard someone coming from everywhere. Maybe several minutes, five minutes, my backup arrived. They drove with the headlights pointing at me and lit me up. He got out of his car, came to me, and asked me, "What should I do?"

What the hell, it was a rookie just a week out on his own. With pain electrifying in my body, I reached up with my right arm and grabbed him by his shirt collar and pulled him to me and whispered to him, "Go down to the alley and look for a guy in a red jacket. If you don't see him, come back here because I don't want to die alone." He ran off.

I could feel the pool of blood inside my bulletproof vest. I laid my head down, this time in an awkward position which made the pain even worse, if that was possible. The rookie returned, no sign of the suspect. He put a yellow rain jacket under my head; he was talking on the radio.

After some time, other patrol units arrived, officers from several different agencies, finally, an ambulance. Officers were running around, making plans, radio going like crazy. Some officers were looking for a bullet hole. The bullet had gone under the shape of my vest, and the hole was not visible.

Finally, one ambulance attendant arrived. Oh no, it was Green. Green had been an officer, but after a few weeks, he was let go 'cause he couldn't cut it. Now he was my attendant. He says he moves me a good manner. I passed out next, and I remember being put into the ambulance. I grabbed Officer Anderson's arm and pulled him to me. I told him to kill that MF. I was pushed up in the ambulance, and the door shut. I was in the back with that idiot Green.

So the gurney was close to the floor. I tried to put my left hand on the floor. The pain was very bad, and I finally got the hand to a position where it didn't hurt too badly. Green was messing around, with his back to me. He turned around, looked like he had an IV needle in his hand. He turned and took a step forward and stepped on my hand on the floor. Oh my gosh, the pain. Again, I couldn't move; finally he moved his foot. My eyes rolled back, and I wanted to kill him.

I don't remember the ride to the hospital. I woke up in a room, and I think I was on a table. Debra, my wife, was standing over me along with Chuck Church, a buddy from the police department. My service belt was still on, and it was very, very uncomfortable. The radio must have been on full blast because it was hurting my ears. I tried to get their attention and tried to move my right hand, but I couldn't. I couldn't move my legs. I must be paralyzed; shit, I am. I could move my lips, my best bet. I moved my lips up and down. Debra finally noticed and put her ear to my lips. I told her to get the belt off me. Chuck reached over and took off the belt, and I got immediate relief.

I waited there, which seemed like hours, and finally people came in and loaded me onto a gurney and pushed me to another room. There I met a doctor, and he explained what a congenital surgery is. He told me I had three holes in my heart. He was going to put a tube in my leg artery and up a tube into my heart and close the holes in my heart. I asked when I was going to get some pain drugs. He told me he did not know because he needed to know where the thing that goes in my artery did not go through the artery wall. I got there and I went to surgery. The doctors found the bullet stuck between t9 and t10. Later, I woke up in the ICU.

Finally I had a little pain, and I could move everything but my left arm and hand. I was out of the hospital in seven days and back to work in six months. During that time, I rode a motorcycle, and on a traffic stop and while standing at the door, I looked between the driver's seat and the door. I saw what looked like the top of a receiver of a shotgun. I opened the door and pushed the driver into the passenger seat. I saw a shotgun with a shortened barrel. I pulled out my .45 and realized the safety was on and pointed at the driver and asked him to step out. I got him cuffed and seated him on the curb. A car officer picked him up and took him to the station.

By this time, I was shaking and my heart was pounding like crazy and I was short of breath. I calmed down in about half an hour. I then rode to the station and went into the captain's office and told him I can't go out there anymore because I'm going to kill somebody that doesn't need killing. I was sent to see the company shrink. He said I should leave the police department 'cause I was going to die an early death because of stress.

So I got a nice settlement and retired. The rest of the story is easy.

CHAPTER TWENTY-FIVE

Mike Wolski

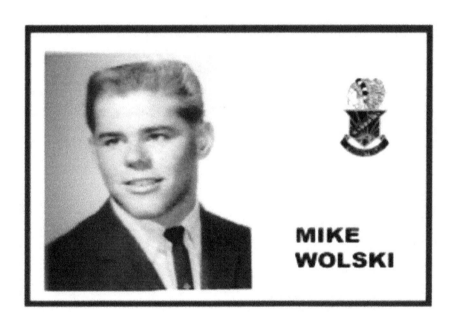

MIKE
WOLSKI

Dinner with the Astronauts

by Mike Wolski

My dad was a huge fan of the space program. He spotted the Sputnik in the desert skies the day after it was launched by the Russians. It was the wee hours of the morning, and he woke me up to come and see it. He told me it was the very first thing in space and asked me never to forget this moment. I haven't. He also woke me for each and every one of the Mercury program launches that were manned by the original seven astronauts. Launches from Cape Canaveral took place at two or three in the morning our time. I willingly got out of bed to watch those launches on TV at that early hour. Why wouldn't I? I had a stake in all of this—I had dinner with the original seven astronauts.

Until I was thirteen years old, I lived in the Mojave Desert in a little town named Quartz Hill. Quartz Hill had two gas stations, one market, a small café, a mid-sized café, and the finest dinner house in the entire Antelope Valley. The name of this dinner house was the Antelope Valley Dude Ranch, and it was here that I had dinner with the original seven astronauts.

The Dude Ranch was owned by Jack and Bobbi Young. It featured elegant white tablecloth dining, cocktails, live music, and dancing every night of the week. The interior of the place was divided into small rooms and meeting rooms for intimate dining, but the cocktail bar and dance floor were huge, roughly thirty feet wide by fifty feet long. My mom worked at the Dude for twelve years.

Because of the popularity of the Dude Ranch, people came from great distances to dance, drink, and dine. There were Hollywood actors, musical greats, and politicians as well as local folks and test pilots from Edwards Air Force Base. People from Edwards socializing at the Dude caused great concern for the US government after the successful Sputnik launch and the advent of the space race. Most of the people from Edwards AFB were working in secret or top-secret classified positions.

As a result, the FBI scoured the Antelope Valley and completed background checks on restaurants, owners, and staffs of selected establishments. The Dude Ranch was one of those selected, was searched for listening devices, and everyone from dishwasher to owner got FBI background checks and security clearances. After a favorable rating was received, all Edwards's personnel were allowed to frequent the Dude, which explains why astronauts were even at the Dude.

I have three sisters who are all older than me. The youngest sister is eight years older than I am. They were all either in high school or married. Since the Dude Ranch was a dinner-only place, Mom worked evenings *until midnight* and sometimes until closing *at 2:00 a.m.* Dad was in construction and worked out of town much of the time. This created a situation where I spent a lot of time alone at night.

The evening that I dined with the astronauts, I was home along with my three dogs. We were watching TV when the phone rang. It was Hal Borg, who owned the one market in town, was a next-door neighbor and president of the local Lions Club. "Mikie," he said with urgency, "change into your best clothes and come over to the Dude Ranch right now!" It was dark out, and I said "But, but, but—" He interrupted me and said, "Don't worry. I already asked your mom, and it's OK with her."

I was somewhere around *9 1/2* years old then. Being that age with no one home but dogs to advise me, my nine-year-old mind told me a clean pair of Levi's and my best flannel shirt would do just fine. So I changed my clothes, washed my face and hands, then went out the unlocked front door into the night. A latchkey kid? What key? I had no key, and nobody locked their doors or windows there in those days.

The Dude Ranch was only three doors east of my house on the opposite side of the road. But everyone had property in those days, and each lot was about an acre. Because of the size of lots back then, the distance to the place was about an eighth of a mile, but it was still a spooky walk in the desert at night. When I got to the front entrance of the Dude, the door swung open, and I was met by Bobbi Young. She had been waiting for me.

Bobbi was probably in her mid to late fifties, had beautiful silver-gray hair and wore gorgeous gowns and sparkling jewelry every night. She greeted everyone who came through the door. She was friendly and socially outgoing and always had a winning smile on her face. But this night, she had a stern look on her face and something felt more urgent. "Follow me, Mikie," she said, and I obediently did. I felt like I was being taken to the principal's office.

We wound our way through all those little dining rooms and finally came to the door of the far north dining room. We stopped at the door, and Bobbi was now smiling at me. Then she opened the door, and told me to have fun. I reluctantly walked through the door then glanced to the right and then to the left, and immediately forgot about my dogs, my house, the phone call, the walk in the night, and the fact that this room was full of men in suits. Just to the left of the door was a standing upright mannequin in a shiny silver space suit. I felt like it was my birthday, and all this was a giant surprise party.

Up until that moment, I had only seen something like that in comic books. I couldn't contain myself and said out loud, "Wow!" The whole Quartz Hill Lions Club broke into loud, extended laughter. The laughter startled me a little and brought me immediately back to earth. Then I heard Hal Borg's voice. "Mikie," he said, "come up here."

I looked in the direction that his voice came from, to try to locate him. The meeting room was long and thin. Tables were placed end to end and formed a really big U with very long sides. In the middle of the bottom of the U sat Hal Borg with a giant smile on his face. On each side of Hal were four chairs. All but one of the chairs, the one on the left end, had someone sitting in them.

I walked up to the head table, and as I got there, Hal stood and escorted me to the empty chair on the end. He pulled the chair out, and I sat down a little confused and wondering why I was there. Then Hal began introducing me to the four men on his left and the three on his right. I didn't remember who was who except for the man who sat directly on my left: Alan Shepard.

Besides the amazing space suit, which I kept staring at, the one thing I can tell you with certainty about that night is that Alan Shepard was a kid person. In between questions from the Lions Club members, he was telling me jokes, poking my ribs, and playing tic-tac-toe with me. He was fun and kind and very funny. It was a long evening, but I had not one moment of boredom sitting next to him.

After the space race began with the successful launch of Sputnik, it was almost impossible to live in that desert and not have the space program touch you in some way. It was amazingly common to be touched somehow by these soon-to-be historical figures. My mom and older sister met Chuck Yeager. I got to meet Scott Crossfield, a test pilot who had his own TV show, and one of my Little League coaches was Joe Walker, an X-15 pilot. His son Tommy was our first baseman. Joe was not only the first man to fly an X-15, but also one who the records for flying it the fastest and the highest. I just knew him as Coach Joe until Mom picked me up from practice one day, recognized him, and told me who he was. There is now a middle school in Quartz Hill named after Coach Joe.

In Antelope Valley, Lockheed and Convair had huge facilities in Palmdale. Randomly, in the night there were giant flashes of light or bursts of massive engine noises coming from the direction of their facilities. There were often unusual lights in the sky, a minimum of ten sonic booms daily, and occasionally on the major highways, traffic would come to a stop because everyone was outside their car, watching the X-15 drop from the underwing of a B-52 bomber. There were giant runways at Convair and Edwards Air Force Base, and I don't ever remember a day that there wasn't a fighter or bomber or X-15 in the sky.

Alan Shepard was the first American in space. His flight lasted fifteen minutes. They shot him into the atmosphere, where he pierced the edge of space then reentered to splash down 300 miles away from where he lifted off just fifteen minutes earlier. About an hour before Alan Shepard lifted off, I was sleeping. "Mike, get up!" my dad yelled. "You gotta watch this launch—it's history!" Indeed, it was history. For the next hour, just knowing that the guy who was poking me and joking with me and telling me jokes, and who I ate dinner with, was sitting in that capsule on that launch pad made me feel tighter than I can even remember feeling. As the countdown continued, I became more and more anxious. By the time they said, "Liftoff," I was holding my breath, and I was panicked and almost crying. When I was certain he wasn't going to crash or blow up, I felt like I could breathe again.

As they switched coverage from the launch pad to the aircraft carrier, the realization struck me that he was going to splash into the ocean in the middle of nowhere with the carrier nowhere in sight. I began holding my breath again. I was talking to God, angels, relatives who had passed, spirits—anyone who would listen and help Alan survive this. Then came the announcement that the capsule had splashed down. I could breathe again except then came the announcement that they were attempting to locate the capsule, and I held my breath again. Finally, I saw him get out of a helicopter and walk onto the deck of the USS *Lake Champlain*. From splashdown to recovery, it took the navy eleven minutes to locate him. For me, it felt like hours and hours.

Deke Slayton was the only member of the original seven astronauts who did not fly in the Mercury program. There were a total of six manned flights, and Deke flew later in the Apollo program. I saw all six of the Mercury program flights, thanks to my dad yelling at me in the middle of the night to get up and watch history being made. To this day, if there is a launch, I either watch it or listen to other media coverage about it.

The original seven astronauts were Alan Shepard, Gus Grissom, John Glenn, Scott Carpenter, Gordon Cooper, Wally Schirra, and Deke Slayton. I met them all, but I felt like one of them was a good friend. I watched all their missions. I had dinner with them.

As president of the Lions Club, Hal Borg organized this entire event. He was an adult and, unlike me, understood the importance and significance of these men attending this event. He must have been experiencing a little stress on this evening, trying to ensure a successful outcome. Why, in the middle of all that, he was able to see one empty chair and think of me will forever be a mystery. He's one of my heroes, and I had dinner with him too.

Odd, but I have spent most of my life barely remembering this significant event. Finally at this age, I appreciate and, in fact, am in awe of my amazing luck in being raised in the middle of all the incredible human endeavors happening in the early days of America in space. And I owe gratitude to my dad. He was wise enough to recognize the importance of this time and place in history, and he dragged me along with him.

Mike and Colleen Wolski's trip to NASA in Houston, 1993

CHAPTER TWENTY-SIX

Lewis Pozzebon

Lewis Pozzebon

Carpinteria High School Class of 1967

Carpinteria roots—reflecting on the small, seemingly insignificant life circumstances/events/people whose influences have amazingly synthesized into opportunities and experiences

Both sides of my family are of Italian descent. Interestingly, all my grandparents immigrated following World War I to the United States from a small area in Northern Italy, between Milan and Venice. Their influences on social/familial relationships, language, music, cooking, and religion have made major impacts on my life.

Another major influence on my life was being raised on the thirty-two-acre Pozzebon property in the foothills behind Summerland. When I was born, it was a dairy, later an avocado/vegetable farm/ranch, and then my dad's excavating business base. Dairy life was a 24/7 job for my paternal grandparents and my parents. The Holstein cows had to be milked twice a day, with my dad getting up at four each morning. He also delivered the milk to a creamery in Ventura, then cut fresh hay, loading it on the truck and returning to the dairy in time to milk the cows again in the afternoon. My mom struggled with the demands of the dairy life, and I believe this motivated her to stress the importance of education on me and my siblings (two sisters and a brother). The difference in my parents' life after the dairy closed was evidenced by the free time that was made available for them to take us on vacations (Marineland, Disneyland, Sea World) and their enjoyment of social life (community dances, clubs).

Farm life also provided a wide range of experiences and responsibilities. Animal husbandry for cattle (dairy and beef), pigs, chickens, turkeys, and later a horse gave me an appreciation for what it takes to put food on the table and being personally accountable for the health and well-being of others. Chores were assigned and expected to be completed without reminders (collecting eggs, feeding and watering, cleaning pens, etc.). Our family also did slaughtering on the farm, which provided more experiences as well as broadening culinary knowledge. Both my mom and dad loved to cook, so it was always a family affair observing the preparation of meals and it influenced my interest in cooking and eating.

I learned a lot from my dad, whose wide range of abilities besides dairying included being an equipment operator, mechanic, plumber, electrician, welder, carpenter, butcher, food preserver, master gardener, and even winemaker. My mom likes to say that my dad is a jack-of-all-trades and a master of none. I especially enjoyed being taught how to drive a tractor at a very young age. Besides operating tractors and trucks on the ranch before I had a driver's license, I was dropped off by my dad with a wheeled tractor to shred weeds on vacant lots or a D2 Caterpillar tractor to disc. I also helped on jobs loading dirt with a skip-loader tractor. And during the winter, we would be sawing and splitting firewood.

The dairy/ranch was a great place to grow up, but it did have its hazards. I barely remember putting my hand into the belt of a table saw that my dad was using. I was two or three, and it left a permanent notch in the middle finger on my right hand. I also remember the barn owls that nested in the hay barns. I recall my dad scaring them out, and I had dreams of them for a long time. There was barbed wire on the fences, boards with nails, weeds with sticker, an occasional rattlesnake, aggressive animals, etc. And there was the incident when my sister Nancy and I were riding on the Ford tractor with Dad and somehow she got her big toe caught in the rear wheel drum. It tore part of her toe off, and she has had trouble with it ever since.

Growing up on a thirty-two-acre dairy included three large hay barns, perfect for fort making and a nearby creek for pollywogs and frogs. The downside was the remoteness from same-age friends and the distance to town and beaches. Also, there was limited technology. The phone system we had was a party line. We had a phone number but we shared the phone line with other people in the area. Two different people could not use the phone at the same time. When you picked up the phone (rotary dial) sometimes, you heard someone having a conversation. You had to wait until they hung up before you could make a call. We didn't have a television until I was seven or eight. Before that, I remember we would go to one of the neighbors who had a television to watch boxing or wrestling. Even when we did get a television, the reception was very poor. The antenna could only pick up one or two stations.

I have great memories of family and get-togethers. The get-togethers included aunts, uncles, cousins, and Italian friends. There was always lots of storytelling, Italian food and music, teasing, and laughing.

Both my mom and dad stressed how important school was, especially Mom. Dad graduated from high school, but my mom's parents pushed her to leave school early and go to work to help with family finances. She worked as a waitress in Santa Barbara. I have many memories of how much she encouraged me by being excited for each school year, taking us shopping for new school clothes, reviewing assignments and report cards, and later helping me type term papers. They really encouraged me to be the first in the family to go to college.

I remember the excitement of going to kindergarten. It was a big deal because we lived four or five miles from Montecito Union Elementary School, so I would have to take a bus from the bottom of our driveway. Part of the big deal was both my mom and dad had gone to the same school. In fact, one of the teachers, Ms. Irene Sawyer, taught both my mom and dad, and she was still teaching when I went there. Ms. Sawyer took a special interest in me, telling me how much she was looking forward to me being in her third-grade class. Her compliments about me being a good student gave me a lot of inspiration to do well in school. I remember the cardboard mats we used to take naps on in kindergarten. I also remember a field trip my mom set up with the teacher. A bus took our class to the dairy, and my mom and dad set up a demonstration on how to churn butter. We got to eat the butter we made, on fresh bread. The class got a big kick out of it, and I was very proud of my parents.

My fourth grade teacher focused on English. She read *Moby Dick* in class and seemed to bring the book to life. This experience led to my lifelong enjoyment of reading, from suspense novels to historical to Western, and both fiction and nonfiction books.

When I was in the sixth grade, our teacher was Mr. Craig. He was very athletic, and every day in class, he would have us do exercises next to our desks. At the end of the year, there was always a special event for the graduating class. We went on a picnic to a neighboring private school that had a pool. There were picnic tables that were covered with white paper, and at each place setting, Mr. Craig had drawn a caricature of each of the students with their name underneath. When I found mine, it was a caricature of me as Jack LaLanne, the famous bodybuilder who was on TV doing exercise shows. I guess I made an impression on him by taking those daily exercises seriously then and continuing through life.

After the sixth grade, I was supposed to go to Santa Barbara Junior High School, but the school district changed the boundaries and Ladera Lane became the boundary between Santa Barbara and Carpinteria school districts. So I ended up going to Carpinteria, where the junior and high schools were much smaller. My senior class graduated with 120 students. The bottom of our driveway became the local bus stop for first a bus and later an eight-passenger van. The van driver took us and some other neighbor kids to Summerland, where we waited for a school bus to pick us up. We waited next to a gas station, and I remember the daily games of pitching coins against the gas station wall. Closest to the wall won all the other coins pitched. We had to agree on the denomination of the coin to be pitched. It was a big deal if it was quarters. The bus took junior high and high school kids from Summerland and the nearby area to Carpinteria Junior High and High School, which were across the street from each other.

It was a little tough transitioning to junior high because I didn't know very many kids. A lot of the Carpinteria kids were into surfing, which I never really tried. The beach was quite a ways from the ranch, and surfboards were very expensive. When we did go to the beach, Mom would drive us either to Butterfly Beach in Montecito or

Summerland beach. Sometimes my grandmother (Nona) would agree to go and keep an eye on us. I can still remember Nona all covered up with a big hat and shawl to keep out of the sun. We had fun building sand castles and digging for sand crabs. Later a family friend from Summerland taught me how to bodysurf, which I thought was the greatest feeling, to be pulled by the wave to shore.

The summer between the seventh and eighth grades, I was able to spend a very special summer in Italy. My mom's dad had returned to Italy following the death of my grandmother. My mom and dad decided they would send me along with my mom's brother to stay with my grandfather and other relative. My mom was fluent in Italian, and growing up, she would write our families in Italy and often send them things (coffee, clothes, etc.). In 1961, part of the idea was that I would get to see and experience Italy's history and culture. It was an overwhelming idea for me, having never been away from home for that long, never been on an airplane, and not speaking Italian very much. Living close by my grandparents, who spoke almost only Italian, helped, and at least I could understand what they were saying, but speaking complete thoughts and sentences was always a challenge.

When we arrived in Venice, the family had arranged for a driver and a car to pick us up. My grandfather lived in an old two-story house in the countryside. There was no running water in the house or bathrooms. We had to use the pit privy that was about 100 feet from the house. One of my chores was to fill pails of water from a faucet near the garden and bring the water into the house for food preparation, washing dishes, and heating water for baths. There was a big cherry tree next to the house (during the summer, I had a great time climbing into the tree and eating cherries) and a large garden. There was also an attached house next door that another family lived in. They had an attached barn with bo (oxen) on the first floor and a hayloft on the second. The oxen were used to pull a large wagon and farm implements.

A car and driver were arranged periodically for short trips to locations in northern Italy: Venice, Verona, Lago d'Como, Cortina del

Ampezzo (1960 Winter Olympics), Monte Grappa, Asolo, Pedavena Brewery, etc. I also got to meet relatives on both sides of my family, which gave me a significant feeling of roots and helped me learn the dialect of the Veneto area of northern Italy. I have returned to see the families several times over the years, and each time, they have been very special events.

Attending Carpinteria High School from 1963 to '67 were some very interesting times and experiences. I reflect back on the great teachers, special friends, and the ups and downs of being a teenager. First experiences such as dating, political discussions, getting a driver's license were all significant. The Kennedy assassination was a major shock. I felt fortunate to go to a high school with 500 students, which meant you got to know almost everyone. It helped me start to break out of my shyness. I joined Key Club, a service program, and met local Kiwanis members. One of them was a local dentist who inspired me to pursue a career in dentistry and helped me to get a scholarship. He had received his dental degree from the University of Southern California (USC), and when I graduated from Carpinteria, I applied and was accepted to attend USC undergraduate school. Although I was unable to get into dental school, going to USC provided many great memories.

The Vietnam War was a huge factor during this time. One of my friends from Key Club was killed in Vietnam. Attending his funeral with the other Key Club members left an indelible impression of the impact of war and the fragility of life. Another friend was killed from a motorcycle accident while I was in high school.

While I was in college, I met my first wife on a blind date during my junior year. When I graduated, I lost my deferment. I had received a low number in the draft lottery, so I was notified that I would be drafted during the summer. Fortunately, a friend of my fiancé had a boyfriend that joined the Coast Guard. I was interested in the Coast Guard from the years reading about Santa Barbara news outlets reporting search and rescues. But during the Vietnam War, I had read that there was a long (two-year) waiting list to be accepted. I drove to Los Angeles and spoke with a Coast Guard recruiter. He said that they no longer had a waiting list because many of the people on the list had been drafted. He offered to set me up for an aptitude test the next day, and if I passed, there was an opening for boot camp the following Monday. The aptitude test turned out to be a combination of education and practical knowledge. The education I had received and the experiences working on the ranch were a great help in passing the test. I was accepted for a reserve program of six months active duty and six years of reserve duty. I spent nine weeks in boot camp in Alameda, California, and the rest of the six months in Yorktown, Virginia, and in New York City, being trained as a port security specialist. I was assigned to the Santa Barbara Coast Guard Reserve Group, and I extended my enlistment several times and retired with twenty-one years of service. My duties over the years included search and rescue on the Point Judith eighty-two-foot cutter, marine safety inspections, marine accident reviews, and spill response.

After my active duty time, I was trying to figure out employment opportunities. I wanted to find something in the Santa Barbara area, but there were no real opportunities. While I was evaluating jobs, I worked for my dad, operating heavy equipment. USC had a job placement office on campus, and one day, I went there to look at the catalog for science majors. I found one job bulleting that described working for Los Angeles County as an assistant sanitarian. The position included being trained as a health inspector of restaurants, housing, water systems, etc. I applied in January of 1972 and had an interview. I learned there was a list that could mean as much as a two-year wait to be hired. I got married in September 1972. We rented an apartment in Carpinteria, but when we got back from our honeymoon, I was notified by Los Angeles County that I could start work in October. We moved to the San Gabriel Valley, where we raised three talented and wonderful sons and lived for twenty-six years.

I had worked in environmental health for thirteen years for LA County when one of my supervisors recommended that I look at a job opportunity with the City of Vernon Health Department. Vernon is a unique city five miles south of the City of Los Angeles. It was

271

founded in 1905 with the intent of being all-industrial. In 5 1/2 square miles, there were 1,500 businesses and less than 100 residents. Vernon was developing a hazardous materials program, which fit with my training and experience in the Coast Guard. I started as a hazardous materials specialist and spent twenty-six years there, the last nineteen as the director of the Health Department. It was a fascinating and challenging job, working to assure compliance with environmental laws and regulations with many different businesses, their employees, technical consultants, and Vernon departments (Community Services, Fire, Light and Power, Police, Water) and their staffs. The businesses included food processing establishments, chemical plants, hazardous waste treatment facilities, glass manufacturing operations, slaughterhouses, recycling facilities, rendering plants, wholesale companies, and many others. As a result of the thirty-nine total years of my public service that were initiated based on a single visit to the USC job placement office, I was able to establish a lifetime pension along with health and dental benefits.

I met an amazing second wife through work and learned we have many common interests and traits. She has an Italian family background, is passionate about environmental health, loves cooking, enjoys nature, traveling, gardening, and family. We were married in 2004, and I helped raise a stepdaughter first in Carlsbad, California, until we moved to Arroyo Grande, California, in 2016. I retired in 2012, and I have enjoyed having the time to play senior softball, to golf, barbecue, read, garden, and travel. I am looking forward to my wife completing her career so we can spend more time visiting with our children and grandchildren.

Louis Pozzebon & Nancy 1954

Louis Pozzebon 1957

Louis Pozzebon in 1958 Classroom Photo at Montecito Elementary School.

Eric Miller

ERIC
MILLER

By Eric Miller

All through CHS, I was always working at my father's Enco/Esso gas station in Isla Vista, doing engine tune-ups, car servicing, sales of gas, tires, batteries, etc. or at Cottage Hospital in the mail room and later the pharmacy, managing the delivery and inventory of nursing-station controlled drugs. I also part-timed at the Knapp College of nursing running the audiovisual (instructional) films for the classes. More about this later, as this was a learning opportunity. I also worked at Parsons airport in Carpinteria for Bill Swain, as a mechanics helper, aircraft fueler, washer-parts chaser pilot, etc. This led to me riding Greyhound buses all over SoCal to pick up airplanes for maintenance at Parsons or delivering planes back to owners from maintenance, and bussing back to Carpinteria. While doing this, I was also helping my father maintain his WWII Goodyear FG-1D Corsair at the Santa Barbara airport in Goleta.

I had the opportunity to fly a large variety of aircraft and meet some famous personalities in aviation, movies, etc. I met Bob Hope when I was assigned the honor of flying the baggage helicopter when Bob Hope, Joey Heatherton, Lola Falana did their USO RVN Holiday Show. It was a great show and morale builder for all the troops. After his time on stage, Mr. Hope walked back up to where we parked the Hueys. I had just strung up the hammock I carried for a quick nap when in the field. He asked me a lot of questions about the helicopter and how I felt about the war; I let him sit in the aircraft commander's seat and answered his very good questions about our time over there. We talked for over an hour. Just before I rotated out of Vietnam, I carried the USO show crew again. Fast-forward fourteen years. One day, I was assigned to a Bum Phillips pro- am golf tournament in Port Arthur, Texas, as pilot with helicopter in case of a medical emergency. There I was, napping in the seat again, and Mr. Hope walked up, woke me up, remembered my name and unit in RVN. The

PR people went bananas when I was introduced to the TV crowd re: Vietnam/USO connection story.

Fast-forward another ten years later, when I was flying corporate jets for Halliburton and the company annual board meeting was in Palm Springs. All of our executives and jets were there. Bob Hope walked in the lounge area, recognized me, remembered my name, etc. All the CEO/golf guys came over, Bob started popping jokes. He had a simply encyclopedic memory for jokes and names and places. He mentioned that we'd met four or five times, in RVN etc. He always made sure that I was OK with the publicity-privacy thing. I had to pass on a lunch invite at his home the next day there in Palm Springs, because we had an early morning flight back to corporate headquarters.

Over the years, I met General Jimmy Doolittle (WWII Tokyo raider), Fitzhugh Fulton (XB-70 test pilot), Bob Hoover (test pilot and air show performer), and a few US presidents and vice presidents. I was lucky to have the opportunity for extended discussions one on one with these people; they were really generous with their time. I learned a lot about flying, people, and politics from their knowledge and experiences.

The Knapp College of Nursing turned out to be a learning experience as I got to know most of the student nurses. The girls always wanted to go out evenings and weekends, and I was invited along, probably because I was quiet and shy (and having a guy along reduced the other guys coming on to a group of girls when they showed up at the Fiesta Bowl after classes for a drink). If the music was good, I'd get invited to dance and never got carded. It was great to learn how to get comfortable talking to women, dancing, and having a beer.

I began flying at fourteen and worked for Bill Swain, who ran Parsons Airpark just over the hill by Rincon. I would ride the Greyhound bus down into Los Angeles and pick up owners' aircraft and fly them back to Parsons for maintenance/inspections or repair, and then deliver them back to the owner in LA and take the bus home. While I worked at Parsons, a local pilot, Sandy Wheeler (father of Bill Wheeler, a CHS '67 classmate), gave me my first helicopter ride. Little did I know that just a year after CHS, I would be drafted out of City College into the army, most probably because I wasn't really motivated to perform (not taking a full course load) at City College. I thought surfing and flying was so much more interesting and cool! That was a *big* mistake! Then that pesky draft notice came along and the army made me an offer: either carry a rifle as an infantry soldier in Vietnam or army flight school and then (as an officer) fly combat helicopters in SE Asia. I chose flight school and served in Vietnam, Laos, and Cambodia.

I was lucky, even though my aircraft was damaged/shot down several times—once we crashed (it burned to a charred hulk) near the landing zone, no injuries to anyone aboard. Another, I was able to nurse it home and the helicopter was declared a total loss, never to fly again. I also had my copilot get shot in the chest and arm, his ticket home—he fully recovered, but we never heard from him again.

I lost my best friend in Vietnam. His name was Stanley Dean Struble. He was always getting us in some type of trouble. He was from Castana, Iowa, and was shot down and died November 19, 1970, flying an (OH-6A) Scout helicopter. A good man and a very good pilot, gone so young. I had seen him only a week before, as I was leaving for a week's R & R in Sydney, Australia. I didn't find out about his death until almost two weeks after he died.

On another flight, the kid sitting behind me sustained a groin wound. I over-torqued every aircraft engine and flight limitation parameter all the way to the Ahn-Khe base hospital. The kid simply bled out before I could get him to the hospital. A redheaded, freckle-faced farm kid. He didn't realize how badly he was wounded—every time I turned to see him, he would smile and give us a thumbs-up. He thought he was going home and he did, but it was in a flag-draped casket. I never learned his name, and this is the first time I've written of the event. It is always with me.

War ravages us in different ways. We all pay a price. A family feels a lot of joy when their father, son, or even daughter returns from war. But sometimes, it's only to find that even though they are home safe, the war has not left their loved one.

After Vietnam, I attended the medical evacuation training course and spent three years flying medevac missions in Texas and then four years in Stuttgart, Germany. I met a cute lieutenant named Penny, and between riding my BMW motorcycle, flying, skiing, and travel, we saw most of western and southern Europe. Leaving Europe, a few more years back at medevac flying in the Carmel/Santa Cruz and San Francisco/Sausalito area and we decided it was time to leave the military, get married, and start a family. We married (in Carpinteria) in 1978.

Back in the civilian world, I spent a few years teaching aerobatics in the Napa-Sonoma valley area before accepting a helicopter job flying out to super tankers and oil-drilling rigs in the Gulf of Mexico. Two great daughters later, I decided that risky flying would better be replaced with international corporate jet operations. We had many transatlantic and transpacific flights with operations into Africa, India, Egypt, China, Russia, Venezuela, etc.

One of the most memorable flights was returning to India from China in the middle of a beautiful clear moonlit night. Our Chinese air traffic control asked us to change altitude for some military traffic. We told them we preferred not to descend for fuel consumption reasons. They asked if we could climb above our present altitude (forty-one thousand feet), and we said yes, if needed we could climb to fifty-one thousand. They cleared us up to fifty-one K. At that altitude, the curvature of the earth is visible, and with the beautiful clear moonlight as we crossed the world's largest mountain plateau (Himalayan) in Tibet and Nepal, we could clearly see Mount Everest (29,028 feet) and the Everest climbers' base camp with all the colorful tents lit up. (835)

Another interesting trip was to Norway in August 2000. We found a small friendly city (Alta) that supports several northern fishing fleets. Alta is far enough north (236 miles from the Arctic Circle) that the sun is up (does not set) in midsummer. All the hotels have heavy thick drapes to block out the sun so customers can get sleep. You can get a lot of hiking/exploring/touring done when the sun stays up almost all the time. After we landed and our passengers departed to their hotels, a few friendly locals were curious about the big private jet that landed at their airport, so to be friendly, we invited them inside for a tour of a corporate jet interior and cockpit. They said thanks for the tour and after asking what hotel we were staying at, they said, "We will see you again," and four hours later, we did! They came to the hotel, picked us up and then they and their friends made it their job to provide tour guide services the whole nine days we were there. They drove us up to early Viking historical sites, to the city of Hammerfest the farthest northern year round occupied city in the world! We donned hip waders and picked cloudberries in berry bogs along the fjords and sampled many of the local refreshments. Very nice people and a great mini-vacation!

Another unusual thing that is part of Norwegian culture is that if you are going to go out and have an alcoholic beverage, you take a taxi—at a blood alcohol of 0.02, the fine is one month's salary and a one year license suspension; at 0.15, it costs you one and a half month's salary, three weeks in jail, and a two-year license suspension. So when people party and drink, they walk, or taxi if you can find one—remember, small town and few taxis. So when the bar closes, everyone walks to the town square and waits for a taxi to come and take them home. Guess what they like to do while they wait. Here it's helpful to remember that Norway is where the real Vikings came from—these guys are huge! So they politely ask you if you want to fight! Picture a town square the size of two to three football fields, with dozens of guys fighting or watching fights while conversing and waiting for the taxis. It's all just fun for them, and if they find out you are a foreigner, they want to see if you fight differently than them. There also are policemen around, and it's just a social activity for everyone, just good fun. If there aren't many taxis, it can last hours. I have never been politely asked if I want to fight so many times ever! Our local friends would just explain to them that Americans don't fight for social fun. Nice people, polite, huge! With a great sense of humor. A great trip!

Another trip was from India to Egypt with a few days in Ankara, Turkey, and then to Cairo, Egypt. We had the opportunity to drive the entire length of the Nile River and see just about every single ancient city, camels, museums, pyramids, Valley of the Kings (and queens), tombs, and sellers of ancient artifacts in the country. It was interesting but tiring and hot, from Alexandria on the Mediterranean Sea all the way to Abu Simbel near Aswan and the border of Sudan.

Three days after we arrived at a small Norwegian seaside town, serious events happened. The world's largest nuclear submarine, Russia's *Kursk*, experienced an explosion and sank. The *Kursk* was the most dangerous submarine in the world at the time. All crew members (118 sailors) died. Alta was the closest seaport and airport. Alta went from a quiet seaport town to completely overwhelmed by NATO and Russian military rescue crews and worldwide news/media reporters within twenty-four hours. Google it or watch the movie.

During our transatlantic hops, we would occasionally stop for fuel, catering, or just a day or two to get a rest break if our next passenger pickup was within a few days rather than go all the way back to home base, only to immediately turn around and start a return leg to the original pickup point. If you saw the movie *Mitty*, its Iceland location shots are exactly true, an interesting place. The people are very friendly—especially if they have a common interest (like airplanes). Iceland has the world's highest ratio of aircraft to number of citizens. One summer day, we were awakened in the hotel by the local aviation club and invited to an annual fly out and luncheon. We loaded into cars, and off to the airport we went for a quick tour of our large corporate jet and then into a local ex-Icelandic Airlines DC-3 that a retired captain had bought from the company when the type was retired by Icelandic Air. Quite a nice retirement toy! The variety of planes went from Piper J-3s up to turbine-powered seaplanes and the DC-3. Everyone flew up to a saddle between two volcano cones, where the blankets and lunches were brought out for picnics. Lots of discussions about airplanes, corporations, and worldwide flight operations. Iceland has the clearest air and waters I've ever seen—the coldest too! Returning to Keflavik, we hangared the DC-3 and then were treated to watching the kids at soccer, and checking out the local beer and desserts. We were sunburned and tired, but what a pleasant and unexpected day off!

After a few years, I got a job offer flying a large turboprop airliner and flying the CEO in his private helicopter in Austin, Texas, then got a job offer with Halliburton Corp., flying medium and large corporate jets worldwide. After seven years, I accepted a contract with a foreign corporation flying Global Express jets into China, Russia, India, Turkey, Norway, Sweden, Holland, Luxembourg, and Egypt. When I returned to the good old USA, I took a job training and supporting DEA flight operations worldwide (airplane and helicopter) out of Fort Worth, Texas. It involved flight training, maintenance testing, experimental test and type evaluation on seventeen different aircraft types. Then one day, they told me I was going to Afghanistan—another war zone! My question was why, and at what salary, since it was not mentioned in my current contract. The DEA aviation manager said, "Oh! No change—same salary." I said *no* (and quit). Shortly thereafter, I got a late-night phone call from an old RVN friend asking me if I remembered the stuff we used to do in Vietnam. I said yes. He asked me if I wanted to do it again. I said, "No way, I've already fought one war for minimum wage." He said, "Whoa! It pays really well," so after an interview in Washington DC, several T/S security clearances were renewed/weapon requalifications completed, I accepted a contract in Afghanistan flying ISR (intelligence/surveillance/recon) aircraft in support of our troops there. After about two weeks in Afghanistan, guess who I met in the mess hall in Kandahar—the very same DEA aviation manager who had tried to force me into doing the job with no salary increase. He said, "Well, look who we have here." My reply was "I didn't say I wouldn't do it, I said not for the pay you offered" (no increase), so he asked what my pay was now. I said, "About three times what you're getting!" End of that discussion!

After two rotations there in Afghanistan, I decided to retire—the old Vietnam stresses and stuff started coming back. They don't call it Kill TV for nothing. I really wanted to support our troops there, but the stress/cost was just too high. So I decided to retire—full-time flying for fifty-four years was enough!

So now, I just want to cruise around in our RV and see (up close) our country and enjoy it. I hope this COVID-19 pandemic doesn't mess that up! I hope I'll get a chance to see a bunch of the CHS ('67) gang, on the way.

Eric in Vietnam

CHAPTER TWENTY-EIGHT

Mary Hotchkiss

MARY HOTCHKISS

Two Brothers

by Mary Hotchkiss Moore

March 12th is a date that floods my mind with memories of my twin brothers. This year would have been their seventy-third birthday. They were the oldest of the siblings in my large family and very much a huge part of my life. As the oldest girl, I looked up to the twins, the oldest boys of the family, my big brothers.

George, Called Georgie by Those That Loved Him Dearly

George was the firstborn twin, being five minutes older than Gerald, according to our mother. This would be his hold over Gerald (not appreciated). When I was growing up as their younger sibling and a girl, George was very protective. George took the responsibility given him by our father, to look after the younger siblings, very seriously. If you knew George, you knew he was the fun-loving brother most of the time.

George was very imaginative and loved to build things. My brothers built an entire fort in the canyon behind our home in Summerland. No girls allowed, of course—well, until Mother ended that rule. It was a really cool fort that looked like it came off the set of *Robinson Crusoe*. To this day, I have always loved tree houses!

George liked to restore cars, rebuild engines and anything mechanical. He was a great mechanic and could figure out how to fix just about anything. He took auto shop and machine shop in school, along with the usual subjects. He had a thirst for learning what made things tick and all things automotive.

My first experience with driving was with George. He was sixteen and I was fourteen. He had been driving for a couple of years already. He had a Jeep Willys 4×4 that he had rebuilt in auto shop. We would head to the back roads behind Carpinteria so I could drive.

I told him I needed to drive so I could cruise State Street in Santa Barbara—that was every kid's dream when they got old enough. He was never worried about my driving or damaging his Jeep. He would say that he could fix it!

He loved the beach. He took us surfing and would help us with bonfires. Those were really good days. Remember the grunion runs? They came in on a full moon to breed on the beach. We would stay late into the night just to catch them. These are among the many memories of my brother that I will always cherish.

Shortly after high school, George enlisted in the air force, and within four months, he would be in the Vietnam conflict, stationed in Thailand, a mechanic for the air force. This would be the beginning of a long career that he loved. He ended up serving twenty-five years, retiring a master sergeant. Upon retirement, George returned to Santa Barbara and opened his own auto repair shop. This allowed him to follow his passion of restoring old Model Ts.

But all too soon, his life was tragically taken from us on November 11, 1995, at the age of forty-eight. This left a large empty space in our family. My big, fun-loving brother was gone. Time has helped to lessen the pain of his loss, and his memories live on!

Gerald, Known to Many as Jerry

Gerald was the younger twin, the serious one. He would take on any challenge with sheer determination. It would be this determination that would sustain him through some tough times in his life.

He had an endless need to explore and learn about people and places. We went on several trips exploring ghost towns and historical sites. These trips were never spur-of-the-moment; every detail was well planned, as even though some would see this as a fun activity, to the serious twin, this was an exploration.

He was the brother that could answer any homework problem, especially math. Jerry was also very protective of his siblings in high school, sometimes too much so! But it was great to be able to ask him for help, still knowing that help would come with a lecture. His philosophy was "do as I say, not as I do." Believe me, my brothers were not perfect.

He played football in high school and the football players played a lot of pranks at school. I remember one time, they picked up a teacher's car and carried it into the hallway of the school and left it there. He definitely enjoyed high school, excelling in all his classes. It was his junior year that he would join the naval reserves.

Gerald would be sent to Vietnam shortly after graduation. He was proud to serve his country. He was the helmsman on a landing craft that carried Marines up the river, to the front lines of the conflict. This was very dangerous; they were fired upon by the Viet Cong and sprayed with Agent Orange. The Agent Orange would rain down upon them as Jerry piloted them up the river, where the soldiers would join in the battle.

Jerry returned home after the Fall of Saigon. He soon learned how unpopular the war was and that veterans were not respected. We were lucky to live in a small town by the beach; our town was very supportive of our troops. Heck, we knew them all by name. The boys from our town that served would receive a proper welcome home in Summerland. This made transition to civilian life easier.

Gerald joined my father's heavy-equipment company shortly after his return. He would operate bulldozers and backhoes. He was an excellent operator and could make moving dirt look like spreading butter. He came by the skill naturally.

On October 6, 1971, Jerry would find himself fighting for his life and the lives of others. Not all would survive. My dad's equipment company would be sent out as wildfire control and containment operations. This day, they were working an arson fire that had been burning for about a week in the foothills behind Santa Barbara, close to the Romero Canyon. This fire had a lot of fuel and suddenly took off, driven by the winds created in the canyon. Jerry and the other operator from Dad's crew, Red, along with a US Forest Service spotter that rode on each tractor, were cutting a fire line along the top edge of Santa Monica Canyon, just north of Carpinteria.

On this day, doing what they were well trained to do and operating with their spotters, no one could have imagined that within four hours, four men would die and two others be severely burned on that mountain ridge. My brother Gerald and Red were those men that sustained severe burns. My dad had heard from an independent operator that the winds had become erratic and that they needed to pull off. My dad ordered his men out. The US Forest Service men did not want to leave. As my brother began to leave, the fire hit the top of the ridge, leaving them to fight for their lives. Red left his tractor and went to Jerry's. Jerry dug in with his blade, leaving the engine running to give them air; this created a space in which they would seek refuge under the tractor, constantly moving to stay alive as the fire raged over them, engulfing the machine. This would seem like an eternity. They survived but were badly burned. The US Forest Service men that were down at the point of the ridge perished.

It would be a long and painful recovery for my brother. But Jerry, being Jerry, was determined to face this challenge head on and get back to work. After his recovery, he started his own construction company in Carpinteria. He built my house pad on Mountain Drive in Santa Barbara in 1974. Jerry was now married and living in Carpinteria. He had two children.

Fast-forward twenty years and his life would be hit by another series of cruel events. He would face his son having a serious and debilitating disease, and caring for him. His granddaughter being born with the serious medical condition of spina bifida and watching her go through medical emergency after medical emergency. And he would soon develop multiple diseases related to Agent Orange exposure in Vietnam. Jerry, being Jerry, would do as he had done before: he would face this enemy head on. He fought long and hard to be here for his family, but on September 11, 2017, he lost the battle.

I have always admired his spirit and the fight that was in him. He never complained, even when he could not move or stand up without excruciating pain. He really was a strong man with a spirit that never broke.

I miss my brothers, their smiles, their laughter, and just the way they were there for us. They are at rest, but truly missed. They will be in my heart forever, someday to meet again.

Postscript

I would like to stop and honor another group of heroes I admire: the men and women who serve as our country's health-care workers, the doctors, nurses, phlebotomists, and all others that are putting their lives on the line, fighting the COVID-19 coronavirus, the worst pandemic to ever hit our world. We have lost over a half a million lives as of this writing. The number of cases is nearly fifteen million with daily cases growing by 250,000 each day. Each of those lives lost was someone's loved one. Let us take a moment to remember the precious souls lost. I pray that this pandemic will soon be over and that we can get back to our "new normal" lives.

Finally, most of us have made it through wars, recessions, gas crises, hippies' free love, fires, and the pandemic of 2020 because we are the Warriors of the class of 1967!

CHAPTER TWENTY-NINE

Gloria Martinez

Chapters of Our Lives

This is the story of my life since graduating from Carpinteria High School. But first of all, I want to back up a little. I was born in Tulare, California, but raised in San Fernando up to my sixth grade. We then moved to Goleta, California, and I did seventh grade in La Colina Junior High School for a very short time. From there, we moved to Santa Barbara California. And I graduated from ninth grade at Santa Barbara Junior High School and went on to Santa Barbara High School, tenth grade. That was short-lived; my parents bought a house in Carpinteria.

So this is where I started Carpinteria High School, all the way to twelfth grade and graduation. I am pretty sure my parents bought the house for $15,000, payments of around $100 a month, brand spanking new. Boy, that seemed like a lot of money back in 1964/1965. Carpinteria was relatively a small town and school, compared to Santa Barbara High School. I was a shy girl, only had a few friends; kids seemed really nice there, and everyone knew I was a new student. I kept a low profile, never got in trouble. I can say I was a good student.

I remember when Sonny and Cher first came on in the '60s, some kids at school would call me Cher, because I had long dark hair and long bangs and I was very slender. I was not trying to look like Cher. I already had that style before Sonny and Cher became popular. I thought that was pretty funny though.

At Santa Barbara High, we had dressed up a little more, whereas Carpinteria High had a more casual look, being a beach town community. After graduation, I did not go to college; instead, I got a job at Josten. I worked there for a short time, then got a job in Goleta at Robinson's. I graduated in 1967 in June and got married in February 1969.

After one year of marriage, we suddenly moved to Indiana. My husband's parents came to visit that year, and after they convinced my husband to move back to Indiana and drive back with them, I was dumbfounded and could not believe what was happening. After my parents found out we were moving in a few days, we did a lot of crying. I was homesick for a long time.

My daughter, my firstborn, was born in Indiana in 1970. After being there for a year, we bought some land and a beautiful mobile home brand new. We had the biggest garden and it was beautiful. We had like five rows of corn, green beans, tomatoes, green onions, radishes. I made sure our garden always looked beautiful. I would go out and hoe the weeds and turn the dirt over, nice soil. My daughter, when she was three years old, would go out in the garden and help me pick some vegetables for dinner. I learned to can food. We also had two big cherry trees, at the back end of our mobile home, which was near our bedroom. I would pick the cherries and make jam and put in jars with parfait wax and seal. I would send some to Mom and tell her I made this jam. I was proud of myself. So I was a true homemaker. I made my daughter's dresses and mine too so we could match. I learned how to sew in high school. Everything I cooked was from scratch from my *Better Homes New Cook Book* from high school, when I had home economies in school. I still have that cookbook, fifty-three years later, ha ha, although I don't use it as much as I used to in my younger years. Being seventy years old (and it's just me and my husband), well, I do as little cooking as possible. We're very simple eaters, and I am constantly watching my weight as I always have been.

After living in Indiana for four and a half years, we sold everything, our land and mobile home. In April of 1974, we were hit by a tornado that came ripping right in our path. We lived in a very, very small town called Thornhope. It flipped our home over. I had just picked up my husband from work, a thirty-mile drive. It had been storming and thundering all day long. I cranked all the windows open. My husband was taking a nap before dinner; my sister was visiting. My daughter was four years old. I told my husband, "Wake up, it's hailing real hard." I told my daughter and sister, "Go in the bathroom and stay there."

My husband ran toward the front door, and I followed him; he was putting his raincoat on. He opened the door and quickly closed it and said, "Quick, run to the bathroom."

As I was running to the bathroom, I turned my head, looking out the window, and I remember seeing this big dark, dark black cloud rolling on the ground toward our direction. My husband was running right behind me, and as soon as we got in the bathroom, I yelled out, "Get on the floor!" We were all on our knees, and just as soon as we did that, our mobile home was rocking and lifting. Of course, we were screaming. When it flipped over, I could hear the shatter of glass breaking. It was a horrendous sound as it flipped over (we had a huge bathroom with double sinks and a huge mirror, also a washer and dryer). I could hear the wind blowing on my face. Everyone landed on me as our mobile home flipped over. I was afraid to open my eyes. I literally thought we were up in the air (like the movie *The Wizard of Oz*). I opened my eyes, and I could see the sky. The washer fell on my husband's back, and the toilet and sink and tub I could see above me. I was now lying down on the ceiling; everything was upside down. Through this turmoil, my daughter got a cut on her knee. She will be fifty years old in December and still has that scar. She was only four years old and remembers a little bit of what happened; she remembers being in the ambulance. I had bruises; my sister escaped injuries. I was thankful for that. We were all taken to the hospital. Our mobile home was destroyed. The front, from living room to kitchen, was all leveled to the ground; the mobile home was twisted. The two big cherry trees we had saved us from being killed. The back end of our mobile home landed on the cherry trees. It was a good thing my husband was not still sleeping since the limbs of the trees came right through the windows against the bed.

So the insurance replaced our mobile home with our choice of pick. We were happy to be alive and in our brand-new mobile home, but whenever a storm came passing by (and that was quite often), we were reminded of our horrific incident. We took a vacation to California, and we had forgotten how beautiful California is, the ocean and mountains. By that time, I was pregnant. We sold everything in Indiana and bought a house in Oxnard, where my parents lived.

My son was born in 1975. My second son was born in 1977, but by the time he was born, my husband and I had separated, and I filed for divorce after seven years of married life with him, two months after my second son was born.

I remarried five years later. I learned a lot from my second husband; he was unique, he was a hobbyist and a rock hound. He was a dental technician and made my wedding ring. He collected rocks and made gems. He also liked to make model airplanes, so the kids learned to build airplanes from balsa wood. By that time, my daughter was a teenager and my youngest was five, and oldest boy seven. He had a son who was six years old. Unfortunately, this marriage also lasted only seven years. Boy oh boy, seven-year itch, so we divorced.

About one year later, I met this wonderful man and we dated for fourteen years. He was not the marrying type; we lived separately, but it worked for us. He loved dancing and so did I. He had a sailboat, and we sailed a lot to Anacapa Island, day sails, and sailed to Catalina Island for a few days; it was a twelve-hour sail. By that time, my kids were growing up fast. I spent my weekends with my boyfriend; every Friday, we dressed up and hit the nightclubs. So it was all a different experience for me and I loved it.

After fourteen years together, we broke up and I wanted more than what he offered me. So I met my present husband and we got engaged. By that time, my ex-boyfriend wanted to get married, but it was too late. I had already found someone else who was not afraid of commitment.

By this time, my kids had all gone their own way. My daughter got married and got her bachelor's degree and master's. My oldest son got married, had his own business. And my youngest son is a DJ and manager of a club and has a fourteen-year-old son and loves the single life.

My husband and I got married in Las Vegas at the Little White Chapel. We just had our fifteen-year anniversary in April. Whoop whoop! He is very fond of my kids, and the grandkids are like his own. He has no children. He was forty-six and I was fifty-five years old when we met, and we hit it off right away. He loves hiking in the Sierras and Mammoth, another new experience for me, something I have never done. I love hiking at 11,000 feet elevation; we take our backpacks and do a seven-hour hike. We have even taken my kids and grandkids every year. Ever since we have been married, we go about four or five days each year; there is so much to do there and so many trails. He has a cabin there, so it's always great to come back the following year. He has taken me to Yosemite, and we have hiked Vernal Falls and Nevada Falls. I love the steepness and switchbacks. One time he took me on a twelve-hour hike to this beautiful place in Mammoth. I was wiped out. We went back to the cabin, and after our showers, he started the fireplace going, we made pasta and relaxed, until the next day another different hike.

It was all a different new experience for me, and my kids loved it too and the day hikes. There are so many different places to hike and the beautiful lakes. My oldest son and my husband climbed Half Dome. I am afraid of heights like that; climbing a granite dome, I could not do that.

My husband is very savvy: he is a handy man, knows a lot about cars, computers, he is also a photographer, and he's even showed me a little bit about photography. He is truly a sweetheart. If I want something, he never says no. Three years ago, I bought a 2017 GLC 300 Mercedes 4 Matic Turbo. This one is a keeper. He saw on my face that big smile I had not had since my mother died two months earlier in 2017.

So at present, I am still working, and since my husband is nine years younger than me, he plans to retire in four and a half years. So I will continue working until he retires, I will be seventy-four and a half years old then. I have worked at Skyworks for twenty-one years—a good job, 401K and stocks. We will settle in Washington State. My husband will continue working for a short time after that. I will watch out for the bears and take up drawing, and relaxation; we can buy a nice place where there are trees everywhere and greenery and do some traveling.

So for now, this is the story of my life in a nutshell since graduating from Carpinteria High School. I have lived an interesting and fulfilled life, have learned a lot about different aspects of life from the different men in my life. I have three beautiful children from my first husband (I adore them and would not have it any other way), five grandchildren, and two great-grandchildren.

My mother passed away three years ago, May 2017, and my father passed away in June 2020. How do you carry on and move on with life with your parents no longer around? It's very difficult, but you have to think of your kids and grandkids and family, be there for them. Crying is good and I do that a lot. I miss them terribly but think of how lucky I was to have had great parents and a good upbringing, and the great memories and how they were always there for me and supportive when things got tough in my life. But in the end, they knew I found happiness, and that is how a parent wants to see their children.

My name as it was in high school, then first marriage, second marriage, and third marriage is Gloria Martinez, Shuey, Jameson, and Johnson.

CHAPTER THIRTY

Jeanne Smith

JEANNE
SMITH

The World through Digital Eyes

by Jeanne Smith Bowles

I love photography and always have, even as a kid. My mom would sometimes let me hold her camera and take a few pictures, and I acquired my own box-type camera in high school. Those were the days of film cameras and the little cubes that had four flashes to one cube. The flashes would pop and get quite hot. The film, of course, had to be developed, so pictures were planned to the last detail to save costs. That didn't stop me much, but I had to pay for developing out of my allowance and babysitting earnings. I proceeded to dabble for a decade with photography, and aside from brief trips to Canada and Mexico, my first trip farther away to another country occurred when I was twenty-nine. I became hooked on travel after this journey with my housemate to her native Scotland. Oh my goodness, was I ever hooked! I must have come home with eight 36-shot rolls of film, which now all reside under my bed in plastic bins.

That didn't end my passion for traveling. And how I enjoyed seeing the finished product come from the drugstore. At present, I have been to 108 countries. I find the plants, animals, people, scenery, and colorful marketplaces fascinating. I've been to all seven continents, and while the cameras still held film, they were upgraded whenever possible.

I married in 1987. My husband Tom is a physicist, which had some extra bonuses, even though I would have married him, no matter what. Physicists hold many international conferences and meetings, and our deal was that if I wanted to travel to a country where he was going, I would go as well. After retirement, I traveled with girlfriends or on my own.

Having my first digital camera met with some resistance on my part. It didn't take me long to take to the idea of taking as many photos as I wanted, since they all went on reusable cards. Our first trip, a family trip (yes, we had a sixteen-year-old daughter at the time), was to Costa Rica. I'll share with you a few trips in my allotted space, and of course, like film cameras, technology developed, and I upgraded at every opportunity. I hope you enjoy a small glimpse of what makes me happiest in life.

Costa Rica

The camera gave me great pleasure as we drove around the country. We enjoyed this excursion on a boat in the shallow part of a river. Now, I know this particular man works with this particular alligator day in and day out, but imagine my unsuspecting delight when I discovered I'd actually captured the alligator with his mouth wide open and the raw chicken in mid-air. We stayed in a condo, and other activities included nature walks, zip-lining, whitewater rafting, and plenty of beach time. The beach time put an end to any more photos I might have taken. We spent a day taking a boat to one of the small islands on the Pacific side of the country, where we picnicked under a ramada-like canvas tent. Tom and I decided to go exploring along the sandy beach. After lunch, we decided to swim around the rocks. While we swam, we didn't recognize how fast the tides came in. I had unwittingly put my camera in the pocket of my shorts, and it was quickly soaked. That was where it was left behind. Argh!

Easter Island

Easter Island provided a lot of photographic opportunities. The island belongs to Chile, though it is over 2,000 miles from mainland Chile. It lies at the extreme right corner of the Polynesian Triangle in the Pacific and is occupied by nearly 8,000 inhabitants, half of whom are indigenous to the island. The main attraction for most people is all the moai, which are monolithic human figures carved from rock between the years 1250 and 1500. The atmosphere of the island is so relaxed in attitude.

It is where our daughter Katie learned to drive a stick shift when she was underage and where she also learned to scuba dive after only a ten-minute lesson. At our accommodation, the lawn was mowed by a horse, and the bounty of horses on the island met the task. We had a resident cat that loved sleeping on our folded towels.

Antarctica

Let's travel south for a moment. The trip to Antarctica is quite arduous. We were on a Russian ice cutter, and it took two days to cross the Drake Passage, the roughest waters in the world. I made this trip with a friend, who needed tending to as she was ill all the way across. I, on the other hand, loved the high seas and ran around the deck like Rose in the movie *Titanic*. After the crossing, we began to see icebergs, birds, and other signs of life. For the six days we were there, we sailed among the floating icebergs, big and small, blue and green, and navigated the islands and listened to the squawking of penguins. The penguins were allowed to approach us if they initiated it; however, we were not allowed to pursue a penguin under any circumstances. Yet when sitting on the ice, they would approach and explore what humans were all about. Some of the predatory birds would steal eggs whenever possible, setting the colony to verbally object. We also entered an active volcano where the sand was warm, so we all left the ship for a dip in the sea.

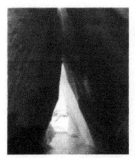 

There is one creature that is not to be messed with, the leopard seal. He is predatory and has a mouth the size of a basketball hoop when open, with lots of sharp teeth, more than I can even photograph. We were told never to move closer than fifty feet. Our mode of transportation during the day was by Zodiac rafts, and we would either stop on a beach to observe penguins and other wildlife, or cruise among the icebergs. Each time we had been out of the rafts, we had to return to the ship's deck for a boot bath in an antiseptic solution. The purpose was to stop the spread of wildlife diseases between the islands.

Indonesia

Our trip to Indonesia was divided into three parts—Komodo Island, Borneo, and Sulawesi. Tom and I flew into Bali and used it as a base between the different parts of the trip. You can likely guess the reason for going to Komodo Island. We rented a houseboat, manned by two, one the driver and the other a steward of sorts. We had our meals on board and slept on the floor in a small room at the back of the boat. The Komodo dragon is the largest lizard in the world, at between seven and nine feet long and 150 to 250 pounds, depending on gender. They can run up to twelve miles per hour, compared to a human, who can run about twice that speed. There are only four islands where the dragon lizards live (Indonesia has more than 17,000 islands in total), and we found the dragons at each one. The lizards have a truly toxic bacteria in their mouths, and one bite is enough to kill a living creature. The bite festers, and the wound becomes infected. Even small children were reported to have been stolen from the villages by the dragons. The tour leader always carries a stick with two prongs for poking dragon eyes in case of their attack.

We stayed on the boat offshore but made time for a lovely walk through the village. The people are Muslim and are very friendly. Their life approach is different from that of many cultures. Instead of being frightened that the camera will rob them of their spirit, they welcome having their photos taken and believe that their spirit will travel the world through the photograph. We were warmly welcomed and shown every aspect of village life. The carved dragons especially caught my fancy.

Our next experience in Indonesia was to visit the island of Borneo. The purpose was to visit an orangutan refuge that was established in 1971. Farmers are destroying the jungle by planting commercial palm oil, and the animals are either killed or find their way to places where they will be taken care of until they can be relocated. We met the organization's leader, Mary Galdikas, who answered our many questions and accompanied us on our outings. To reach the national park, we traveled by boat through the mouth of the Kumai River and into the Sekonyer River. We didn't arrive at the ecolodge until twilight. Camp Leakey (Galdikas was a student of Louis Leakey) was even further up the river. While we began to see wild orangutans, it wasn't until we approached the camp that we saw some of the camp residents. In the rushes, we came across Mario, a baby who was willing to come aboard for food. Um, don't think so. At the camp, we observed many family groups—females with young, and awesome to behold, Tom (his name), the dominant male in the FAST. On the third day, we were allowed to visit the nursery, where the very tiny babies were learning how to play and eat.

The third part of our Indonesia excursion was a snorkeling resort on a small island off the coast of Sulawesi, one of the bigger islands. Actually, it was a scuba resort called Wakatobi, which also accommodated snorkelers. There were cabanas along the shore and a main dining room. We were not allowed to wear shoes for a whole week. Each cabana had a footbath in front for rinsing sand.

There were several boats (perhaps four) and two hour-long scheduled dives a day for each person. The snorkeling was the most spectacular we had ever seen in our lives. Fortunately, I had purchased a small underwater camera. It was nothing like the big rigs of the scuba divers, but it was fun, and some of my pictures were colorful and fanciful. When a krait passed by Tom's head, we were startled to learn that the snakes were actually land animals and liked to sleep in the footbaths at night. We never walked through that footbath without a flashlight again. The one activity we did not enjoy was snorkeling at night. It was quite a scary atmosphere in the dark. The underwater world is definitely a fascinating and totally gorgeous place.

Hudson Bay, Manitoba, Canada

Our destination for this trip was Churchill, which is one of the few places in the Arctic where the polar bears gather. We traveled with another couple on a Natural Habitat excursion. Seeing the bears is a matter of perfect timing. Because the ice on Hudson Bay does not always freeze at the same time each year, the bears are dependent on the solid surface of the ice to leave the tundra to hunt in the winter waters. The only time to see the bears is before the ice forms, and we were extra lucky to have a late season when the bears were abundant. Our day started early, with a trip by bus to the launching pad. From there, we traveled miles in what was called a tundra buggy. These were equipped with toilets, potbellied stoves, and observation decks to get more up close and personal with the bears. It was cold in the vehicle because the windows were often down for a clearer view with cameras. Those stoves felt mighty good!

Churchill is a small town, with dark skies most of the time during winter. The residents leave their doors unlocked in case of marauding or curious bears. Anyone can take refuge in one another's houses. This is a built-in safety net.

Out on the tundra, one activity we were fortunate enough to observe was the older male bears teaching the younger ones how to fight. The pairs spar and knock each other around, and it is really quite amusing: standoff, knock down, mock fight for hours on end, as many as a dozen times. Hey, even polar bears like to lie spread-eagled on the ice after playing so hard.

To us, it is unbelievably cold, but with all that fur and all that activity, they get hot.

By the way, did you know that under their fur, the polar bear has black skin?

Tanzania

Of all the times that I have been to Africa, my favorite place is Tanzania and, in particular, the Serengeti National Park, which actually extends across both Tanzania and Kenya. The variety of wildlife is extraordinary, and if that weren't enough, the Masai people inhabit the area. They are a colorful and friendly society and made the place magical.

Camping in the Serengeti National Park is unlike any camping experience. We had tents with toilets actually inside them, and we were able to take showers with the help of camp assistants who supplied warm water for us. The camps are moved regularly to have as little impact as possible on the land. Beyond that, it was exciting, if not unnerving, for the vulnerable tourist to have a jackal, lion, or even an elephant tromping around your tent walls. We had a central cooking and eating location. And food was not allowed in the tents. (Duh!)

If I were to show you a photograph of each and every animal we saw on our safaris, I would probably take up at least ten pages. Choosing was difficult, but at least you may get a feel for it. Our jeeps were open to the air, and the land was ever expansive. We would set out at sunrise and come back at sunset. It seemed that we had different adventures on each outing. The animals in their natural habitat were something to behold. We saw animals drinking from the river, and there was even a large (smelly, almost like sewage) pool where the hippos congregated. There were valleys, hills, rock formations, and all sorts of places to explore.

Almost any camp where you will stay in southeastern Africa will have guards who will escort you to and from your tent. Some guards carry rifles, some do not. Any animal can pass through the camp. The most fun in the Serengeti was seeing adult animals with their young. As I said, Tanzania was my favorite of any African trips. With Mt. Kilimanjaro in the background, it provides a place of peace and refuge. I would return there whenever I have the resources, to be sure!

Scandinavia

When someone says they want to go to Norway and Sweden in winter, they must be nuts, right? Our main reason we chose to do this was our attempt to see the Northern Lights. We traveled by ship, train, and bus to get to northern Sweden, and we had a fine adventure, even if we hadn't seen the Lights. We went dogsledding for hours, ice fishing, snowmobiling, and out of nowhere, something extraordinary happened. While snowmobiling at night, we were standing on a frozen lake, and suddenly the sky changed and these curtains of light fell around us. The lights were green and pink and purple and shimmered in the darkness. It was breathtaking!

We also stayed a night at the Ice Hotel, with its blue ice and ice sculptures. In the Ice Hotel, there were no restrooms, so if you *had* to get up, you had to walk to the warm area. There was also a bar where there were glasses literally made from ice. The record number of drinks from one glass before melting was twenty-seven.

This is a good place to say good night and goodbye for the moment. I hope I will have other opportunities to share my travels.

CHAPTER THIRTY-ONE

Maureen Reyes

MAUREEN
REYES

Maureen Reyes-Kispersky

When I was seven, my family loaded all our worldly possessions into my dad's pickup truck and headed for California in search of a better life. West Texas was not a great place to get ahead at that time if you were Mexican or non-union. After a three-day trip, we arrived on the west coast somewhere near La Jolla. I will never forget the first time I saw the ocean. I had *never* seen or even imagined anything so vast. It took my breath away. That was the first of many wonderful things about our new home that we would find. My dad, who was a carpenter, checked employment opportunities as we worked our way north on the 101 and finally settled on trying Carpinteria. How very lucky for us! Such a beautiful little community with friendly people and great weather. My sister Doris and I went to Aliso School, which was within walking distance from our house. We made friends there who are still friends some sixty years later—great school. When I was in the fifth grade, my parents sent us to Catholic school, for which we had to take a bus to Montecito. A great school with delightful nuns.

My dad worked mostly in Santa Barbara, and my mom did housekeeping locally, taking my little sister Valeria to work with her. My mother was a French war bride, having married my dad, an American soldier, at the end of World War II. Unfortunately, my sisters and I didn't learn much French, but later in life, we all did go to visit my mom's country. Our French cousins have visited us, as well.

We went back to public school for high school, where I remember having great teachers. Among them, Mr. McKown, Ms. Holmes, Mr. Feiock, and of course, Dorothy Bear-Cat Tripp, the art teacher. My fondest class memories are from her class.

During my senior year, I married Mike Cundith. Two years later, he left for Australia to go surfing, but never came back.

In 1980, I married Phil Kispersky from Cambria and found myself once again settling down in a beautiful, friendly little town just south of Hearst Castle located in a thick pine forest. My husband, a contractor, has had his own heating and cooling business for over forty-five years.

In 1981, we had a son named Paul, and in 1984, we had a daughter named Rachael. As with most people, our lives and experiences revolved around our kids and their activities. We also managed to take some pretty great vacations. Three were to Europe and we stayed with my mother's family, based just outside of Paris. A few times, we went to Hawaii, had a great time in Costa Rica, Mexico, and Florida. One of our family phases involved dirt biking, so we did a lot of desert camping. For several years, we houseboated every summer on Lake Powell. It was a lot of fun.

These days, we're not so active anymore. We live in Morrow Bay. Our house is a stone's throw from the harbor water, and Morrow Rock fills our front windows—very nice view.

I've recently been diagnosed with Parkinson's and I also managed to crack my pelvis in a couple places, so I kind of have to take it easy. I'm pretty good at that.

I so enjoyed our fifty-year class reunion (fifty years, gasp!). I especially loved how everyone picked up conversing with one another as though it were only five years and not fifty!

Luckily for me, I have a loving and supportive husband and daughter looking after me and an incredible son who cares for me with boundless patience and love.

I am so looking forward to reading the stories of my fellow classmates. I want to thank my good buddy Linda Fryer (friends since the third grade) for helping me submit this chapter.

CHAPTER THIRTY-TWO

Bob Walsh

BOB
WALSH

The Caribbean aboard a Cat:
An Exceptional Playground

No one said it was going to be easy. But nobody told us it was going to be so much fun! My wife Lynne and I, and our five-year-old Aussie mix dog Mollie, have been living aboard our Antares forty-four-foot sailing catamaran *Leap of Faith* in the eastern Caribbean for the past two years.

In October of 2007, we decided we were ready to head for the tropics. The passage from Annapolis, Maryland, to Ft. Lauderdale, Florida, was relatively uneventful. We'd sail the Atlantic when weather permitted, and motor down the Intracoastal Waterway (ICW) when the weather turned foul. Our goal for the season was to sail our boat to the Caribbean by way of the Thorny Path, using Bruce van Sant's invaluable guide to help us. We would make our crossing from Ft. Lauderdale over to the part of West End on Grand Bahamas Island. After watching the weather closely for weeks, we crossed the notoriously treacherous Gulf Stream in the early hours on December 5th and sailed across under full sail, accompanied by a bright full moon, with ten knots on the beam and calm seas.

THE BAHAMAS ISLANDS

We arrived in the beautiful Bahamas a mere ten hours later. The elation we felt in finally hitting the tropics was thus far unparalleled! We were like kids in the proverbial candy store: running on the perfect white sand beaches, snorkeling for hours in the crystal-clear waters, napping under gently swaying palm trees, and enjoying fresh fish and lobster that Bob's spearfishing prowess produced from the ocean. It was the paradise we had always imagined! Six months earlier, Lynne and I retired from building custom homes in the beautiful but cold and snowy tundra of Sandpoint, Idaho. We sold the home, the cars, and the toys, to set out on the adventure of a lifetime. We love the mountains of northern Idaho, but we knew the time had come for a change to a gentler climate. Finding the right boat for us was a labor of love. During the Miami 2004 boat show, we finally stepped onto the Antares 44 and knew instantly that we'd found what we had been looking for. The layout was the first thing that connected for me. The cockpit can be wide open or fully enclosed when the Strataglass panels are attached, and the spacious helm station makes it comfortable for long passages. Additionally, with the galley down in the port hull, it allows for an unusually large and well-appointed galley, as well as making the saloon feel more like a typical living room. The fit and finish was especially crucial for us having been custom-home builders. The level of detail that is built into our boat makes us feel as if we still live in a custom home, but at sea!

We slowly worked our way through the Bahamas, enjoying those magnificent and completely unspoiled islands. We made it to Georgetown, also known as chicken harbor because so many cruisers with intentions of sailing to the Caribbean chicken out once they hit Georgetown. It's the last stop before the real passage-making work begins, but we pressed on. We soon discover how aptly named the Thorny Path is, as it was a very grueling four months of motor-sailing, beating to wind in heavy easterly winds and seas. Many night passages were required because the wind would be more likely to moderate during that period. Admittedly, we had purchased a sailing vessel—we wanted to sail and grew somewhat discouraged by the amount of motoring that was required. We beat from the Bahamas to the Turks and Caicos, down to the Dominican Republic, along the north shore of the DA, crossed the Mona Passage to Puerto Rico, and then made our way along the south side of Puerto Rico. Then we crossed the Vieques Passage to the Spanish Virgins, on to the US Virgins, and finally into the British Virgin Islands.

VIRGIN ISLANDS

The research we had done before embarking on the Thorny Path leg of the adventure had not prepared us for the reality of the level of determination that was required to push our way southeast to the Caribbean. However, once we made landfall in the Virgin Islands, we knew all the hard work had been well worth it.

Returning to the British Virgin Islands was like coming home again. We'd forgotten how beautiful and clear the waters were. While the islands predominantly lie east to west, the north-to-south orientation of them relative to the Sir Francis Drake Channel allows for fantastic sailing as the easterly trades are ever present, while the majority of easterly swells and wind-driven chop are blocked by Virgin Gorda Island. The real bonus is that there are a plethora of islands close enough together that day sailing from one to another is almost always available, regardless of conditions.

Having thus far spent the majority of our time beating to wind, we really hadn't had much opportunity to sail downwind. The BVIs provide this opportunity. The layout of the islands allowed us ample opportunity to sail on many points of sail. This was the first time we'd had a chance finally to hoist our custom-made spinnaker while sailing both to and from Anegada Island. Unquestionably, the spinnaker made a spectacular sight, and we love to hoist it and hear it snap open. However, rigging it took between twenty and thirty minutes, and the effort would be for naught if we failed to have accurate weather forecasting to determine its suitability for the day's conditions. Eventually, we discovered that the 635 sq. ft. screecher on a roller furling (standard sail included with our boat) made just as good a downwind sail as our spinnaker. Best of all, it was always rigged and ready right there on our bowsprit. There was no need to blanket the sail with the main sail in order to dowse it safely; no one is required to go forward to the bow. We had no worries about a squall sneaking up behind us while daydreaming at the helm (as happened to us one day while sailing from Guadeloupe to Montserrat). You can simply roll up the screecher, and you're done! We've discovered that with twelve to fifteen knots of apparent wind, we could average seven to eight knots of boat speed. No need to even set the main sail, not bad in our book!

Both the USVIs and VBIs offer the easy lifestyle. In the BVIs, you can easily sail into Road Harbor, Tortola, walk from the anchorage to a selection of markets, provision your boat, and be back on the boat within an hour. Set sail and another hour later, you're dangling on the hook in a quiet anchorage, appreciating another beautiful sunset with a cool drink. The real allure of the Virgin Islands for us is the fine and easy sailing, fantastic snorkeling, abundant scuba diving, great kayaking, and hiking on the many trails ashore. This last year, we were able to spend enough time there to discover out-of-the-way anchorages that felt as if time had simply forgotten about them. We'd share these locations with you, but then they'd lose their undiscovered charm.

We hauled *Leap of Faith* out in Trinidad for the hurricane season, but when we returned in early November, we were able to spend a great deal of time lazily exploring the Leewards, Windwards, and Grenadines, and are often asked which island is our favorite. The Caribbean Islands offer such a variety of experiences it is impossible to choose, for they all have their own allure. But we must admit that the French Islands are among our top rated with their incredible patisseries, delectable assortment of imported chesses, and excellent fashion shopping. The locals have proven to be quite gracious by maintaining a friendly and helpful demeanor in spite of us inadvertently butchering their beautiful language!

A prime example is our first visit to Isle des Saintes. We were on our way to meet friends ashore for cocktails, when we noticed that we were running low on dinghy fuel. Not speaking a word of French, we found ourselves standing in front of the pumps and looking for gasoline. We had a choice between *gazole* (diesel) and *essence* (gasoline). After several moments of head scratching, guess which one we chose? Yep, *gazole*. Sounds more like gasoline than *essence*, doesn't it? We can tell you for a fact that diesel does not care to be run in Honda gasoline outboards! We made it just for enough to get ourselves to the middle of the anchorage before our dinghy let out a great belch of black smoke and quit. Luckily, our friends saw us and towed us in for cocktail hour. Why get towed back to the boat when we knew we'd have hours of work (and much cursing) ahead of us to get that diesel fuel out of our gasoline engine! Now, we carry a fantastic guide titled *French for Cruisers* by Kathy Parsons, and we are learning the lovely but difficult French language.

One of our favorite aspects of cruising is the gift of seeing ocean life in its splendor. Recently, while sailing in the BVIs just north of Jost Van Dyke, a pod of whales were breaching off our port side. Another great brush with sea life occurred as we were departing Trinidad for the lovely isle of Tobago. We left the anchorage at 2:00 a.m. to ensure we'd reach Tobago with plenty of sunlight in our favor. I was sitting in the starboard bow seat with the searchlight, keeping a lookout for unmarked obstructions, when we acquired a delightful escort, a pod of about twenty large dolphins. They were bow surfing, as they're known to do. Suddenly, I heard several loud, rhythmic thumps just below me and felt the boat vibrate with each thump. Shining the light down onto the dolphins, I was able to see a particularly large one swimming alongside, whacking our hull with his powerful tail. This went on for several minutes until Bob frantically called to me to come take the helm while he checked the engines. Apparently, the sound and vibration created by the hull-thumping dolphin was so extreme it made Bob fear some engine catastrophe had just occurred!

THE RESCUE

Before departing our very structured and admittedly mundane lives back in Idaho, we agreed that safety at sea was essential, knowing it would primarily be just Bob and I aboard our Antares, we both got our CPR certifications. Recently, Bob had cause to use his when our dog Mollie, while making a routine beach landing, inadvertently herded a wild goat straight into the ocean. Realizing too late what had occurred, we immediately called her back to allow the goat to swim back to the shore. However, the goat proceeded to swim further out to sea! Bob, fearing the goat was too panicked to find its way back, ran to the dinghy, fired it up, and chased down the goat to herd it back to the safety of the beach. All was looking very successful, when just two feet from shore, the goat went under. Bob jumped from the dinghy and hauled the goat back onto the rocky shore. It was not breathing, so Bob began CPR by pumping his chest and slapping face. (No, mouth to mouth was *not* an option!) Immediately the goat coughed up salt water, but then passed out again. I continued CPR efforts until finally the goat let out a little "baaayyyy," and we both felt tremendous relief. We continued to soothe and stroke him until he finally was able to regain his wobbly legs. He stood, turned to us, and let out a tremendous "BBBAAAYY" as if to scold us for our inattentiveness, and teetered off into the bushes. He was right to berate us, and Mollie will never again be allowed to roam the beaches off-leash when wildlife is present.

The following morning, we took a hike to find the goat and assure ourselves that he was OK. We found him not far from the location of the dastardly deed, where he approached us quite readily and appeared very healthy. Luckily, we were able to sail on, knowing he was safe and sound.

I must admit that living aboard a boat is unlike anything I ever expected. It has its difficulties, to be sure, but the rewards of being able to explore the many beautiful islands are unparalleled. Each day offers a new look into their rich histories, and the chance to meet the friendly local people. I've learned to identify and shop for the exotic fruits and vegetables, and learned to prepare the local Caribbean dishes, except breadfruit—that's a toughie. We never tire of swimming in the clean, clear turquoise waters. But best of all, we've developed friendships with fellow cruisers that will hopefully last a lifetime. These gifts are far greater than we ever expected, and it's all here for the taking, if one only has the temerity to take their own leap of faith.

CHAPTER THIRTY-THREE

Stanley Thayer

My name is Stanley Shepard Thayer. I will now endeavor to put my life in a chapter. I was born on July 2, 1948, at about five o'clock in the morning at St. Francis Hospital in Santa Barbara. My dad's name was Frank Thayer, and my mom's name was Marilyn Shepard Thayer. I was named after my mom's dad, Stanley Shepard. He lived on Shepards Mesa in Carpinteria; we lived on one of his avocado ranches on Casitas Pass Rd. about two miles from town. I have an older brother, Frank, and a younger brother, Bill. We had a lot of fun when we were kids; we went to the beach a lot and had a whole orchard to play in. There were fruit trees down by the creek—apricot, peach, and an apple tree. I loved to sit by the creek when the water was roaring and eat that fruit. My dad had a big hothouse, where he grew avocado seedlings. I loved to go in there. It was always warm and smelled good.

We also had a couple of horses, which we boarded at a friend's ranch. I loved to ride. I got bucked off one time. I was riding a mare; we named her Ava, probably after Ava Gardner. My dad taught us how to shoot with the bow and arrow, and I could hit a lemon swinging from a tree. I also had a BB gun. It was a pump, four or five pumps, and it was powerful. I would shoot the little birds in the fruit trees, thinking I was doing good. I would never do that now.

My dad would take my older brother and me on deer-hunting trips, along with my dad's friends and their sons. I was probably between eleven and thirteen; my brother was three years older than me. We would go hiking and keep ourselves busy. All the men would be drinking and playing poker. They would have us go out into the bush and flush deer out. It worked. When I got older, I brought my shotgun; we all had shotguns. I remember one hunting trip, about dusk, we were down by the creek and two rattlesnakes were getting a drink. We shot them and skinned them and ate them. They were good, tasted kinda like chicken.

I always liked playing sports: football, basketball, and baseball. Basketball was my favorite as I was going into high school. I would practice every day. We had a large cement patio in the back of the house, with a basketball hoop connected to the fascia board. I wanted to be tall and play on the varsity team. I knew that I would.

I got a little ahead of myself. I want to talk more about my grandpa, my mom's dad, whom I was named after. He had three daughters, my mom being the oldest. He taught them how to fish and they went camping a lot and my mom was good with a shotgun. I am sure he also would have liked a son. Well, my mom gave him three grandsons, and Bonnie, my aunt, gave him one and a granddaughter, so he took the three of us hunting and fishing. My younger brother was too young to go. We had some great times together. All of us grandkids called him Daddy Boom. Now the story behind that: what I heard is, when he was going to school, he was a big kid, and when he walked into the room, all the kids would say, "Boom boom," and the *daddy* probably came from my mom and her sister calling him daddy, so he was Daddy Boom to us. He was 6'2". He wasn't overweight; he looked good. I sure loved that man.

My grandma we called Gom; her real name was Madge. The way I understand it, when we were young, when we tried to call her Grandma, it came out Gom, so it stayed that way. She was only 4'11" tall and spunky and so much fun, and I loved her so.

I remember one time, Daddy Boom took my cousin Greg, Frank my brother, and me fishing in his small motorboat. We shoved off in Santa Barbara Harbor; it wasn't long before we started catching fish, but not just any fish. We ran right into the middle of a school of bonito. We were catching tuna left and right, what a blast we had. Daddy Boom wasn't fishing; he was smiling from ear to ear and taking pictures. We had many great trips and lasting experiences together. I miss him so. Gom and I were like two peas in a pod; we would make each other laugh hysterically. I miss her wonderful personality.

I think it's time to go to high school. I wasn't the greatest student; studying came hard to me, but I sure liked sports. My best sport was basketball, and I excelled at it. I practiced all the time.

My dream came true. I was on the varsity basketball team; my senior year was the best. I even received a few trophies, and my teammates were the greatest. What wonderful times they were, and I thank God I was in the class of '67. What a wonderful group of people, we had great times together. After I graduated, I hung around Carp for a while. I got a job at Loops Restaurant as a busboy and dishwasher. Loops was a hangout for everybody. My friends and I would sit there and drink coffee and smoke cigarettes and laugh a lot. I became friends with the hostess; her name was Laurie. She had the most beautiful blue eyes I have ever seen. We hit it off and started going out. We really liked each other, but we were both too young to get serious. I was only eighteen and she was seventeen. Besides, I was kind of wild. I drank and had a lot of wild oats to sow. I used to come to her parents' house late at night, and she would open the side door to her bedroom and let me in. We would talk a lot and kiss, but that was all. We were very intimate but never had sex. About that time, my cousin was killed in Vietnam, and I sure did not want to be drafted, so I joined the Navy Reserve in Santa Barbara. After a year, I went active, so after boot camp, I went to the Naval Base in San Diego, waiting for a ship to be assigned to. The day came. When they posted it on the wall, I looked at my name, and beside it said MCB4. I turned to my friend and said, "What kind of ship is MCB4?"

He said, "That's not a ship. It's a mobile construction battalion. They go to Vietnam and build airports and make roads."

Well, you can imagine what I said! There was one good thing about it. I was stationed at Port Hueneme Naval Base, only half an hour from Carpinteria, so when I didn't have duty on the weekends, I went home. Laurie and continued to see each other. My duties at the base were a lot of guard duty and working the armory. I was learning how to take apart a MIG rifle, and I cleaned a lot of them. That was gonna be my job. I was a gunner's mate, so I worked in the armory in Vietnam and took care of the weapons. In 1969, we flew over to Vietnam and were stationed at Da Nang. In the early morning, 3:45, we were trucked into Camp Adenir; as I think back, it was kind of scary. We lived in Quonset huts. The first night the

Viet Cong welcomed MCB4 to Vietnam, I heard a siren and a lot of noise. I ran outside. It was just beginning to get dark. I didn't know what to do. I didn't see any bunkers. I saw a few sandbags. I stubbed my big toe and knelt down by them. I remember the pain. I think it was the first time I really prayed. I said, "God, don't let me die." The next morning, I walked down to the latrine, a big outhouse. In the attack last night, four men got hit; they all lived but some lost arms and legs. I remember looking at the outhouse and seeing all the holes made by the shrapnel and thinking it sure was good that no one was in there at that time. As time went on, there were more mortar attacks, but I knew where the bunkers were. After we were there for a while, they put me on guard duty in the watchtowers. I would sit up there at night and look through a starlight scope. I remember one night the mortars were coming right at the tower I was in, one after another in a straight line. I pushed the button for the siren and fell to the floor. They missed the tower, thank God. One morning, I got up, went to the armory, and found out that my boss, my friend whom I greatly respected, got killed that night; it devastated me. I didn't work that day. I stayed on my bunk.

Now it was time to leave Vietnam. What a great day! Everyone was happy to see me at home. Laurie and I were so happy to be together, we dated a lot. But then I started to date other girls, but we still went out together. Now it was time for a tour in Okinawa. We stayed in touch, but then we both stopped writing. Nixon gave a three-month cut, so I got out of the navy early, I was happy about that. I stayed in Carp for a while, drank a lot, took some drugs, lived a wild life. My mom and dad had moved to Rancho Mirage down in the Palm Springs area, so I drove down to live with them for a while. They were happy to have me. They had a little guesthouse in the back; it was nice. I was twenty-two, was still drinking a lot.

I didn't know what I wanted to do. I worked for a gardener for a while, and then I used my GI bill to go to the College of the Desert to learn air conditioning. You had to take math, English, and all these other requirements, and I wasn't the greatest student, so three months, that was it for me. So now what did I do? Still living with my parents, still drinking and other things! I needed a good job. My parents had a friend who was a painting contractor. They had drinks with him at the bar, and he said, "Send him over." My first day on the job I wore my cowboy boots. Well, you can imagine what the workers thought of me! But they all drank, so I fit right in; they took me under their wing and taught me how to paint. I was about twenty-four then. I met a guy at the bar who was looking for a roommate. We became good friends; he just got a divorce, so we rented a house. I was making good money. I was in the union and had good benefits, so it was wine, women, and song. The years went by; it was party and girlfriends. When I was twenty-nine, I met this gal who was a barmaid. We hit it off, so we dated, and after a while, she became pregnant. We lived together, and we had our son Shawn.

Years went by. My drinking and drugs were coming to an end; even smoking had to go. It made me sick to drink and hurt my throat to smoke, and forget drugs. I was thirty years old. Now what do I do? I was looking for God. One day after work, my friend from work gave me a tape about Jesus and his return to take his church with him. As I listened, my heart was stirred, and I was under conviction. I didn't know then, but it was the Holy Spirit ministering to my heart that I needed Jesus. I had never heard John 3:16, "for God so loved the world that he gave his one and only son, that whoever believes in him shall not perish but have eternal life." That night, I could not sleep. Finally, I lifted my head off the pillow and said, "Jesus, come into my life." I fell back and slept like a baby.

The next morning, I knew something had happened. I was different. Some of the things I used to do, I had no desire to do anymore. I didn't know then, but found out later that I was born again, like Jesus said in John 3:3, except a man be born again, he cannot see the kingdom of God. So my spirit became alive to God. I was spiritually born again. So what do I do now? My girlfriend's name was Diane. I didn't know it, but she was brought up in the church but didn't walk the walk, so we went to church. I knew we were living in sin. We needed to be married; finally, I asked her. We were married on May 28, 1982; my son was five years old. I had a great marriage; we loved each other. We lived in Palm Desert for a while, and then moved to Desert Hot Springs.

My mom lived in Rancho Mirage, which was about fifteen miles from where we lived. She needed help and asked us if we would move in with her and take care of her, so we moved in. We took care of her for four years, then she died. We then moved to Yucca Valley and bought a house there. I still worked for a painting company in the lower desert, so I had to drive an hour down the hill to go to work. Yucca Valley elevation was about 3,369 feet. Also, our church we attended was in the lower desert. Our son also became a painter. He got married and had a son, whom they named Larry, after his wife's dad, so I have a grandson; he is twenty-four right now. In April 2011, I was playing a video game with him at the house. My son came into the room and said, "Mom doesn't feel good." I went to her; she was having a heart attack. I called an ambulance; they came and took her. She was gone within an hour, went to hospital, and they told me she died in the ambulance. You know, everyone loses their parents and it's painful, but losing a spouse is so much more. I grieved for a while, but at least I knew where she was, and I knew she was so full of joy and had perfect peace. We just missed by one month being married twenty-nine years.

After about a year and half, I went to Carpinteria to see some old friends. My younger brother would be there; we had a good time. Then it was time for me to leave. Remember that girl I dated when I was eighteen and she was seventeen? Well, she still lived there! It had been forty years since I saw her! On the way home, I got a phone call from my brother. Apparently, he was in a store, talking with someone, and he said my name. Well, it just happened that Laurie was in the store and heard my name, so she went to him and said, "Did you say Stan Thayer?" and right away, he said, "Laurie!" and she said, "Bill!" That was the beginning of the miracle, so on the phone going home, he sent me a picture of her. Wow, did she look good! In the next three months, we called each other twice. It must have not been God's timing, because nothing came of it.

One night I was sitting in my La-Z-Boy chair, watching TV, and I got a phone call from a friend I hadn't seen since high school. We used to play basketball together, and he wanted to have a reunion with two others of my friends in Carp. At first I said no, and then I prayed about what God wanted me to do. After about a week went by, he called again and said, "You're comin'." I said "OK," so I rented a car, called my aunt in Carp, and she said I could stay there. So off I went, and as I stepped out my door, I said "It's just you and me, Lord," meaning I didn't need a woman or anyone to share my life with. The Lord was enough for me.

We met at the Palms. Well, I quit drinking when I was thirty. Everyone was having a good time; it was good seeing them again. As the night went on, one passed out. I took my other friend back to the hotel. He couldn't drive, so the night was over. The next morning, we all went to breakfast, then everyone went home. The next morning, I walked to the beach, and after walking for a while, I had this thought to find the house where Laurie lived, where I used to come and see her. It was across from Fosters Freeze; I was on the sidewalk, but I didn't see it. I called Laurie, but all I got was a voice message, so I walked back to my aunt's home. The next day, I walked to the beach again. After a while, I had the same thought, so I walked up the street to houses across from Fosters Freeze. I was standing on the sidewalk, and I called Laurie, but once again, I got a voice message. I was getting discouraged. I had to go home in two days. I started to walk, but then I stopped. I said, "Lord, I can't leave without seeing her," and I prayed, "Lord, show me where her church is." The first church I came to, I was driving on Foothill Rd., and it was the First Baptist Church. I saw the sign. I said, "I know that's where she goes." It was on a Saturday, and the church was open. I went in, and there was a man standing in the front hallway, I asked him if Laurie Foster went to this church. He said, "The pastor is in his office. Ask him." So I went in and met the pastor, and he said, "Yes, she does," so we talked for quite a while. He was checking me out, and that's a good thing. He said, "Come to church tomorrow. She will be here," and I said I would. He had me close out in prayer, and I left.

I was at church Sunday morning, sitting there, waiting to see her, when the pastor walked by and said, "Laurie's not coming. She didn't feel good." I knew I would call her later. Just then, the pastor's wife came up to me, talking to Laurie on the phone. She handed the phone to me, and Laurie and I had a short talk. Church was about to begin. I told her I would call her after church.

After church, I drove up Casitas Pass Rd. and found some shade trees. I called Laurie and we talked for a while, she told me she was dog sitting—that was why she wasn't home. She said she was tired and had a headache. We both agreed to meet at Carl's Jr. I got there early. I was excited about seeing her again. Then she came through the door, and our eyes met. Wow, did she look good. She told me much later that when she first saw me, it felt like she was home. To sort of break the ice, she brought a photo album of us when we were together. What a blessed time we had. We talked for four hours! And then I walked her to her car. I asked her if she would have lunch with me. She said yes, we hugged, and I asked her for another hug. I got it.

The next day, we went to the Garden Restaurant on Santa Claus Lane. After that, we went to the beach. We found a big rock and sat on it. We talked and watched the birds. Soon, I had my arm around her and gave her a little kiss. After a while, we walked back to the car. We drove to her car. I let her out. She had to be at church at five, for she was a leader in Celebrate Recovery. I kissed her and then she kissed me. I felt the same way I did when we were teenagers.

The next day, I packed up, said thanks to my aunt, and took off. On the way home, I thought, how could this work? Two hundred miles away from each other—she had her life there, and I had mine and family here. I called a friend over for a Bible study. When he got there, he said I looked like I lost my best friend. I told him about her, and he said, "Call her." I don't know what I was waiting for. We talked and I was joyful again. We never missed one day in talking with each other, and every night, we would pray and say goodnight.

For two years, we dated. I would come down and stay with some friends, and she and I would see each other every day and every night—what a romance. I found love at sixty-five. She never got married; she was engaged a couple of times, but it didn't work out. She said when she saw Stanley Steemer, she always thought of me. We went to the movies, dinner, breakfast, romantic places. We held hands and did a lot of kissing; we were crazy about each other. After about a month and a half, we were sitting on her couch, and I said I loved her, and she said she loved me too. After another month, on her couch again, I asked her to marry me. She said yes. I would drive to Carpinteria and pick her up. She stayed at Super Eight in Yucca Valley, and we did that several times, and every time she cried on the way home. She went home on the train. One of the times she visited me, we went to the Red Lobster for dinner. After dinner, I got on my knees with a ring and proposed to her. It was like a Hallmark movie. Our waitress was watching and crying; people congratulated us. It was an amazing evening!

We had a two-year engagement. I wouldn't change a thing. We were two people in love, and it was better than any romantic movie. We both knew God had put us together, and so did our pastors, so we set a date for November 14, 2015, to be married at her church and by her pastor. It was a beautiful wedding, and many people attended. At the wedding reception, there was a lot of rejoicing, and everyone was so happy. We loved it, but we were so excited about starting our marriage and going on our honeymoon to Pismo Beach. We are now coming up on our fifth anniversary, and our love for each other is stronger than ever. And I get to look at the most beautiful blue eyes forever. We both are so thankful to Jesus for what he has done for us, and what he is doing in us every day. Thank God for his amazing grace.

Newlyweds Stanley and Laurie, 2018

Stanley and Laurie, 1968

CHAPTER THIRTY-FOUR

Esther Cerda

Front Summary

Remembering When . . .

I remember graduation day like it was yesterday. Class of 1967 made memories. We were the last class to graduate from the old high school. The following year, the building would be used as a middle school. My graduating class members want to put together a book of memoirs of accomplishments. So what did high school prepare me for?

First Event

I wanted to go to school, but I realized I needed transportation, so I went to work to earn money to buy a car. I enjoyed helping and being around people, so I looked for a job working and helping people. I found myself at nineteen working for Community Action Commission. This is a nonprofit organization helping low-income families or families in need. I was bilingual, which helped, and had good local references. I became a community development director for Carpinteria at the age of nineteen.

My job entailed working closely with schools, preschools, local agencies, helping families in need. My bilingual skills came in handy. In October 1969, we had a bad fire in the mountains that came down almost to Highway 192—back road. This fire wiped out a lot of structures and buildings. I helped coordinate clothing, housing, and food for families in need. That late December came the rains. I remember so well. The road on which I lived on was wiped out by the downpour. Also, local nurseries lost a lot of their plants. You could actually find plants on the sand of the beach. The road I lived on was wiped out. Cramer Circle on the north end of Carpinteria was wiped out by the torrid rain. Also, my family was fine, so I went to work with families who had lost everything. Carpinteria was declared a disaster. I started reaching out to the local community and Santa Barbara for necessities for families who lost all. Food, clothing was donated, and I was able to find some housing. The connection I created with local organizations really helped. In all the chaos at the time, I was notified by the local mayor that the governor of California would be coming to town, and the mayor wanted me to ride in the bus with the governor. Guess who? Ronald Reagan.

I got so excited that I wore my new white tennis shoes. The mayor said, "Wear good walking shoes." Did I know that the governor would actually walk in the Cramer Circle neighborhood? My white tennis shoes were no longer white but black and full of mud. I greeted the governor, shook hands, and deep down, I was upset I wore the wrong shoes.

I received feedback from the mayor. The governor was impressed how quickly the community got together to help the needy. I received a plaque from the mayor for all I did—just doing my job helping those in need.

This governor became the fortieth president of our nation later in time. Who can say they rode in a bus with our fortieth president? Little ole me from Carpinteria High School.

Second Event

My life was not just work. One needs pleasure also. I have always been interested into my roots from Mexico even though I am a full-born American. In the last fifteen years, I have gotten to know some great known musicians. I love mariachi music just like I love my oldies but goodies. I have met some great friends from southern California, Arizona, Texas, and Pennsylvania. We all have something in common: mariachi music.

In 2005, my husband planned on going to Guadalajara, Mexico, to attend the International Mariachi Festival. One month before, I lost an office staff, and I couldn't go. My son went in my place. He had so much fun mixing with the mariachi groups from California as well as with the friends we met. Guess what? The following years, I swore I needed to go.

It was August 2006, fiesta time. My brother John became president of fiestas for the Mariachi Festival in Santa Barbara. He brought to the bowl Mariachi Vargas from Tecalitlán and Mariachi Los Camperos of Nati Cano. That night after the concert, both groups came to my home for an after drink.

Now mind you, if you don't know mariachi. Mariachi Vargas is known as the world's *best* mariachi. They are from Mexico City. They have many CDs and play backup for Luis Miguel, a Mexican artist. I even rode on their bus to my house that night and had breakfast with them the next morning. These are memories that you never forget. We have met up in Guadalajara, Mexico, and San Antonio, Texas. We greeted each other with grace. So guess who is my favorite mariachi? Mariachi Vargas de Tecalitlán.

I have no complaints for my life since graduation, successful in education, in the workforce, and even in retirement. I am still living the life anytime I can. God has been good to me, even in meeting up with my high school classmates at our fiftieth celebration and again to establish a book. Thank you, Joe Lovett, Terry, and Cori.

CHAPTER THIRTY-FIVE
Linda Kohnke

Books, seashells, coins, antiques, correspondences, Pueblo Indian pots, dust, CDs/cassettes tapes, image of the Virgin Mary, photographs, buttons, lint, holy cards, fabric, cut glass, Depression glass, quotes and phrases, linens, DVDs, mason jars, Avon perfume bottles, Dodger posters, Christmas tree ornaments, and all those artistic masterpieces created by my children and grandchildren. This is a list, though partial it may be, of the things I have collected over the years. Ah, some heads are nodding. You too have a collection. Maybe it's antiques, or books, or macaroni ornaments? Some of my items I've relinquished, while others I just keep collecting, like *dust*, for example.

By far the largest of my collections would be quotes and phrases. It's more than quotes and phrases really. It includes notes from classes and lectures, words not in my everyday vocabulary but I thought they should be, lyrics to my favorite songs. I have spiral notepads, spiral notebooks, steno pads, journals, and scraps of paper where I've written down what I've heard or read along the years. I have framed quotations hanging on my walls and propped up in my bookcase. Idioms can be found magnetized to my fridge, and Occam's razor is written with lipstick on my bathroom mirror.

I do this because I find these quotes and phrases to be profound, even spiritual, while others just make me laugh. For me, they are great communication tools. Some never leave my head but just stay there at the helm, helping me steer my course through life.

If you don't have something nice to say, don't say anything at all.

This is a quote I remember my dad saying. He must have said it a lot if I'm remembering it all these years later. Honestly, I wasn't good at following these words, but I do remember this one time I did.

In the early 1980s, I was teaching at the preschool where my children attended. One scruffy little boy, whom I'll call Max, was a real challenge to the staff and to all his little preschool mates. It seemed to them that Max was being corrected constantly. So keeping my dad's words in mind, I vowed to myself that nothing negative would pass my lips when I next encountered Max.

What could I say? "Good job hijacking Billy's tricycle" or "Hurray! Only one bucket of sand flushed down the toilet today"? Eventually, I saw Max in the play yard, and with profound joy, I said, "Max, I really like your red shoes!" Well, he locked eyes with me, and from that day on, he looked for me in the play yard. We became buddies, boogers and all.

> *Perhaps this is the moment for which you*
> *have been created.* (Esther 4:14)

Sometime later, staff learned of the suffering Max was having to endure in his little life. I learned a lot in preschool.

> *Be kinder than necessary because everyone you*
> *meet is fighting some kind of battle.—*
> J. M. Barrie

My dad always had a footlocker. He acquired his first footlocker in 1933 while in the Civilian Conservation Corps, one of President FDR's work relief programs during the Great Depression. I remember Dad stored his footlocker under our basement stairs when we lived in Chicago. Once when home alone, I think I was probably aged ten, I broke into his footlocker.

> *Sometimes you just have to do something stupid.*

Well really, how long can one live with a big mysterious box under the stairs?

> *A girl's gotta do what a girl's gotta do.*

The contents, as I recall, consisted of mostly brown-and-white photographs of people I didn't recognize. There was a painting of beets my sister created in first grade. Some grainy black-and-white photos were scattered about. One photo of me in an inner tube at Sand Lake with Dad standing in water halfway up his calf. My memories are of the water being much, much deeper than that!

The real treasure was fining the photo album of our family road trip when I was eight years old. Our destination was California, but Albuquerque was as far as we got. I don't blame my parents for cutting the trip short; they were trapped in our Pontiac with two teenagers. One angelic eight-year-old can't offset that. I'm certain I was angelic. This was pre-burgle footlockers days!

It's not how far you fall but how high you bound back.—Ziglar

Most of the pics in the photo album were taken in New Mexico, where we stopped at some tourist trap and bought a trunk-load of souvenirs. The place was pretty big, and there was a lot of stuff, a buckboard, some horses and tepees just like on TV, only in *color*! One photo in the album was a real-life Wells Fargo stagecoach. Wow! My brother loved that. Another photo had my sister leaning against a hitching rail, headscarf tied at the chin, arms folded in front— teenager on vacation.

Stick a fork in me 'cause I'm done.

One of my favorite photos was of Native American hoop dancers. Another favorite was with my brother and me each wearing a headdress. We were standing beside a Native American "chief" dressed in full regalia, teaching us sign language. Oh, the chief was majestic. But I was disturbed by the fake arrow attached to his headdress that made him look like he was shot through the head— natural reaction as Jay Silverheels was my heartthrob at that time. On TV, he played Tonto, sidekick to the Lone Ranger.

*Better to have loved and lost than to have
never loved at all.*—Lord Tennyson

Having concluded this sentimental journey through the photo
album, I must have felt that I was working on borrowed time. So I
closed up the footlocker—mystery solved!

Some three or so years later, we finally made it to California.
Dad's employer relocated us to a new home in Carpinteria, and
footlocker I moved with us. The home not having a basement,
footlocker I was stored in the garage. How long footlocker I reigned
there before relinquishing its position to footlocker II, I do not know.

Only the rocks live forever.—James A. Michener

What I do know is that footlocker II has been reigning in my
garage for the last seventeen years, ever since the passing of Mom
and Dad.

After turning seventy, I thought it best to start organizing family
photos and memorabilia. This meant looking in footlocker II.

*You must do the very thing you thing you
cannot do.*—Eleanor Roosevelt

What I expected was there: snapshots of the hoop dancers and
Chief Arrow Through the Head, brown-and-white photos—who
are those people? Further inspection revealed the unexpected. I
found correspondences that my parents had saved. Some of these
correspondences were between the two of them, dating back to the
late 1930s. My parents were in love!

The real discovery was the collection of spiral notepads, steno
pads, and three ring binders. The contents all written in Dad's hand.
Included were notes from classes he'd taken, tips on self-improvement,
words of wisdom, quotes and phrases, all the verses to his favorite
songs. It was almost eerie. I had no prior knowledge that this was a
habit of his. The first twenty years of my life, I lived with him. Plus,

the last twenty-two years of his life, he and Mom were my neighbors, just two houses down the street from me. Never saw a spiral notepad about the house. (He was a neatnik for sure.) Yet here we had this commonality. How did that happen?

No seen every sees the flower.

The person that he formed himself to be floated off the pages of his notepads.

Be careful of the words you speak, make them soft and sweet.
You never know from day to day, which ones you'll have to eat.

Indeed, Dad always chose words of kindness and encouragement. I can only hope that when the time comes whoever finds my notepads can say the same about me. Then again that might be

As likely as rocking-horse manure.

Thought I'd mention that in one of Dad's notepads, he'd written copious notes on how to win at blackjack and craps.

Every coin has two sides.

I want to leave you with some of my favorite quotes. Enjoy.

How far you go in life depends on your being tender with the
young, compassionate with the aged, sympathetic with the striving
and tolerant of the weak and the strong. Because someday in life
you will have been all of these.—George Washington Carver

When you come to a fork in the road, take it! —Yogi Berra

Most folks are 'bout as happy as they make up
their minds to be.—Abraham Lincoln

You cannot make yourself feel something you do not feel, but you can make yourself do right in spite of your feelings.—Pearl S. Buck

Hoist by my own petard!—Hamlet

Those who give light must endure burning.—Viktor Frankl

To do is to be.—Descartes

To be is to do.—Sartre

Do-be-do-be-do.—Sinatra

Goodnight, Mrs. Calabash, wherever you are.—Jimmy Durante

Linda Kohnke Husted
Class of '67

July 1957, Longhorn Ranch, NM
Linda (8), brother John (13)

CHAPTER THIRTY-SIX

Barbara Swing

Ocean . . . River . . . Tears

The sky is summer blue, the Channel Islands are hazy in the distance, not like in the fall when they are seen, crisp as the air, on the horizon. I bob in the ocean, just past the break, riding the breath of the sea, the swell, peak, and trough . . . breathe in, breathe out. Or so it seems. The water is perfect, special, this day. It is so clear I marvel that I can see the ripples of the sand below. It is cool, not cold, and words fail to describe the feeling of it, on my skin and my whole being, suspended as I am. The moment is what I recall vividly these many, many years later. Something that, in my life, was of that place and time and of no other.

Moving toward the shore, I let the swell take, the gentle break carries me, and with the assist of my yellow-and-blue Churchill fins, I ride the wave toward the shore. Did I take this for granted? Perhaps, but loved the doing of it, not knowing then that it was something I was leaving behind, only to live in a visceral way in my memory. I was never an accomplished boy surfer, but that didn't matter. I loved being in the ocean and was lucky to know the gentle ocean of Carpinteria. It was there, over the years, I became a water baby. I so appreciated those of my friends that loved the water too, to be in it, groove to it—shout out to my wonderful then-friend Shelley. No fluff, no hairdo perfection or bathing suit sitting-strut-beach-towel-groovy for us (the '67 yearbook endpaper staged-photo notwithstanding). Nope, just ocean and warm sand and the being in the moment in the joy of the waves.

I left this beloved beach town sometime in 1968 and headed, with my then-husband Greg Skinner (married three days after my eighteenth birthday in September '67 . . . a whole other tale!), to the far, far north of Humboldt County, yet carried with me so many memories growing up in an enchanted place. It was a good move, though, to this wild, wild place of forests and bay and beaches and lagoons and rivers, but not the friendly ocean I'd come to love. No, it was cold and untamed by sentinel offshore islands . . . frigid and wild. The first time, maybe in about '68 or '69, that I tried going in, a sunny, warm day, College Cove, I think, just north of Trinidad. I waded in and dove into the waves. No, no, no, you can dive in, come up gasping, but you can't stay. For humans without thick wetsuits and surfboards, this is hostile territory. I retreated to the beach with profound respect for mother ocean. This was just a different neighborhood that I would have to get used to. So now I wade in the surf of those somewhat gentle local beaches or, at low tide, have collected edible seaweed in the tide pools if the conditions are safe. You also learn not to turn your back to the ocean here, no matter how much you love it, as not all beaches are considered gentle, even if they appear so.

I started, here, to write about how I came to love our rivers, but a tragic tale, forever lodged in my heart, kept interrupting my thoughts, nudging as I put these words down, insisting, so acquiescing to the memory, I shall share it. The ocean here is achingly beautiful and changes with the landscape, there are miles-long beaches you must trudge over big dunes to get to, the ocean there with seemingly endless rolling breakers (no surfing there!) or the beaches where a sand spit separates the sea from the lagoons (Big Lagoon, Freshwater Lagoon, Stone Lagoon), where dramatic breaches, at Big and Stone, ocean overtopping the spit to invade the lagoon, sometimes at very high tides or storm conditions or swollen by the creeks that feed them—or all three in a perfect storm, like pulling the plug in a bathtub, the lagoon water rushes, carving a channel to the sea until equilibrium is restored. Then there are beaches where the forest-covered tall cliffs meet the sand, steep ocean shore drops off and often a huge, powerful, shore break. Sometimes the lay of the land is just right, and the cliffs give way to sheltered coves, with gentle slope, that produce the perfect wave break and are where to find those clad in thick wetsuits, paddling out to meet the curl. The ocean here is wild, glorious, indifferent, and can take what you love in the blink of an eye. So this I am sharing.

My dear friends, on Thanksgiving weekend in 2012, were walking the beach, along the spit between Big Lagoon and the sea. Howard and Mary were accomplished outdoor enthusiasts, hikers, skiers, mountain climbers, kayakers, and they taught their kids Olivia and Geddie (Greg) to love adventuring too. As they walked, their dog Fran got caught up in a sneaker wave, and Geddie went into the surf to rescue her. Geddie was soon in trouble, so Howard went after him. Mary then went in after Howard. Olivia was held back by friends on the beach, or she might have been lost too. It does not take much for the ocean here to overpower you, even in very shallow water. Neither Howard or Mary, once rescued from the waves, could be revived, and Geddie was never recovered, lost to the sea. Fran, the dog, made it safely out of the shore break, back to the life forever changed. I found out by watching the evening news; first the name Mary Scott was spoken. My head snapped up, stunned, but I thought, wait, that's not such an unusual name. Then came the names Howard Kuljian and Greg Kuljian, erasing any doubt. By then, I was sobbing and screaming at the TV, helpless and in shock. Both Howard and Mary would have known the dangers, but it didn't stop them. To me, it will always be that they died for love. Their tragic end belies their beautiful souls and that they were the kind of people you'd want to surround yourself with. Lucky to count them as friends, I carry them with me always. Lordy, this was hard to write, as it brings me back to those moments. I am glad, at last, that thoughts of them now bring the happy memories, not just the shock and trauma of their passing.

They were well loved in the community and many of us volunteered to help at the estate sale to help raise funds to Olivia, then in her freshman year at college. She had extended family living far away, and now that she had lost her entire family, they expected she would come live with them. No, she said, this is where I belong. With the outpouring of support to those far-flung family members who gathered here to deal with the loss (opening homes to them, organizing volunteers to provide home-cooked dinners to be delivered each night as they faced the daunting task of funerals and settling the estate), they came to see what this close-knit community meant to Olivia. Her uncle said, "Finally, I understand, this *is* home." The Kuljian family was in the midst of a rehab on their Victorian-era rural house in the small community of Freshwater, and a number of the estate sale volunteers looked at each other and said, "We've got this." Thus, it came to be that group of about twenty-plus folks, friends and neighbors, pitched in when they could, and over about a month or so, we stripped old wallpaper, scraped and painted, laid flooring and carpet, did plumbing and electrical work. Dear friends of Howard from his college days finished with great craftsmanship and roughed-in staircase with oak treads and risers, and beautiful balusters and railing. We did yard work and plantings to make the house sale-ready in an effort to give Olivia a nest egg with which to finish college. Local retailers and others came together and donated materials as well as their time. Being retired by then, I was able to help almost daily and it was sad yet soothing, turning my grief into something meaningful and beautiful, like a prayer. When the task was done, it was hard to let go of being there, my last physical link to them. Every so often these days, I make the trek up to Freshwater and pass the house, where a new family lives and I mark the changes they are making, settling in and creating a life there. I slow down as I pass by and think that if the spirits of Mary, Howard, and Geddie hover there, the current occupants have the *best ghosts ever.*

Yes, the ocean here is so very different than in Carpinteria—the world's safest beach! And one learns quickly to read its moods and to never let your guard down, even on seemingly calm days. Because I craved the water, and the ocean could no longer give me that essential experience, early on I came to know and love the rivers and tributary streams of the north coast and became mostly a river-rat instead. Rivers, too, have their perils and will claim the unwary or unfortunate, so one must learn the character of each, the moods, and how they change with the seasons. It's been a while now; getting older has slowed me down (dang knees—but thank you for your many years of carrying me on adventures!), but for many years, I used to carry those same Churchill fins and face mask and walk upriver some miles—mostly the Mad River, as it's in my backyard—and short the river down in a sort of free-dive float, loads of fun on par, sort of, with riding waves in Carp. Ha ha ha, no itchy salt water dried on my skin, or sand in the suit—small blessings indeed. The Mad runs through my little town of Blue Lake (yes, there was a lake here once upon a time, fed by the river, but its course changed and the lake was gone, but to the confusion of visitors still, the name remains). It is a small, peaceful river, except in a very wet-winter flood stage, and reminds me of the gentleness of the beaches in Carpinteria. The north fork on the Mad is smaller still, more creek-like than river and can run dry, or underground, in the late summer.

One special memory I have of wading in the north fork was years before I moved inland—about twelve miles from the coast—to Blue Lake, with the town motto "Sunshine and Sea Air." Walking east along the levy and then scrambling down to the river, swollen with the late fall rain and wading in knee deep, standing very still, many salmon, fat from their time at sea and migrating to spawn upriver, slipped past me, brushing my legs as I stood marveling at their passage. Living here in this tiny town, now for thirty-some years as I put these words down, I have not experienced this again. I don't know if the salmon migration has changed or if my timing is off, but that was a singular experience and marvelous. I take that back, I do know, at least some of it. Time makes its mark on everything, but so does man, and not always in a good way, though there are those who strive to live sustainably and encourage and teach others to as well, within the web of life, and not have dominion over it. Many did not take heed for a long time; some still don't, and damage was done, but we're hopefully learning to do, to be better.

Other rivers here, to the north and east, are more mountain rivers with pronounced sections of rapid—lots of whitewater kayaking and rafting—and some great, great swimming holes when the river stills and deepens. One of my favorites is the Smith River in Del Norte county to the north, one of the last free-flowing rivers in California, and much of it runs along the northern border of Jedediah Smith State Park with its hush-quiet stands of old-growth redwoods, the understory carpeted by Western sword fern, native rhododendrons, salal, elderberry, huckleberry and vine maple. The land there has lots of blue-green serpentine rock, and the color of the river always reminds me of tropical ocean pictures—that crystal-clear pale to deep blue-green.

The rivers are the most swimmable of the waters, depending on the time of year, but the bay and the lagoons have their own water adventures. While I have swum in them too any number of times, for me, kayaking them is the most fun. Humboldt Bay is a working bay, so boating safety and paying attention to other watercraft is essential. So too is paying attention to the tides if you are on the north or south edges of the bay, or you may find yourself literally stuck in the mud until the next high tide frees you. Paddle past the downtown Eureka side, with its shops and industries, or across the channel to working docks of Woodley Island Maria, or a bit south to the Eureka Marina—mostly fishing boats, few pleasure craft—and with much caution, by the big ships from faraway places lading timber or wood chips. Though this too is changing as the timber industry becomes more sustainable and the region diversifies its industries. Read that as leaving some trees for later or just leaving many alone to be, well, trees doing their thing sustaining whole ecosystems. Head then toward the bay opening, being cautious of the strong currents and ship traffic, and nose around the historic Coast Guard station, giving them a thumbs-up as you pass by for the lifesaving work they do.

The lagoons too each have their own personality. Big Lagoon is, well, big. Fun to paddle and folks with small sailboats play in the stiff breezes coming off the ocean. Sitting low on the water in a kayak is an almost immersive experience (except if you capsize, then it's totally immersive) and allows for delightful explorations of the shoreline, or paddling up the creek that feeds the lagoon, sometimes past grazing herds of Roosevelt elk, or the humble feeling of being in the middle of the watery expanse, bracketed by forested hillsides and ocean vistas. Stone Lagoon, to the north, is smaller, more intimate but is my favorite, with its paddle-in campground, pretty much accessible only by water, fun to explore, and headland trails if you need a bit of a walkabout to stretch your legs.

There is so much water here, in many guises, to explore and experience. Oh, I forgot to mention the rain lots of rain, late fall through spring. Coastal fog too. That's way we have the rivers and lagoons and redwood forests. It's only in writing this, do I realize how I've unwittingly defined much of my life by that life element, water, first nurtured in the waves of Carpinteria beaches. In my fifty-plus years of living here, so far from the beaches of my youth, I have come to love this place and call it home. Rural, friendly, wonderful vistas and adventures...a great place to experience all that life throws at you. However, hometown will always be Carpinteria, however untethered from it I am now, with many memories grown hazy, a magical place to grow up and come of age, a sort of benchmark that I gauge other places by. And I guess why, though so very different in many ways, Humboldt County met that mark, and here I took root (well watered!) and thrived.

Barbara Swing/Skinner/Keating
December 2020

CHAPTER THIRTY-SEVEN

Reynae Pearson

REYNAE AILEEN
(PEARSON) LOMELI

Reynae was born in Long Beach, California. She was raised in Midway City, near Disneyland. She developed a love for Disneyland that lasted well into her life. Her father worked for Standard Oil, and he was transferred to Carpinteria and rented a house on Carpinteria Ave. near the Standard Oil road that led to the pier. She was able to bring her horse and kept it on the property. While living in Midway City, she had a paper route where she rode her horse to deliver them.

Reynae enjoyed the pleasure of living in a beach community. She was a sun worshipper that went to the beach to be with friends and develop that tan that was so becoming on her. Her teenage years were typical of most Carpinteria teenagers. Her father was a Mason, so she participated in the Rainbow Girls activities sponsored by the Masonic Temple. In high school, she was a song leader. In 1966, her father was transferred again by Standard Oil. She finished her junior year of high school in Carpinteria and then had to move to Santa Maria. She left a lasting impression on all her Carpinteria friends that still exists today. Even though she finished high school in Santa Maria, her heart was still at Carpinteria High School. She epitomized "Warrior spirit never dies."

Living in Santa Maria brought Reynae some major life changes. Her oldest daughter, Denette, was born in 1967, and she got married to her first husband. She also went to cosmetology school to get her license. She was rather proud of that because she always renewed the license with the state. She did that up to the time she moved to Virginia. Stacie, her second daughter, was born in 1972. She was pretty much a stay-at-home mom even though she did a small amount of hair cutting on the side. She always loved horses, and she was able to have a horse while living in Santa Maria. Her husband was eventually transferred to Carpinteria to be the manager of the Safeway store. The family relocated to Carpinteria when Denette was in eighth grade and Stacie was in grammar school.

Life in Carpinteria was a big change from Santa Maria. She no longer had her horse, so she settled in being a stay-at-home mom. The girls kept her busy with their various activities. She had Denette in Rainbow Girls. Stacie, the ever jock, played various sports. Reynae was always at all their events. After being in Carpinteria for several years, her marriage ended in divorce. This created another big change for her. She started working while raising the girls. She worked at several different places. Her last job while living in Carpinteria was at Mission Industries as the administrative assistant to the VP of marketing.

In 1983, Reynae ran into Greg Lomeli at the Palms after the Russell Cup track meet. Several weeks later, they went on their first date. They dated for three years prior to getting married. She was working at Mission Industries, and Greg was teaching at Carpinteria Junior High. They bought a condo at Franciscan Village and settled in with both girls. Denette had graduated from high school by then, and Stacie was just finishing junior high. Stacie kept her busy with all her sports activities especially when she entered high school. The ever-faithful mom, Reynae never missed a game. Stacie also started hostessing at the Big Yellow House in Summerland, which meant Reynae was an Uber driver. In 1995, Greg accepted a middle school principalship in the Corona-Norco School District. They relocated to Temecula, California.

Just prior to moving to Temecula, Reynae became a grandmother. She was way beyond excited and found her true calling. She was with Stacie when she gave birth, and Reynae was able to cut the umbilical cord because Stacie's husband was stationed in Korea. Thus, this started the unique bond between Reynae and Lorenzo. Within the next four years, two more grandchildren were on board. Marco came first and then Monica. To say the grandkids brought much joy to Reynae is an understatement. She was still young and vibrant, so when she was with the grandkids, nothing stopped her from doing whatever they wanted her to do. She played basketball, chased them around, and even tried to play soccer. She had great times playing dress-up with Monica when she was young. In 2004, Denette blessed Reynae with a set of twins. Isaac and Isabella were born in Massachusetts. By this time, both girls were living out of state. Stacie's husband was in the military, and they were stationed in various bases, the last being in Virginia. Denette has lived in Milford, Massachusetts, for twenty-plus years.

Living in Temecula was a good time for Reynae. She worked a few temporary jobs for about two years and then settled into being a stay-at-home wife. She truly enjoyed not having to work, and this allowed her to visit her daughter if a need arose. Shopping was a hobby that she perfected. Many a day she would go to the mall in Escondido for a day of retail therapy. She was great about hitting all the sales but never went overboard on her spending. The Temecula house was large enough that it allowed both daughters and family to visit at the same time. Christmastime with all the kids was always a tremendous amount of fun and left many lasting memories. Reynae got involved with women's Bible study at Rancho Community Church. She was also active in MOPS through the church. She was able to form some strong friendships through these activities. All these experiences solidified her Christian life and values.

Reynae had a uniquely strong bond with her sister Marilyn. There was a four-year difference in age between the sisters, but that didn't impact their relationship. Both girls enjoyed getting together with their mother for some shopping and of course a nice lunch. Their mother passed prior to their father. After her passing, the girls made a point to spend as much quality time with their father as possible. Marilyn's husband ran a successful masonry business, and they always invited Reynae and Greg to join them on their vacations. The vacation time created lasting memories that are still shared to this day.

Christmas time for Reynae was so, so special. She would start preparing a list of what she was going to purchase in July! She kept a detailed list of what she had purchased and was great at hiding the presents from everyone so no one would know what they were going to receive for Christmas. Then when the grandchildren came into the picture, she upped her game to ensure that all of them got something really nice from Grandma. With the large house in Temecula, both families were able to stay at the house numerous times for Christmas. The pictures of the times are hilarious especially with all the girls wearing matching pajamas. The house was always decorated inside and out for the season. Reynae and Christmas went together so well that even today, the family still experiences a strong emptiness during the season.

In 2006, Reynae was diagnosed with stage 4 breast cancer. She received her results of a biopsy on a Friday, and the following Tuesday, she was having surgery. This started a ten-year battle that she fought valiantly. Throughout the whole ordeal, she was a tower of strength. She endured numerous chemo treatments and radiation. She never let it get her down to where she just wanted to stop living. The opposite was the norm; she continued to do everything she was accustomed to doing. She never stopped attending her Bible study group or her MOPS activities. She was able to counsel several women who were going through the same struggles. The number of women that reached out to her was incredible. Over time, the disease remained relentless.

Reynae decided that she wanted to be closer to her precious daughters in 2015. Since both lived on the east coast and were well rooted where they were living, it only made sense for the move. The move to Virginia was in 2016. Reynae continued getting treatment for the cancer through VCU Massey Cancer Center in Richmond, Virginia. The time she had in Virginia was extremely special for her and both of the girls. They were blessed to have had a wonderful mother that loved them unconditionally. She showered them with much love and guidance. Funny how she got smarter as the girls got older and they had their own children. Reynae might be gone from this earth, but the entire family knows that she is in heaven. Being a true follower of Jesus Christ gave Reynae much peace because she knew where she was headed. As a family, we miss her every day, but she set an example for us on how to live our lives with humility and dignity. Her legacy is her daughters, who are living to follow her example of what it is to be a loving mother, loving wife, and most of all, have a strong spiritual conviction of being followers of Jesus Christ.

My mom was an amazing woman. She helped me realize that it is more fun to give than to receive. So today, I take tremendous joy in this tribute legacy letter.

She taught me about love, patience, grace, and God. My mom, Reynae, taught me how to pray and have a relationship with God, and she was always led by example. My mom was and is the most precious gift from God—so much beauty, grace, and love.

She touched my heart and my family in so many ways. Her strength and smile even on the darkest days made me realize I have an angel beside me. When she was diagnosed with the breast cancer and she talked to us about it, I would ask myself, "Why, God, why my mom?" When I posed the same question to her, I remember she would say, "Why not me?" God's will, not mine, will be done.

She was a God-fearing Christian woman till the day she passed. If I could say one thing about her, it's that she loved Jesus and wanted me to know him so when my time comes, we can see each other again in paradise. I am so glad I was raised by a strong woman like her. Seeing her, I have learned to get up each time I am knocked down in my life.

She gave me strength and inspiration, plus she taught me to believe in myself and help others. Such valuable lessons helped me in my life. I am sorry for all the times I made her worry but thanked her for all those moments when she was there for me. Even though she is not here on earth with me, I continue to hold on to all those precious moments we shared and still feel her guiding and supporting me from heaven. She gave me courage to go on this chosen path.

She might not have left millions in her bank account, but she left a legacy worth so much more. I am happily married now for twenty-seven years. We have raised three wonderful kids: one is completing his master's degree, one is steadily employed at the Naval Shipyards, and the youngest is currently enrolled at ODU, working toward her dental hygiene degree. I truly believe that her legacy is living through each and every one who knew her. She touched every person she ever talked to.

I love you forever, Mom.

Love,
your daughter Stacie

What I remember the most about my mom is that she made every occasion, holiday, celebration memorable. That is the one thing I wish I did more for my kids. I have such wonderful memories of her always decorating the house for all the holidays and fun birthday parties. She always made everything so special. She had a great eye for decoration and fashion.

When having conversations with my kids and helping them navigate through life today, I try to think back on the conversations we had growing up and her advice to me. What should she say? How should I say it?

She loved being involved in all the grandchildren's lives. She enjoyed watching them play sports and being their biggest cheerleader. She loved doing their hair and nails and playing games with them.

Right before she passed, we were able to take a family vacation together, I know that filled her heart, to see us all together laughing and having fun together.

I can't believe how hard she fought right up until the end, always with a smile on her face and kept her sense of humor and never complained. You could tell she was at peace to where she was going.

I miss being able to tell her what is going on with the kids now; she would be so proud of them. I know she is looking down and smiling at us.

Dear Reynae,

If you were here today, I would tell you how you helped me transition to my new school and new friends when I first moved to Carpinteria. At the age of thirteen, I found it pretty rough to leave behind my friends and relatives.

You were one in the group that welcomed me in the hallway outside homeroom at Carpinteria Junior High School, September 1962. Thank you for that.

I remember that same year, you came to my house on horseback. Afterward, I wrote to friends and relatives back in Chicago to share my excitement about my visit from you and Patches.

Such things are important to a young person. You helped me fit in.

Also, you were one of the first people I knew to appear on television. It was pretty exciting to see you and the other Carp. kids dancing on *The Lloyd Thaxton Show*, like *American Bandstand* with a touch of zaniness.

You were a fun person to be around, full of laughter and joy. It was a blessing for me to have known you, Reynae.

With gratitude,
Linda Kohnke Husted

CHAPTER THIRTY-EIGHT

Dolores Echeverria

In Memory of Dolores Echeverria

Dolores Echeverria was born at Cottage Hospital in Santa Barbara, California, on December 26, 1948, to Miguel and Emma Goena Echeverria. Dolores was also known as Lola, Loli, and Dolly. What a gift she was to her six sisters and parents. They lived on Cramer Road, where Miguel bought our four properties, in which there were eight rentals. Miguel built their first new three-bedroom home on Cramer Road in 1955, and life was good. Dolores went to Our Lady of Mount Carmel School from first through eighth grades, graduating with Maria Chagolla, Diane Darcy, and others.

In 1962, Miguel became the groundskeeper at the Santa Barbara Polo Fields and moved his family to the residence on the site. Dolores loved horseback riding and got a job hot-walking polo ponies. The likes of Buddy Ebsen, Fess Parker, Jill St. John, Jayne Mansfield, Lance Reventlow, and Robert Wagner were just a few of the movie stars that frequented the polo games; it was glamorous and a fun place to live. In 1963, the family bought a home on Andrea Street behind Canalino School, with neighbors the Reimers, Campos, May, Blaise, and Gonzalez families. Dolores was a Girl Scout and, in high school, joined Mariners, and with Pam Cleveland, Linda Fryer, Irene Ortiz, Leslie Statham, and other girls who sailed to Catalina Island for a weeklong trip.

Dolores married Jack Reimers while in high school and delivered daughter Silvia on May 29th. Although high school administration wrote that she could not walk in the graduation ceremony or attend prom, Miguel and Emma fought for her right to do so, and she graduated with her class and attended prom with Jack.

Second daughter Denise was born two years later. Dolores worked a paper route for the *Santa Barbara News-Press* and worked at Santa Claus Lane in the souvenir shop, which was owned by Jack and Lois Reimers. Jack operated the train. In 1973, after Dolores divorced Jack, she joined sister Silvia in South Lake Tahoe to work at Harrah's Casino as a cocktail waitress. There she met and married her second husband, Michael Hilsz, a bartender at the casino. They purchased their home and raised the girls, but later divorced when the girls were grown. Sister Martha worked cocktails at Harrah's as well, but she and Silvia both returned to Carpinteria in 1974. Dolores retired from Harrah's after thirty years in cocktails, part of that time in management. She was a great cocktail waitress, had the best sense of humor, and of course, always told a funny joke.

Dolores started collecting early on: Bauer pottery, chenille bedspreads, green Depression glass, old signage, vintage purses, '50s linens and records, vintage vases and lamps, old marbles. She loved garage sales and thrift shops and always found amazing items, which she gifted to her sisters when she would visit.

Reading was also a passion, and volunteering at the bookstore on Tahoe Boulevard was her love. She read hundreds of books, as well as listening to all types of music; she loved to dance and laugh. She was an avid knitter and crocheted, making afghans for her nieces and nephews. Dolores helped raise her four grandchildren and doted on her two great-grandchildren. She wanted to come home to see her family before she passed away of cancer at Cottage Hospital on November 25, 2018, with her sisters Silvia and Martha at her side.

Echeverria Sisters Sylvia & Dolores

Dolores sailing to Santa Catalina with Mariners (Irene
Ortiz, Linda Fryer, Leslie Statham, Cheryl Capes and Pam Cleveland)

CHAPTER THIRTY-NINE

Steve Wright

Life Following Graduation

After graduating from high school, I wanted to continue my education in the field of civil engineering. With that said, I decided to enroll in college in Santa Barbara, but after about a year and a half, I was bored with college, not stimulating or interesting enough. One day while wandering around Santa Barbara, I came across the navy recruiting office. Knowing only a little about the navy from my dad's stories of his time in the navy, I found it interesting. I went into the recruiter's office and told the chief I wanted to join the navy. He asked what field most interested me. Again, because of my lack of knowledge concerning naval rating, I made my selection by which rating badge I liked the most. It turns out that was a Data System Technician (DS). The rating badge was an atomic symbol with three arrows pointing in and one pointing out, looked very cool. It also turned out that was an advanced field, which required passing an aptitude test, followed by an initial enlistment of six years. Seems I did extremely well on the aptitude test and was offered any one of five ratings in the advanced fields. I chose DS.

Next came questions about how long I wanted to wait before reporting to boot camp. It was possible to delay it 120 days, but being eager to start my new adventure, I selected two weeks. And two weeks later, March of 1969, I was in boot camp in San Diego, CA. Not to bore you with the details of boot camp, suffice to say that period was fourteen weeks of learning, sacrifice, and a little pain.

One interesting story: after about six weeks of boot camp, the first class in charge of our company told me to report to sick bay for a submarine physical. I informed him I didn't sign up for sub duty, to which he replied, "It wasn't a question and didn't require a response. Just get your #*&% over there and get a physical." The first trip over, sick bay was closed, which I reported to the first class. He directed me to return to sick bay the following day and get my physical. The next day, I went near sick bay, hung out for about forty-five minutes, and returned to my company. Again, the first class asked if I had gotten my physical, to which I replied, "Yes, and they will contact you if I qualified for sub duty." Needless to say, I was a little nervous for the last eight weeks of boot camp.

At the end of boot camp, you get orders and find out which field/ job rating you will be pursuing. I was one of very few selected to continue as a data systems technician. The ironic part was after leaving college because it was not challenging and I was tired of school, I learned I would be attending three different phases of electronics and IT schools for the next two years. Boy, was I excited. They did have a great incentive study plan: flunk three tests and you were straight to the fleet or Vietnam as an unrated sailor. That meant you would get every lousy detail available.

After almost two years of intense schooling in San Diego, Mare Island, and Washington DC, I graduated as a petty officer third class, data systems technician. My first and only duty station was in Hawaii on the island of Oahu. I spent almost four years there as a sailor and about one more year after my discharge.

I was a cave sailor, spending the remainder of my enlistment in an underground facility. There were many adventures and stories from that period, but not knowing the age of all readers, I will save many of those for another book.

Fast-forward to 1975, the year I was discharged from the navy and enjoying life as a civilian but, after a short while, needing something else to pursue. I ended up accepting a position as a supervisor in the Operations Control and Date Systems Centers aboard a USNS government missile-tracking ship. I spent four years running around the Pacific performing range safety for missile operations. I was still single for about half of that time, so it was a little like a cruise ship without the pool, live music, or ladies.

We made several trips to Guam, Hawaii, and up the California coast from our home port in Port Hueneme, California. My most memorable trip on the ship was a six-month deployment in 1978 to the Marshall Islands. Onboard, we had a couple of scientific organizations, a couple of government departments, along with

National Geographic and a navy helicopter detachment from North Island in San Diego, California. The purpose of the trip was to check the residual radiation levels from the Bikini atom bomb test performed in 1954.

Once on station, we homeported in the Kwajalein Atoll and, from there, performed three deployments to the different atolls of the Marshall Islands.

Having no requirement for my crew until the end of the radiological investigation, I hooked up with the navy helicopter detachment and was able to travel to several different islands for exploration and diving. I started diving in Carpinteria and at the Channel Islands, where the visibility was limited and the water was cold. During my time in Oahu, I spent most of my off time in the water, either surfing or diving. I also spent time diving while in Guam. I didn't think water clarity or temperature could get any better, but then I was given the opportunity to dive in the Marshall Islands. The water was extremely clear and the temperature of a warm bath. I fell in love with diving there: giant clams (some over three or four feet across), fish of all colors and sizes, and very large sharks. I believe I got to dive in waters that nobody else had been in. I had a great time while there. It was mesmerizing in the morning from the bow of the ship, watching the flying fish rise above the water and glide for 75 to 100 feet before reentering the water. The nights were also unbelievable; having no streetlights, car lights, or city lights, it was amazing how many stars you could see. Many nights I would set up a cot on the helo deck and sleep outside, under the stars. Every now and then, the night's sleep was interrupted by a passing rain squall, but by morning, I was dry again.

Oh, I forgot to mention I got married before the deployment to the Marshall Islands. The best thing that ever happened to me, but during my trip to the Marshalls, I missed our youngest son's first birthday and, upon my return, was informed by my wife, she dearly loved me but I wasn't playing lost at sea anymore. As it would happen, shortly after I returned from the Marshall Islands, the shop was decommissioned and turned into a fish reef off the California coast—kind of made the decision for me.

After leaving the tracking ship in 1979, I accepted a position with Hughes Aircraft Company as an instrumentation engineer. I ended up working with the navy once again, this time in support of the F-14 and F-18 aircraft weapons systems and electronic warfare systems.

Stepping back in time a moment to 1976—that was the year I met my wife Kay. I met her at a friend's wedding and, shortly thereafter, realized she was the one I wanted to spend the rest of my life with. We've had a lot of great times and our share of rough patches, but through it all, we were side by side. She always brought out the best in me, despite what she might tell someone in a conversation when I'm not present. She is always up for a challenge and game to share any adventure with me. We have two sons and two wonderful granddaughters. I'm very proud of my sons, now grown men with fulfilling lives of their own. The two granddaughters are great; one's already off to college and the other to follow in a couple of years. I can't imagine where I would be if I hadn't met Kay.

Jumping forward again to 1979, when I began what was to be a thirty-year career with Hughes Aircraft Company. Actually, when I started, it was called Hughes Aircraft Company, which was eventually bought by General Motors and then again bought by Raytheon. It was an extremely interesting career, experiencing many sights and adventures most people never see or experience. Climbing in and out and working the cockpits of F-14s, F-18s, and other naval aircraft was a great experience. I was able to work with leading-edge technology and continued my education throughout my entire career.

Observing flight operations from the fight deck of the USS *Eisenhower* was quite a thrill. In fact, just getting to the shop from Puerto Rico was an adventure. We had so much equipment with us that after it was all loaded in the transit aircraft, we couldn't get in through the normal boarding door. We had to get up on the wing and go in through the emergency escape hatch. Once inside, we were supposed to put on life jackets, but there were none big enough to fit me. I asked the crew chief, "What happens if we have to ditch in the ocean?" to which he replied, "No problem, with all this equipment in here with us, we won't be getting out." It made for wonderful forty-five-minute flight to the carrier, but we made it.

After thirty years, I retired in 2009, thinking all this work stuff was behind me. I blissfully enjoyed a great retirement, yearly fishing trips to the Eastern Sierras with my sons and Dad, occasional trips to the desert with our sons and their dirt bikes and off-road vehicles, and many projects with my granddaughter's 4-H organization. I was even fortunate enough to play Santa Claus for a few of the local area schools for eight years. I was returned for almost four years when a defense contractor made me an offer I couldn't refuse. I've been back to work, again with the navy, since 2012 and enjoying every minute of it. Instead of aircraft engineering, it's now shipboard engineering. If all goes well, I should be retiring again at the end of 2021.

Well, folks, that's a compressed look at some of my life events after graduation. I'm very fortunate to have had a career I enjoyed and a loving and supportive family for the last forty-three-plus years. My only hope is that everyone's life was as fulfilling and enjoyable as mine.

INDEX

393

Thayer, Pamela, 204

Thayer, Stanley Shepard, 329

Thorny Path, 321–22

Tom (Jeanne's husband), 303–4, 306

Tomales Bay, 127

Tompkins, Leon, 8–9

Travis Air Force Base, 246

Triple Crown, 72

U

United Airlines 707, 7

United Stated International University (USIU), 13

University of Southern California (USC), 270–71

US Army, 81, 156, 216, 227

US Forest Service Emmett Ranger District, 45

V

Veterans Administration, 46

Veterans Memorial Building, 79

Vietnam, 3, 5, 7, 29, 56, 79–81, 90–91, 138, 167, 245–46, 251, 270, 277–79, 283–84, 289, 331–32, 384

Vietnam War, 14, 90, 138, 167, 216, 270

W

Waimea Bay, 8

Walker, Joe, 260

Walsh, Lynne, 321

Western Airlines, 39–40, 42

Western Offshore Drilling and Exploration Company, 40

West Maui Mountains, 8

Westmont College, 111, 165

Wheeler, Bill, viii, 278

Wheeler, Sandy, 278

White, Cindy, 83

Wien Air Alaska, 42–44

Willamette University, 95

Wolski, Colleen, 143, 150, 262

Wolski, Mike, 143–45, 147–50, 257, 262

Wright, Steve, 206, 381

Y

Yantis, Jackie Niccum, 223, 230

Yater Spoon, 5, 10

Yeager, Chuck, 260

Yeager, Jeana, 226

Young, Bobbi, 257, 259

Young, Jack, 257

Yucca Valley, 334, 337

Lightning Source UK Ltd.
Milton Keynes UK
UKHW041825041122
411674UK00007B/146/J